Don't Wait for Me

Don't Wait For Me

How a Mother Lost her Son to Bipolar Disorder and Drug Abuse

Ros Morris

EDINBURGH AND LONDON

First published in Great Britain in 2008 by
MAINSTREAM PUBLISHING COMPANY
(EDINBURGH) LTD
7 Albany Street
Edinburgh EH1 3UG

ISBN 9781845963422

This book is a work of non-fiction based on the life, experiences and recollections of the author. In some instances, names of people, places, dates, sequences or the detail of events have been changed to protect the privacy of others. The author has stated to the publishers that, except in such respects, not affecting the substantial accuracy of the work, the contents of this book are true

A catalogue record for this book is available from the British Library

Typeset in Bembo and Dearjoe

Printed in Great Britain by
CPI Cox & Wyman, Reading, RG1 8EX

Acknowledgements

This book would not have been written without 'Zach'. He has bravely allowed me to write about his illness. The account has been written from my perspective, although at times the story is told through emails from Zach. In order to protect the fragile identity of my son, the names of all involved, with the exception of the Central Middlesex Hospital, have been changed.

I must specially acknowledge my husband's belief in me. If I had not received his encouragement, I might not have embarked on this project. Without my daughter, who read the manuscript and gave me much advice, it would not have progressed. Both of them have been through much pain and anguish during the years of Zach's illness. Our profound hope is that Zach can somehow come to terms with his condition and eventually create a happy and fulfilling life for himself.

Ros Morris

Contents

Part One

Part Two

Part One

I

Beginnings

October 1997

Yesterday, we came back from the country. It was a splendid late-October Sunday but it was unseasonably hot and the London-bound traffic was unbearable, leaving us limp and ragged by the time we arrived home. Driving along the narrow lane, shielded on both sides by the dying, mottled leaves of autumn, Sam turned left into the driveway and parked the car. I was startled to see Beth and Molly waiting on the doorstep. Was this a welcoming party? For a moment, the thought travelled through my mind that they were standing there because they were happy to see us return. Then our daughter Beth ran towards the car, visibly distressed. Confused by her reaction to our homecoming, I stared searchingly at Molly, Zach's long-standing girlfriend. She appeared agitated, pale and drawn, and she tugged at the limp blonde hair that hung wilting over her forehead.

Beth sobbed. She attempted an explanation. About an hour ago, she recounted between panicky breaths, they had received a phone call from a woman, a social worker. She had explained to Beth that Zachary, our eighteen-year-old son, had been arrested and then taken to the psychiatric ward of a nearby hospital. Beth was so shocked and bewildered by the call that she had been unable to take in what Renata, the social worker, had tried to tell her. She had mentioned Middlesex. Sam and I turned to each other, stunned. Sam threw open the boot of the car and manhandled our baggage into the house, all the time muttering expletives. The dog, Max, followed him, searching for Zach, his favourite human. The house was orderly. The chaos was to follow.

The girls were agitated. They had strange things to tell us, they said – about spaceships and pyramids and bizarre writings on Zach's bedroom walls. He hadn't slept at all, they said. He had stayed up all night, scrabbling around with sheets of paper, scrawling mathematical equations and babbling incoherently about 'the meaning of the universe', incessantly slamming doors and going in and out of his room. He looked weird and manic, almost unrecognisable. He was totally out of control, so much so that they were unable to fathom why. What had he been doing to make him behave like this? His conduct made no sense and they had been profoundly frightened by his illogical actions and then what had happened to him.

While I listened to Beth and Molly, my mind raced. What on earth had happened here this weekend and just what should we do? Should we wait for someone from an anonymous hospital to call us or should we leave now and head out simply in order to do something, anything, to find Zach? I was paralysed, unable to make this decision, but Sam's emotions overrode his patience. He'd junked the bags in the hall, deposited Max in the kitchen and returned outside. He was in a panic and pressing me to leave. 'We've got to search for him!' he shouted. Middlesex? Then, surely, he proclaimed, it had to be the Middlesex Hospital. I told the girls to wait by the phone and to call us on Sam's mobile if they heard more. Reluctantly, and with great foreboding, I got into the car and we hurtled off into the horrid north London Sunday traffic, towards the West End and the Middlesex Hospital.

As far as I could remember, there *was* no psychiatric ward at the Middlesex Hospital. I don't know why I knew that hitherto irrelevant piece of information and I wanted to impart it to Sam but, in his panic, Sam was not absorbing facts. His foot firmly on the accelerator, his hand frequently on the horn, the further south we ventured, the more distraught he became and the longer it took us to make headway. Eventually, we made it to the hospital, Sam running in with me trailing in his wake, not asking questions of relevant staff, not really knowing where he was heading, simply heading somewhere, anywhere, to try to find his son. Then Beth called. He was at the Central Middlesex Hospital in Acton. So the wild goose chase began again. Back in the teeming traffic, we accelerated towards Park Royal, a no-man's-land of industrial estates bordered by the North Circular.

The hospital appeared in a sea of lonely buildings, a high-rise of ungainly dimensions, dwarfing the clutter of suburban housing and unattractive hospital outbuildings. At the doors of the psychiatric department a cluster of young men huddled together, smoking dope and calling to each other in hoarse, strangely aggressive voices. It was not a prepossessing start. Through interminable corridors, we made our way up to a ward where a television bellowed out an indistinguishable programme, watched by two ragged old men. On seeing us searching, bewildered, for someone in charge, a freckle-faced, red-headed young woman came over and introduced herself to us. 'Zach's parents?' she enquired. 'I'm Renata. I've been asked to take care of Zach while he's here.'

Pointing us in the direction of unoccupied space, Renata manoeuvred us into a small room with an internal window shielded by a paisley-print curtain. Loud knocks emanated from beyond, then continuous rapping on the window, followed by banging and rough shouts. The social worker calmly ignored these disturbing noises and explained that Zach had been arrested in Kilburn very early that morning. From what they had managed to elicit from him, he had walked from our house to Kilburn, a distance of about two miles.

Somehow, he had gained entry to a small block of flats off the High Road and then, according to witnesses, had harangued the tenants, explaining that he was 'Jesus, come to save them'. Furious at this intrusion on their somnolent Sunday, they called the police. The police realised that Zach was not a serious criminal and that he was either stoned or mad or both. To their credit, instead of locking him up, they took him to the local hospital. Zach was seriously disturbed, explained Renata. At this time, they were unable to diagnose why. They needed more time. But would we like to see him? He was in the room from where the peculiar knocking, banging and shouting originated.

The room was airless and dank. It was dark and pungent. Zach lay on the floor on a dirty mattress, a glass of water sitting nearby. Excrement and graffiti stained the tiled walls. There was nothing in the room save for the manky mattress. I could hardly believe what was there before my eyes. I was outraged, horrified and disgusted. Although I had seen Zach just a few days earlier, he now appeared shockingly unhealthy, thin and unkempt. His clothes, what there were of them, hung off him, dirty and dishevelled. His hair draped itself in lifeless shards around a face gaunt, colourless and sweaty, his eyes dark-ringed, huge and staring. He got up when he saw us but, instead of our once ebullient, attractive son, he was a madman who raved at us. Arms akimbo, he yelled expletives, standing directly in front of Sam, nose-to-nose, extraordinarily belligerent and threatening. It was wholly unnerving and frightening. None of the threats and shouts made sense, nothing was articulate or lucid. We were unable to comprehend him and reluctantly left the room, convinced he was suffering some kind of drug-induced psychosis. As to what drug had caused it, we had no clue. It was only later that Sunday, when we spoke about the series of events with Dominic's father, that we found out that Zach and Dominic had been ingesting '2CBs'[1] the entire weekend. Dominic was one of Zach's oldest friends and in recent years they had certainly been able to get hold of – or cook up – plenty of revolting mind-altering substances. At this juncture, though, the drugs were a red herring, an obsession of Zach's we were to learn much about over the subsequent years.

The reality hit me. We could not leave Zach here in this godforsaken dungeon. It was too awful, too dirty, too depressing – Third World. It was our first experience of the inadequate mental-health facilities in London; we were novices. We thought that we were privileged in having private health insurance. Surely this would entitle us to something better, something we could recognise as more akin to 'our own'. The least we could do was to move him to another facility, a private hospital with rooms, we hoped, without shit decorating the walls. Renata was helpful. She understood our bewilderment and our predicament. She knew of a private hospital in west London that would be able to help. We only had to call our insurers. She would speak to them on our behalf.

Then, as we were walking along the murky corridor, a doctor approached us, a young Indian psychiatrist. He had interviewed Zach and he agreed that it would be appropriate to have him transferred to another clinic but qualified this by asking a chilling question: 'Is there any history of mental illness in your family?'

Sam and I looked at one another, staggered. 'Mental illness?' we retorted. 'What kind of question is that? Of course not!' His condition had to be drug induced, didn't it? Mental illness?

Why is it that a drug-induced psychosis should be preferable to mental illness? What is it about mental illness that so terrifies us? Is it the lack of self-control or the belief that someone who suffers from such a condition is defined historically by a gibbering, slobbering wreck chained to the wall of a nameless Victorian institution, preserved far away from day-to-day humanity – even though such institutions no longer exist? Reactions to mental illness have been fashioned by countless books and films purporting to expose the terrible suffering in such barbaric edifices. We have been privy to the lives of the eccentric and the mad in the films of Ken Russell. His biopics of Mahler and Tchaikovsky are brimming with intelligence and insight into insanity. We have read of the gradual deterioration in the lives of famous writers such as F. Scott Fitzgerald, Tennessee Williams and Sylvia Plath.[2] Ken Kesey's psychotic Big Nurse Ratched fills us with dread when we think of the treatment she meted out to her vulnerable patients in *One Flew Over the Cuckoo's Nest*, and especially to Jack Nicholson's Randle McMurphy in the film adaptation. Mental illness, therefore, was to be avoided; in fact, it seemed to us far worse than cancer.

Yet the drugs issue was something that compounded our anxieties. Did we really believe that we could control Zach's use of drugs more easily than a psychological illness? We had known since he was about fourteen that he used illegal substances. I had often walked into his room only to be aware of the pervading smell of weed, open windows on freezing nights and furtive hidings of secret packets. On many occasions, I confronted him about it but was met by adolescent hostility and promises to abstain. A few weeks earlier, having returned home from our summer holiday, I noted that Zach was behaving decidedly oddly. His moods moved backwards and forwards from aggressive irritability to short-tempered belligerence and then contrition when he appeared to have a window of insight into his behaviour. The very day we arrived back, he had an awful spat with the man in the video shop where I accompanied him after a rather tetchy lunch. Quite out of character, he swore and shouted at the rather pompous assistant for demanding more in fines than Zach deemed appropriate. After I'd apologised profusely to the man, who thereafter banned Zach from the shop, I asked him why he had been so rude. 'The man's an absolute cunt. I don't need to go there. There's plenty of other places to rent videos. I'm just tired. I was looking forward to seeing you again and now this bastard has spoiled it for me.' Whether he was tired, I didn't know; I put his reaction down to drugs of some kind. He was eighteen and for the first time we had left him to take responsibility for himself and Max, our much-loved dog. Maybe that had been a mistake. In retrospect, it was. But everything is easy in retrospect.

Neither Sam nor I condoned Zach's drug use but nothing appeared to get through that would stop him. We knew that he didn't like to drink and rarely drank too much, preferring to 'inhale'. Sam had occasionally smoked weed when the children were small and I often told him to stop, that the kids would somehow know by osmosis and that this was unacceptable behaviour for a responsible parent. I don't know how prevalent it was among our peer group. Certainly, I knew of parents who indulged in weed and others who did lines of coke at the weekend or on holidays, although Sam never went anywhere near hard drugs and is virulently anti-drugs to this day. We were of the generation for whom it was acceptable to smoke as much as you wanted at university but then, once serious employment loomed and kids were around, you stopped and just overdid the booze – a far more accepted practice, though no less lethal. Sam smoked the occasional joint until Zach was about six and has never touched anything since. He never smoked in front of the kids, only late at night, the same way that others would have a Scotch or a glass of wine or two and realistically, although I could never agree with it, that was all it was, the odd smoke followed by an attack of the munchies and a handful of chocolate-chip cookies.

Some years after the event, Zach related to me what had happened to him during his first Glastonbury experience. He was fifteen. In the middle of the night, while the rest of the drugged-out, fume-filled kids slept or cavorted off their faces, the St John Ambulance volunteers found him running naked in a field, high on acid. They carried him back to a tent where they tried to feed him, clothe him and bring him round to a semblance of normality. Being Zach, he had to experiment far more heavily than his contemporaries, dropping so much LSD that he was out of control; to this day, he still experiences terrifying flashbacks. Over the following months and years, he tried a cocktail of everything, including both cocaine and heroin. 'Never injecting, only smoking,' he informed me. 'That way, it's not habit-forming.'[3] In addition to these undesirable narcotics, he added to the list crack, pills and ecstasy and everything and anything else he could find. However, his favourite of favourites was ketamine, a nasty but not at that time, unfortunately, illegal substance.[4] Many times I would come down to the kitchen early in the morning only to find the microwave caked in tiny, shiny, sticky particles that resembled sugar. I would look at the mess with feelings of irritation and disgust. This was yet another thing that I had to clean up after Zach. I had no idea what the residue was and thus no reason to feel frightened. He later informed me this was the result of 'cooking' ketamine. In its liquid form, it looks like tap water and has no smell. He carried it around with him in a gin bottle or in vials that purported to contain rosewater. (During a later episode, I removed a bottle from his room and dispensed three hundred pounds' worth down the sink. He found this amusing.) Cannabis was a daily dose, so it was easy to believe that this episode was the result of his shambolic drug abuse. It was a demonstrably *preferable* explanation. Preferable, that is, to a mental illness.

I pinched myself. My reverie ended and I found myself back at the Central Middlesex. The doctor continued his explanation as to why he believed that it was not a drugs problem here but something organic and, consequently, far more dangerous. I stood there shakily, nauseous and dry-mouthed. We remained in the corridor. The television blared unremittingly and Zach's shouts became more rasping the longer we talked. The young psychiatrist was quite persistent and guided us to a row of plastic chairs arranged along the wall outside the locked room. He gestured to Sam and me and we sat down. He had a sheaf of notes in his hand and I could see that the black biro in his shirt pocket had leaked ink at the bottom right edge, creating a stain on the otherwise spotless white cotton. He was oblivious to this and the inky stains on his index finger and he now removed the pen so that he could make more notes. While he was talking to us, my mind wandered once more and I pondered why he was here in this grubby hospital in London, so far from home, and how many young men intent on destroying their short lives with these revolting substances he must have dealt with and how many more young patients with acute mental-health problems he must have come across.

'You know,' he continued, 'the symptoms that Zach presents with are not conclusively those of a drug-induced psychosis, although I agree it looks like that.' He consulted his notes once again, looking up at us and smiling. 'I really think that he should stay in hospital so that we can do a complete workout on him.' His smile hooked me, hypnotising me, and at that moment I almost reached out to him, almost consented to leave Zach there. Then suddenly he leaned towards Sam, the pen dropping from his fingers and clattering onto the greasy linoleum. He bent down to retrieve it. 'I'm very worried about Zach,' he said on his way back up to face us. 'You don't know how this will all pan out. He needs the proper help.'

He sounded so plausible and I knew that he was trying his best to convince us, but we were simply not listening. Without having to express it to each other, Sam and I did not want to hear what he was saying. We were in pure, classic denial. There was no way that we were ready to hear about Zach and mental illness or stays on sickening psychiatric wards where human faeces stained the walls and gangs of dissolute young men roamed around, calling and shouting to one another in the chaos of a shadowy asylum. In spite of the doctor's pleas, both Sam and I had decided that it was impossible for Zach to be mad. We insisted that they transfer him to the private clinic later that night. Once removed from the North Circular, he remained in hospital for a further twenty-four hours and then, refusing any more treatment, he came home. Our first mistake.

2

The Way Up

He wasn't a particularly antsy kid. Just like any other, really. The first of the two, so of course I was the neurotic mother, suffering severe post-natal depression for a good two years after his birth. Night after night, I would lie in bed, glassy-eyed, fearful for when Zach would awaken, wondering what on earth I could do with this human whose every breath was reliant on my presence. Mornings, by nine the house was cleaned and sparkling. Floors were vacuumed to perfection and not a dust mite was allowed repose on any piece of furniture. Soup was on the stove, meat in the oven and a pudding in a metal bowl, the beaters cleaned once more and replaced in their pristine environment. Four courses by ten in the morning. Terrycloth nappies, their creases symmetrical, filed away in the airing cupboard. Twelve bottles shiny and upended next to the sink. Of course, I couldn't breastfeed. I was far too anxious and too reticent to ask for help. Was this depression?

I was in agony. Sharp stabbing pains caused me to wince and gasp, and my breath was shallow and anguished. Zach would cry to be fed, to be changed, to be burped, simply to be with someone – but I held back. I did everything that was required for his physical well-being but I was emotionally detached. I loved him but I was frightened and too fearful to bare myself, even to him, a tiny baby. There were myriad occasions when I put him in his pram and walked for hours and hours around the suburb where we lived. I knew no one. We had recently moved into the house and I didn't drive at that time. There was no one I could speak with about him, apart from Sam – and I was too ashamed of myself to tell Sam of my feelings. So I worked like a mad housewife in order not to engage with Zach.

One late spring morning, when I felt that I could no longer take the misery, I called in to our GP and explained my feelings, Zach on my lap, sleeping, content. 'I feel empty,' I told the doctor. 'I have such pain.' I pointed to the pit of my stomach. He looked at me with bemusement, his bushy eyebrows like bats' wings above his eyes. I could determine the irritation in the way he spoke. 'You're low,' he said to me patronisingly. 'You've just had a baby. It takes time. I'll prescribe you some vitamins.' *Vitamins?* It was my turn to look at him with befuddlement, surprise. What could vitamins possibly do to help me with my despair?

My eyes awash with tears and my prescription in my hand, I carried Zach back to his buggy, gently replacing him so that he was warm and snug and safe. Then I walked out of the surgery towards the road. A car approached from a distance. I stopped on the kerb. An indistinct voice in my inner consciousness spoke to me. It would be so easy just to push the pair of us under its wheels. For a moment, the thought shone brightly in my mind, then I gasped with disbelief at myself. How could I even consider it? I stepped back hurriedly, looking around to check whether anyone else had noticed what I was thinking. The world continued playing as it was. No one had seen anything. I hurried home. These thoughts did not occur again. When Beth was born, the awful, terrible feelings and abysmal pains faded away as if they had never been and have since stayed buried deep in my psyche.

Zach was born after a melancholic twenty-two-hour labour, which I had to endure in a grim Victorian hospital stuck on a busy four-lane road in the centre of London. It was a Sunday afternoon in the middle of a bitterly long, cold, grey winter. Snow and slush covered the roads around the grubby pink edifice and when it was time for me to make my way from the car to the labour ward, Sam guided me along, helping me to avoid the deep potholes that pitted the street and not slip or slide and land on my behind, belly up, like an enormous seal.

It was not a busy weekend in the teaching hospital and the delivery room was overflowing with medical students who peered and pondered at my efforts at childbirth, rather as if they were viewing a zoological specimen *in extremis*. Strapped up like a tortured terrorist, I could only pray that my endeavours would soon be over. It took all night and most of the following day. The pain came over me in spiteful waves. Sam's cajoling just irritated me. I hated it all. Him for putting me in this place, me for being so carelessly irresponsible as to allow myself to fall pregnant and everyone else around me for showing so little interest in my well-being. I was simply an object for their further education. When Zach finally made his way into the world, a tiny little human, I could only turn my head away in exhaustion and despair. Not a good omen, in hindsight.

Yet Zach was absolutely delightful. His father adored him from the moment he gave his first cry, peering around the delivery room, unseeing, yet apparently taking it all in. He was not beautiful then. He became more beautiful the more he gained weight and the more interest he showed in his surroundings. From three months onwards, I would be stopped in the street whenever I took him for a walk. 'What a gorgeous baby,' I would be informed by all. 'What a perfect boy!' He slept and ate and did everything the perfect baby would do, apart from the first few weeks, when during the early part of the evening he would cry and cry and cry. He had been fed. He was bathed and burped and was not in obvious pain nor suffering from colic but he cried incessantly. I would go up to his bedroom and peer behind the door, seeing his distress, his bright wet face, his little body scrunched up in the corner of the cot. But I was inert, unable to give him what more he needed. As we were beginners, we listened to other parents and took the advice we were given: 'Let him cry. There's nothing wrong with letting a baby cry, especially when there's nothing wrong.'

But how did I know that nothing was wrong? Why was it *wrong* to pick up a baby when he cried? When I look back now, I hate myself with a visceral loathing. How could I have left him for hours to cry and cry, until he slept, worn out by his exertions? Did he feel then that he was abandoned, that no one out there cared for him and no one ever would? Were those the first feelings that he experienced of the natural world? What heartless, terrible advice. I now ask myself incessantly: who knows whether these feelings of abandonment have impacted on his vulnerability to painful, anxious and stressful situations?

Then, as quickly as it had arrived, the crying stopped and over the following months Zach turned into a bright, happy, precocious toddler. He was joyfully chubby, the long, dark hair that he was born with spilling over his brow in gentle waves, sparkling hazel eyes shining with intelligence. He walked and talked before one year and, of course, he was our 'genius'. Beth was born three years later and he treasured her from the moment that he saw her in hospital on a warm, glorious spring day in a ward suffused with daffodils. She, too, melted when she was around him and he would carry her around the house, his tiny arms holding her tightly around her chest, my heart in my throat with the fear that he would drop her; but he never did and she trusted him implicitly. He was her darling big brother. But there were times during those early years when I was worried for him. He had nightmares, night terrors, when we had to make use of what psychological knowledge we had – and that was scant – and his mood on waking up from an afternoon nap could be gravely bad-tempered and black. He would stand in his cot and cry great lonely tears that would wrench my heart with their ferocity. Only after copious hugs and kisses and drinks and sweet biscuits would he calm down and become the Zach we knew, the unhappiness fading away. Somehow, I think now, those black moods must have been a precursor to those that were to plague him further along.[5]

Our nuclear family survived the toddler years and Zach embarked on his education, starting at nursery school at two years old. He learned well and quickly, made friends and got into fights with other little boys, and became himself. With pangs of acute nostalgia, I look at the birthday cards and Mother's Day cards and Christmas cards that he made me. 'To the best mum in the world,' they would say, all glittery fingerprints, awash with the first handprints and jammy kisses. So sweet and adorable, like the soft downy cheeks that I stroked with the tips of my fingers, wondering about the day when they would be rough with beard. How is it possible that he should ever have changed from that whole being into a fractured shell?

Kids who came to our house and whose houses he played at remain friends to this day. But there were those times when he refused to go to primary school for one reason or another that I was unable to ascertain, when I forcefully propelled him into the classroom, much against his wishes. And there were other times too when his bad temper led to him being excluded from activities. I would look at him and wonder why this beautiful child could not express himself other than through violent tantrums. However, these occurrences were comparatively rare and generally passed over quickly.

Photographs in our albums portray a happy, contented family whose activities were varied and fun. Holidays were spent on horses, trekking in canyons and white-water rafting or skiing. Zach was an excellent athlete and a good footballer. He has a first-rate brain, writes well and is musically gifted. He never really needed prodding to finish homework in his first school and managed, without much effort, to slide into a good secondary school. For the first two years there, he did well. His grades were good and his teachers liked him. His circle of friends extended and we began to see girls in and around his room and outside the door to the house, ringing him up, day and night. But other friends were not so encouraging. They were the guys with faces replete with ear studs, nose studs, lip studs and eyebrow studs. The first tattoo displayed itself and with it came the demands that we let him attend various concerts in and around London and the first of the weekends spent in the amnesiac waste of the acid hit.

Then the A-level years began and homework became much more of a problem. Parents' evenings usually resounded to the refrain 'Zach can do much better'. Yet the teachers who taught his specialist subjects rated him highly and they left him alone, recognising perhaps that if they did so, he would contribute more to their lessons than if they pressurised him. It was all very well to let him be, treat him like an adult and not a recalcitrant child, but did they ever ask him what he was doing those afternoons that he didn't turn up for games or extra periods? Why did no one ever call his parents to tell us that, yet again, he was absent without leave? Only in later years did he inform us that instead of playing football he was sitting on a bench on Hampstead Heath smoking a joint with one or other of his friends, or wandering around the streets of north London in a haze of other noxious substances.

He meandered along, doing the minimum that was required of him academically, despite the school's stated belief that he was 'quite able' to continue on to the most coveted university if only 'he was prepared to put in that little bit extra'. Unfortunately, he was not. With hardly any effort and without even reading the required texts, he managed three Bs and, with much prodding from Sam and me, applied for and was offered a place at a London university. However, further education was the last thing on his mind and, with much cajoling, he persuaded us that he should take a year out before starting his degree, so that he and his band could become 'the next big thing'.

3

Backgrounds

Zach was obsessed with music. Prior to that bleak autumn following his first admission to hospital, he was the pivotal member of his band. He began playing the guitar at fourteen and made steady progress, forming a number of ensembles over the following years. This latest incarnation seemed to be on its way to stardom. He was totally focused on the music, writing choppy, edgy guitar-based melodies. The group had taken on various hues and personalities and was now in its final embodiment. Zach had honed down an assortment of members to those who now stood with him on stage. Two of the guys were old friends. We generally managed to get on well, the band members and us, but one of them, Tosh, the singer, was problematic, an altogether different story. Zach had met him through an ad he had placed in one of the music magazines searching for a 'talented singer'. Tosh came from a broken home, had been living on his own since he was sixteen and had a serious drink problem. We noted that the relationship between the two of them was not a meeting of equals.

Tosh was unlike any of Zach's other friends. Small and weedy, he had a sullen, ashen-faced, fox-like demeanour and expressed his 'angst-ridden artistic bent' in bouts of wild drunkenness. His strangest feature was his eyes: the corneas were misplaced, giving him the appearance of a demonic creature of the night. It was apparent that he loathed and resented Zach's background and family, and regarded Zach's girlfriend Molly as a threat. He was generally uncontrollably and aggressively boorish to her and anyone connected to her. I now believe that he fully intended to destroy Zach and that from the outset he sought to drive a wedge between our son and us. We did not realise the psychotic yet Machiavellian influence that Tosh would have over Zach and how the unhealthy symbiotic relationship would impact on the many who would come into contact with them.

One instance stands out: because of Tosh's negative influence over him, Zach made the curious decision to break up with Molly. 'It's you or Tosh,' he explained to her shamefacedly. Within months, unable to remain apart, they got back together again, to Tosh's profound chagrin. But one setback did not stop him in his war of attrition. Ironically, Tosh would subsequently suffer profound psychological problems, which led to the most horrific outcome – but that was some time in the future. Then, we simply had to contend with his repugnant personality, while Zach insisted that Tosh remain the focal point of his existence.

The combination of Zach's musical composition and the lyrics penned by him and Tosh – together with the talents of the other three guys, one of whom would go on to real stardom – meant that the band was creating a buzz. They were touring and playing gigs on a weekly basis, boasted a loyal fan base and were about to sign with a major record label. But early that autumn, their personalities were in conflict. Things began to unravel and countless unfathomable clashes created vivid tensions between them. Tosh drank too much. Zach smoked far too much cannabis and was using God knows what else. The guys in the band were well aware that something was wrong but they rallied around Zach in an attempt to keep things together. Having him back at home, it was our primary intention to establish the causes for Zach having been arrested in the first place.

* * *

That first chaotic October weekend, friends who owned and managed a small hotel on the edge of Dartmoor had invited Sam and me to the West Country. 'Bring Max,' Archie prompted us. 'He'll have a wonderful time chasing rabbits and going for a swim in the river. And we'll feed him too!' So we packed the car and secured Max in the back. Even though it was almost wintry November, the days were of sparkling autumn finery, dry and warm. It was bucolic. The area was one of sublime beauty. The River Dart coursed through the garden of an unconventionally picturesque lodge, surrounded by the rolling greenery of one of the most glorious counties of Britain. We didn't fish but Archie gave us rough directions and we walked for miles along the river and among the boulders strewn by the meandering path. We became hopelessly lost in spite of following the bends and curves of the streams and brooks adjoining the watercourse. Above us, the sun shone warm and bright but I panicked, wondering whether we would ever regain our way, until we heard the voices of ramblers, who guided us to the right path. Generally, I never panic but there was something, I felt, that was not quite right in the cosmos, something that I was unable to pick out; maybe I was experiencing a little of what was happening in London, the unseen umbilical cord.

How do you know when your life is about to change irrevocably? Beth's experiences that Friday afternoon were a forerunner of events that would occur many more times over the next ten years. On her way back from school, sitting upstairs at the back of the bus, she watched the traffic snaking its way up the Finchley Road. Finally passing the lights, the bus came to a halt and she descended onto the gritty tarmac. She turned left into the close. The road was quiet. So too was the house. No sound, no soul greeted her. She called out to Zach. Silence. She realised that she was alone, so she called Molly. They had made arrangements to go to Brighton that Saturday. Now she wondered whether Molly had any idea where Zach could be hiding out. 'Nope,' replied Molly to Beth's enquiry. 'I haven't spoken with Zach all day. But I'll be around later.' Beth replaced the phone and began to make her way towards the kitchen. She was thirsty.

Suddenly, she heard the door slam and Zach walked into the hall. 'I'm off,' he said to Beth, as if he had just spent the day with her.

'But you've only just got in,' she remonstrated, eyeing him carefully and wondering whether he looked quite right.

'I'm off,' he repeated. 'I'm out of here. I'm going to get a tattoo.'

Beth stopped on her way to the fridge, all thoughts of a Coke vanished. 'What d'you mean, a tattoo?' she asked him.

His eyes glittered. He looked clammy. His hair was greasy and perspiration shone around his nose and chin. 'An atomic bomb,' he replied.

Beth gasped. 'Should you be doing that?' she questioned him hurriedly. 'What will Mum and Dad say?'

Zach looked at her, a bizarre smile playing around his lips. 'I'm gone.'

When Beth was awoken later that night by the pounding sounds of U2 spilling through the walls of her bedroom, the Zach she knew was absent. He was out of the real world. Stoned. Blasted. He lay on the futon in his room, thumping the floor in time to the beat. 'What the fuck are you doing, Zach?' Beth shouted, irate. He looked towards her, unknowing, unfeeling, a blank look in his eyes as if he had somehow shut down. 'Zach?' she asked. Nothing. 'Zach, are you all right?' she asked again. Still no intelligent response. Concerned, Beth walked over to the bed and shook him. His slight body shivered in anticipation of her presence but there was nothing that she could do to elicit a reaction from him. This was not the first time that she had seen him like this, doped up, stoned, but she could usually have some sort of conversation with him, even if he just dissolved into inane giggling. This was more . . . confusing. Sad but angered, she left him and went back to her room. She pulled the covers over her head and slept until Molly rang the doorbell first thing in the morning and the two of them set off for Brighton, leaving Zach snoring on his back, the ashtrays overflowing and a spilled glass of water soaking the sheets as they lay tangled at the foot of his mattress.

The hour was late when, exhausted, the girls arrived back at the house. Notwithstanding their predilection for all things Brighton, the day had not gone to plan. The streets were crammed with students, tourists and day-trippers, and there was a surreal feel to the place. Everywhere they went they were jostled and pushed, and the late-autumn heat frazzled them. They were just happy to be back home. The house was empty. No sign of Zach. Just a mess in the kitchen where he had taken food and left plates and scraps and dirty glasses in the sink for the unknown someone to clean up. The girls stayed up in the hope that he would reappear. Molly had fully expected him to try to see her over the weekend. She was surprised to find him out. Increasing concerns about his moods and his significant drug consumption had led to their breaking up again during the summer months. They had only recently got back together once more.

Exasperated, Beth tidied the kitchen, her small frame darting around the room, shoving the hair out of her eyes while she washed the glasses and took out the rubbish. Molly attempted to establish where Zach could be. She tried calling the usual numbers but apparently none of his friends had seen him. Tired and irritated, she noticed an old photo of Zach on the wall above the washing machine. He grinned out at the camera, holding a football shield, surrounded by a gaggle of little boys punching the air with their fists. She smiled ruefully. 'Where are you, you fool?' she muttered, turning towards Beth. 'I can't find him,' she sighed, stifling a yawn. 'I'm whacked.'

Beth shrugged her shoulders. 'I can't be bothered to wait up for him any longer. He's such an idiot. Let's go to sleep,' she added. 'Maybe he'll just turn up.' They climbed the stairs to Beth's room, where she pulled out the sofa bed. Within minutes, they were asleep but it was a fitful night.

It seemed like moments later. A door slammed shut and then reopened – only to be slammed shut once more. Beth turned over to see Molly sitting up on the other side of the room, rubbing at her eyes. 'Did you hear that?' she whispered. Beth put her hand up, gesturing to Molly to be quiet. She slid her legs out of the bed and tiptoed to the bedroom door. Molly came around and joined her. Another door slammed and they could hear shouts emanating from one of the other bedrooms and a pounding along the wooden landing as if an army in hobnail boots was marching in deadly formation. Tentatively, Beth turned the handle and gently drew the door towards her. What she saw when she opened it horrified her.

An apparition. Standing outside her room, his jeans rolled unevenly over his knees and wearing a ragged sky-blue T-shirt, stood Zach. He was barefoot and his feet were filthy, the toenails bloodied. Sunglasses were perched on top of his head. His face was drenched in sweat, and perspiration had gathered in black patches on the shirt. Beth stared at him. He stared back at her, a strange, crazy *Clockwork Orange* grin leading to wide, wild eyes. Tiny pinprick pupils glinted in the depths. In his left hand he carried a Bible.

Molly gasped and grasped Beth's shoulder. 'Oh, my God,' she whispered. 'What's wrong with him?'

Zach leered at her. 'Game over!' he shouted. He turned and began to pace up and down the corridor, punching at the air as he went. 'Game over!' he repeated, the decibel level increasing. 'I am time.' He slammed at the walls. 'I am time, it just is!' He repeated the refrain. The girls watched, mesmerised, as he retraced his steps. 'Game over!' he yelled again. 'It just is.' He kicked at the wall, leaving a bloody footprint. 'It's JUSTICE!' The sounds echoed frighteningly around the house.

Abruptly, the door to the spare bedroom opened. Tosh, his hair dishevelled and his clothes in disarray, darted into the hallway. 'He's fucking nuts!' he screamed out to Beth, who recoiled in terror. 'He's been fucking doing my head in all night! He won't calm down!'

Striding up to Zach and pulling at his top, Tosh yelled at him, 'What are you fucking *doing*, man?' Zach stopped the mantra, looking about him, but it was as if Beth, Molly and Tosh were invisible. He was in another world, another stratosphere. Stumbling past Tosh, he punched the wall again, agitated, manic, unable to stop the jittery hand movements, sweat dripping onto his chest. Tosh turned to Beth and Molly. 'D'you know what he's been doing all night?' he interrogated them. They shook their heads simultaneously. 'He's been as weird as fuck. I couldn't stand being in the same room as him. He wouldn't sleep and he wouldn't stop talking and shouting and gabbling rubbish.'

Zach was out of control. Beth realised that this insanity was something that she had never experienced before with him. It petrified her. Who was this frantic boy who leered down at her with his horrifying, sweaty face, his staring black eyes and peculiar grin? Molly tried to stop him from the pacing, his muttering and the pounding feet, fearful that he would break a floorboard and damage a tendon. She pursued him along the corridor once more and attempted to lead him back into his room, gently propelling him forwards, her slender arms snaking around his waist. 'Please, Zach,' she begged him, 'please calm down. You're going to hurt yourself!' But she was unable to curtail the movements and he roughly pulled away from her. 'What are we going to do, Beth?' she moaned. 'What's happened to him?'

Beth started to cry, at a loss to know what course of action to take. Tosh was no help and she was ill equipped to handle Zach on her own. 'I don't know what to do. We've got to try and make him go back to sleep.'

'Zach!' she cried to him. 'Zach, go back to bed!' He ignored her. He ignored them all. They watched him closely, with trepidation. Then, unexpectedly, his face changed. It was as if from somewhere he had had a revelation or had heard a voice. He pulled at his jeans belt to tighten them. 'I'm going out,' he said menacingly. 'I'm leaving.

I've got to go. There are things I have to do.' He strode into his bedroom. They heard the banging of wardrobe doors and opening of drawers. Moments later, he ran out into the corridor. They saw that he had pulled on a pair of running shoes. No socks. One trouser leg still rolled up above his knee, his shin white, bloodied and hairy.

'Zach!' called Beth once more. 'Zach, where are you going? You can't go anywhere now. It's first thing in the morning. There's nowhere . . .' Ignoring her, Zach made his way down the stairs, two steps at a time, oblivious to her entreaties. He was oblivious to them all. He pulled open the downstairs door and made to run out into the street, shadowed by Molly. Done in, agitated and venomously angry, Tosh leaned over the landing. 'We've got a fucking band practice today!' he shrieked after Zach. 'You better come back, you bastard!' The door slammed. The windows shuddered throughout the house. 'I'm outta here,' Tosh muttered blackly, pulling a sweater over his head. 'You fucking let me know when the fucker comes back,' he said, directing his venom at Beth. 'Fucking wanker.'

4

This Cancer of the Senses

Devastated, Beth watched as the skinny figure disappeared from sight. The house was now eerily silent. Molly stood in the downstairs hallway, her hands hanging down at her sides, nails scraping at the insides of her palms, her blue eyes red-rimmed, sore. Suddenly, she dropped down onto the bottom stair, the step squeaking as she did so. 'My God! What was that all about? Do you think it was just drugs?' Beth joined her in the passage. One of the pictures that hung above the staircase had been dislodged on Zach's journey downwards and she tried to straighten it, straining to her full height. 'He really appeared to be nuts, didn't he?' she responded. 'I've never seen him like *that* before! I never even heard them come in.' The hair at the nape of her neck was clammy from anxiety and she gathered it into a ball, winding it around her head. 'Should we check his room? Maybe he's left something behind.'

The corridor had borne the brunt of Zach's kicks, and dirty marks blotted the walls where splashes of blood had dried. Molly stood outside the bedroom, fearful of what they would find. She rubbed the residue of tears from her cheeks. Cautiously, Beth opened the door. It creaked. A gust of wind hit her. Every sash window was open to the elements. The curtains were pulled haphazardly across them, so that the bright morning sunlight spilled into the room, illuminating the chaos within Zach's brain. Beth's mouth gaped in disbelief.

The bedroom walls were swathed in magazine covers, CD inserts and fragments of paper glued together haphazardly, so that it was difficult to determine where one finished and the other began. On each and every scrap was written some kind of mathematical equation, strange chaos theory, hieroglyphics or Egyptian diagrams. The writing overran the glossy pullouts onto the wallpaper beneath. The further they ventured into the room, the more bizarre an experience it became. Books on cosmic themes, ancient Egypt, spaceships and planets were displayed as if in a museum or library, stacked one against the other, not randomly but as if there was some kind of organising principle in the confused jumble of Zach's mind. Other books were piled together in towers; his tapes and CDs were arranged in patterns and sequences. Even his guitar was coated in inks and colours and diagrams. Scrawled over the walls, too, interspersed with arrows and geometric shapes, was some kind of algebra. To the uninformed, it would have looked like the result of a mathematical genius's brainstorm. There were even, apparently, conclusive answers to these equations but the writing was illegible and the sums made no sense.

Beth and Molly picked their way through the maze. Screwed-up handwritten scraps of paper littered the floor between the tower blocks of books and CDs, and Zach had unceremoniously yanked his clothes out of the wardrobes, so that they resembled fodder for Third World relief. Drawers were left open and socks and underwear were thrown onto the carpet, bundled together in a jumble. The ubiquitous half-drunk tumblers of Coke and water were placed on every shelf and his sheets and duvet were bunched up in a heap. Molly was the first to break the silence. 'I can't believe he's done this,' she said, brushing against a tower of *National Geographics*. 'It's mad. Do you think it could mean something?' Beth quickly straightened the magazines before they tumbled over. 'Who knows what it means to him. He's obviously done it for some reason or other. He must really be cracked.' Molly's breath came anxiously and she wrung her hands together as if trying to eradicate the fears of the last few hours. 'You know, he's been acting weirdly for months,' she said, now hugging Beth, 'but I never imagined that he could do something like this. There's something really abnormally wrong but I can't get my head around it.'

Beth extricated herself from Molly's anguished embrace. 'I think we should leave it. I don't know what to do here.' She turned to walk out of the room, shivering, as the cold air from the open windows had whipped at her T-shirt, exposing her belly. 'Molly?' Zach's girlfriend wiped at her eyes. Avoiding the debris, she joined Beth in the hallway. 'I'm going home, Beth,' she said quietly. 'Let me know if he comes back, will you? I'll come back later. I'm too spooked.' She collected her bag from Beth's room. At the front door, Beth clasped Molly, holding her just a bit longer than usual, needing the reassurance of someone she knew. She was bewildered by the events, unable to take a decision that no fifteen year old should have to take. 'Do you think I should call my parents?' she asked her friend. Molly's restless, intelligent eyes widened with the recognition that the two of them were still alone in the turmoil. 'Maybe later,' she responded. 'Maybe you should wait a bit.'

In the silence, Beth closed the front door and retraced her steps back up to the comfort of her own room. Her bed. Her things. Later that afternoon, after Molly had returned to maintain a vigil with Beth, the phone rang, the harsh sound punctuating the stillness. Beth lifted the receiver hesitantly. An unknown woman's voice asked her if she was related to Zach. Beth's heart throbbed wildly. 'Yes,' she responded hurriedly. 'What's happened? Is he all right? I haven't seen him since this morning.' She heard noises at the end of the phone, shuffling papers, a Tannoy in the distance. 'It's all right,' the voice said. 'I'm Renata Graham, a social worker. I have Zach here at the . . .' Noises in the background and Beth's panic meant she was unable to hear where exactly Zach was. Something to do with Middlesex. 'The police have brought him to us. He's very confused and distressed and upset.' Beth began to cry, the tears dripping onto the back of her hand. 'He was trying to break into an old lady's flat in Kilburn,' Renata explained. 'The other tenants called the police. It seems that he'd put himself in a dangerous situation there but he was cooperative and the police could see that he was ill, so they didn't take him to the station. They brought him here to us – to the hospital.'

Beth was unable to take in any more information. 'What shall I do?' she begged of the social worker. 'My parents are away but they're on their way home now. We're waiting for them.' Beth sobbed, great shuddering breaths that burned her throat. 'I don't know what to do.'

Then Renata asked Beth a chilling question: 'Has Zach had any other experiences like this?'

* * *

For a week or so after he left hospital, I followed Zach around like a sinister private detective. I tried my best to appear calm and normal and to avoid giving him the impression that I was pursuing him. I made short notes in order to be able to determine how his moods differed. The hospital had not given him any medication, nor had they recommended that I contact another doctor. They had wanted to keep him there, but in a half-hearted manner, so it was quite easy for Zach to make the decision that he was well enough to discharge himself. He was over eighteen and therefore an adult.

The rest of us walked around the house on eggshells, not knowing with which of Zach's moods we would be confronted. That first Sunday evening, before he'd been discharged from hospital, Sam and I were both shocked into silence by the turmoil in his room – the room that Beth and Molly had retreated from in astonishment. Beth and I cleared it of all the detritus – the abundant paper, the filthy glasses and the rubbish strewn about the floor. We tidied the books and CDs and videotapes; we washed the sheets and duvet; we made the bed and rearranged the clothes.

The walls were problematic. Between us, we somehow managed to clean the wallpaper so that only shadows of the diagrams of suns, moons, spaceships and pyramids revealed themselves between the normal boy's-bedroom stripes. It calmed our fevered brows but did not lessen the anxieties brooding in our chests.

To some extent, we believed that we had dealt with this descent into confusion and madness but my notes highlight the daily attrition to our senses. When Zach returned, he complained bitterly to us that we had 'destroyed the balance' of his room. To this day, he has yet to find me blameless.

> ***26th October***
> *One week later. He's still quite high. He's very talkative, although will listen to the other side (me). He walked with Sam last night and told him of his previous police cautions. Would he have been so honest normally? He still believes that he was right in his behaviour (breaking into old people's homes?). He's no longer so threatening with me, but is this because he knows I don't want to hear it? He ate reasonably well but was still up at 1 a.m. Not so manic in presentation as previously but he's still trying hard to please – too much. He said that he had had a long conversation with Dominic's mother, Maggie, and told her that he was 'Perfectly well – in fact, he'd never felt better! In fact, everything was just fine!' He told her that he was 'perfectly happy – never happier'. He appears to have lost his cynical edge. Will it come back? I fear that he will lose his friends if he remains so elated.*

> ***27th October***
> *He was reasonable at 11.30, and then he became quite manic and blames me for throwing away his diagrams and writings and cosmic insights and theories. He's angry and almost delusional and needs to talk about it – constantly. He says he's mad but won't agree to see a psychiatrist – says they're all 'evil and mad' and that the world is run by 'mad, evil people'. He says that he has to move out because he's 'breaking up the family' and finds it 'heartbreaking' to see me like this. Then he adds that he's 'cracked everything'.*

28th October

I didn't see much of him today. He went out last night to the pub and then, much later, he and Tosh and Alexei broke into the park and played football but it was three in the morning and too cold, so they came home. Each time I saw him during the day, he appeared quite lucid, then at seven o'clock he called me from a pub. I asked when he would be back and he replied abrasively, 'Whenever, just whenever.' At least he called. So I waited up for him. He came in at just past midnight. We had a long talk. He's very emotional and veers from tears to hostility in the same sentence.

We realised that we had to seek help. Every day presented us with different problems. Zach hardly slept and he barely ate. Sometimes he showered once a day, on other days he might take two or three baths and showers or he might simply stay for days in the same clothes that he had slept in, not bothering to wash, brush his teeth or shovel down the enormous amounts of food that previously used to disappear into his lanky frame. Our tall, thin, floppy-haired son, who had been, like Harry Enfield's Kevin, a typical teenager, was now a distressed, manic young man whom we no longer recognised. He came in and out of the house at all hours, playing his music loudly and endlessly, stomping up and down the stairs, banging doors and talking to anyone who was willing to speak with him. He couldn't sleep and spent hours on the phone to whoever was up and prepared to listen to long, monotonous harangues. I came to dread those wild nights, lying awake, wishing for the dawn in the hope that Zach would have found some peace. Sam absented himself from us, just wanting it all to go away. He found much to fill his time so that he wouldn't have to be around Zach. Beth and I kept things going and I felt terribly remorseful that she too should have to experience this pain, these responsibilities.

Yet somehow Zach managed to keep some things organised in his head. For months, the band had been booked to perform their set in front of an invited audience of record-company contacts, tour managers, fans and journalists. The gig was to take place in late November and it was meant to be their big chance. A tour of Ireland was in the offing – gigs at universities and colleges up and down the country. They'd released their first recording, a five-track demo, which had been very favourably reviewed and had received much radio airplay. Zach insisted that the band were going to play the showcase. We hoped that if we ferried him to and from practices and rehearsals, we'd be able to keep a sharp eye on him while also taking some of the pressure off him, so Sam and I generally drove Zach and the boys and all the equipment to wherever they were rehearsing. It was punishing and I never had any idea what kind of mood Zach would be in. He was sometimes grateful, sometimes resentful and often angry and irritable. Finally, a friend recommended a psychiatrist, a guy her son had been seeing for anger management. I hoped that maybe he would be the answer.

I persuaded Zach that we had to see someone, putting it to him that he should get help with sleeping, rather than trying to convince him that he needed treatment for a mental illness or drug use. With great reluctance, he agreed to see the highly recommended Dr Goode, remonstrating with me the entire journey to town that it was a complete waste of time and money going to see a psychiatrist and that the money could be put to far better use than going into the pocket of an amoral shrink. With buttoned lips, my head down, I endeavoured to ignore his hostility and drove. I was getting to the very end of my tolerance for these chaotic days. I was emotionally and physically overwhelmed and desperate to get some help. If a so-called miracle worker had been recommended, so be it. Thus we finally made it to the first of the medical profession whose existence is predicated on the insanity of others.

Dr Goode worked out of a series of large, bright rooms in central London. After the initial greetings, he led us into a room containing the requisite scholarly tomes stacked on shelves opposite a tall, old-fashioned coatrack that held a number of hats, coats and walking sticks. There was no clichéd Freudian chaise longue in residence but a smell of cigar smoke pervaded, though the offending item was not to be seen. Three comfortable chairs were placed in front of a spacious, leather-lined antique desk. Large green succulents bookended it, while two boxes of tissues and a pitcher of water were placed conveniently in front of us. Sitting himself behind its splendour, Dr Goode picked up a fine-looking gold-nibbed fountain pen, which he held poised above virgin white notepaper. We were ready to rock and roll.

5

Autumn Heads for Winter

Our first meeting was not encouraging. Zach slouched down in the chair, his shoulders drawn in to his chest. His face was sweaty and grubby, his hair dull and greasy, his clothing in disarray. He kicked out at the carpet, resentful and irrepressibly irritable. He protested that he should not be there and attacked me verbally. I wanted to explain what had happened to Zach and how badly it had affected us, in the hope that somehow Dr Goode would be able to discern the reality of the situation. He asked Zach to explain the circumstances that had caused us so much anxiety.

Fascinatingly, while he spoke with the psychiatrist, Zach's attitude changed. Although his hostility to me did not subside, he became calmer and less argumentative with Dr Goode, all the while reiterating his opposition to my belief that he needed to see a psychiatrist and repeating that there was nothing wrong with him. He had stupidly taken some drugs, he explained, having an allergic reaction that led to him being erroneously arrested and sent to a psychiatric ward. It was all a mistake. Things had got out of hand. He was stressed and hadn't been sleeping properly. Things would now revert to the way they had been prior to the end of October. He wouldn't use drugs again. Mental illness, he argued, was an extraordinary explanation. It was my fault that he was here, for no apparent purpose, and could we please go home?

Dr Goode asked for my response to this diatribe. I struggled to explain to Zach that his behaviour had been inappropriate, that it was not realistic to believe that how he had been behaving was within the bounds of reasonable expectations. I tried not to be antagonistic but it was difficult. Dr Goode asked his questions in a quiet and succinct manner and did not patronise his patient. I got the impression that he wanted Zach to feel that he was a friend. He presumably believed that in order for Zach to do as he advised, he had to persuade Zach to like him. In the end, Zach did not dislike him but neither did he do as he requested.

After about forty minutes, Dr Goode placed his fountain pen on the once unblemished paper, now a spider's web of scrawled notes. He laced his fingers together and looked up at Zach. 'I'm not going to make a formal diagnosis at this time,' he said. 'There's no point. You may still be suffering from a drug-induced psychosis. There may be a mood disorder.' He looked at me. 'I'm going to prescribe Zach some medication. It will calm him down. I'll also give him some pills to help him sleep.' He then spoke to Zach. 'I suggest,' he motioned his head towards me, 'that you try to do as your parents ask. Things will be a lot easier for you then, Zach. Try not to be antagonistic. Eat, sleep and don't use any other drugs. We should then be able to make some sort of headway.' Zach's grin said it all: 'That's what you think!'

Dr Goode wrote for a moment and handed me the prescription: zopiclone for his sleeplessness, lorazepam to address anxiety, and haloperidol, an antipsychotic medication, for his unstable moods. The doctor turned to his diary and made notes. 'We'll meet again next week to see how things go. You can call me at any time. My secretary can always get hold of me if it's an emergency.' I sat on the end of the chair, willing Dr Goode to allay my fears. I felt utterly inarticulate and he did not, it appeared to me, understand why I needed a diagnosis, a reason. I was terrified of going back home again with Zach and resuming these restless, endless nights and days. The most worrying aspect, the drugs, was a separate issue, he posited, a red herring, and at this juncture he would not address Zach's copious narcotic ingestion, sending us home with what seemed to me to be unhelpful suggestions as to how we could best manage the situation.

We were always able to contact Dr Goode. He apparently worked seven days a week, rarely taking a holiday, except for the usual deadly August break,[6] but I felt he never really got to the bottom of Zach's increasing mental distress. At no time over the next three years did he write us a report on Zach's condition and treatment, nor provide us with a copy of the notes that I assume he sent to our GP. We saw him often, Sam and I together or Zach alone or the three of us sitting in front of him, although I would not describe our meetings as family therapy. That would not come until much further along the line. In hindsight, family therapy would have been enormously beneficial but he never suggested it to me, although I requested it. He prescribed an array of medication with varying effects, telling us that Zach was suffering a psychotic illness with manic tendencies that *could* be manic depression. It took a good year before Zach was given a definite diagnosis of manic depression.

Between shuttling Zach and the band and the equipment to practices, I struggled to persuade him to at least try to be a part of our lives. Once or twice, he came with me to walk the dog but I could tell he was falling apart, somehow disappearing as a person. He felt generally unwell, he said. He looked absolutely awful. His face was lifeless, his eyes dull. He held himself as though he had no desire to remain upright. He complained that the ground was uneven, that noises were louder, that colours were brighter, more frightening. He talked obsessively about the end of the world and the melting of the polar ice caps, his omniscience and how he was 'suffering for everyone'. It was rare that what he said made sense. He repeated sentences he'd gleaned from magazines and newspapers, and quoted passages from books; he rhymed and riddled and distorted poetry. It was utterly distressing. He shambled through the days, his shoulders hunched, his head down, his hands shaking, fearful that he would not be able to play his guitar. Although he was taking the sleeping pills, his sleep was disturbed and he would get up countless times during the night, having had, he explained, the most terrifying nightmares. At this stage, he had been prescribed the sleeping pills, a mild tranquilliser and the antipsychotic medication but nothing appeared to help him; all they seemed to do was give him horrid side effects: an unhealthy, sweaty pallor, a runny nose and unnatural facial movements. We were very frightened for him.

How we endured the next two to three weeks, I really do not remember. All appears to be opaque and then, unpredictably, the fog clears to reveal vivid flashes like splintered glass. Everything was geared towards the gig but none of us believed that Zach would be able, even with our help, to hold it together enough to play the set in front of a capacity crowd. We handled him as gently as we could, all the time endeavouring to avoid his distress. Sam, Beth and I tried to live as normal a life as possible. Christmas was upon us. It was exceptionally cold and the nights were long and brutal. Beth saw her friends but her heart wasn't in it. Sam was busy with work and networking and parties. My life revolved around Zach and the house and those friends whom I felt able to see. And all the time, Zach disintegrated further. Visits to Dr Goode seemed pointless. He played around with the medication and the advice he advanced to Zach but Zach was absent. My notes reveal the turmoil:

24th November
He was up very early and burbling some rubbish or other. Obviously little sleep. Very worrying. He's anxious. Manic. Up and down. I called Dr Goode. He told me to bring him over. He had a window. Twenty minutes. Although severely agitated and unable to remain calm and still, Zach was quite quiet in the car. After seeing him, Dr Goode said he was 'As high as a kite!' In the evening I gave him one tablet. He seemed slightly better. After that he went out. I couldn't stop him. Said he was going to go to Molly's but he didn't turn up.

It was a freezing cold evening and he told me later that he walked around Hampstead. He withdrew £200 from his bank account, then discarded his jacket, sweater, bag and wallet somewhere, God knows where, and, he said, 'I went to Wembley Stadium and broke in. There was no one there, no security, nothing. I scaled the peaks and went onto the turf.' This was rubbish, surely? Could you believe it? Was it actually possible?

At midnight, agitated, extremely emotional and panicking, he called Molly to tell her what he had done. She told him to get a taxi and to go home. She immediately rang Beth to tell her where he was and what had happened and Beth ran up to my bedroom to tell me, her face a mask of anxiety. He finally arrived home at 1.00 a.m., icy cold, wet through, distraught, in a complete state. He cried pitifully and said that it was the worst night of his life. He said he'd been running up and down Finchley Road and that the owner of one of the kebab shops had run into the street when he saw him and tried to give him something to eat! But he was afraid to stop. So bizarre . . .

He wanted to sleep with Max, in his basket. I persuaded him to eat some pizza and to go to bed, smothering him with his duvet and extra blankets. He slept until quite late, utterly worn out.

25th November

I kept on opening and closing his door to make sure that he was still there, asleep. I didn't know whether I wanted him to stay in bed all day and then be up all night or to be up and driving us mad with his manic energy. He was finally up at 12.30 p.m. and seemed quite reasonable. I received a phone call from a woman who had found his wallet. He had discarded it along with his clothes in a cul-de-sac around the corner from us. Fortunately his address and telephone number were in it. She said she would bring it round to us. She did so later. There are good people. There are human beings, like the kebab man and this woman, who recognise when kids are out of kilter. When she arrived with his things he put on a charming act, pretending to be the recalcitrant child. She explained to me that he had also broken into a house where they were holding a prayer meeting for someone who had recently died and the mourners had been obliged to eject him from the premises because his behaviour was so outrageous and frightening. I was mortified. He laughed and apologised to her, 'Silly me, I'm such a naughty boy!' I told her how thankful we were to her. She appeared to understand my distress. I managed to get her address from her so that I could at least take her around a bunch of flowers. I didn't give him any more medication. Dr Goode said not to until after the show. But he's not yet down. Why so up? Why this constant trip?

The afternoon of the major gig, Zach surprisingly made it to the venue. We watched every journey he made, in and out of the car with the equipment, to and from the club for drinks or food. We would not let him out of our sight. I'm not sure how much of this he was aware of. He was generally oblivious to our reality and appeared to be functioning on a completely different level. Only the music induced him to weld together so that he did not splinter. It was a weird juxtaposition, his psychotic persona and his musical abilities. The medication had slowed him down but the mania continued apace. How was he going to perform his set, which was physically demanding even under normal circumstances?

The others arrived one by one. They set up the equipment, bantering with one another while fixing leads and microphones. Tosh was typically late and displayed his toxic characteristics in his usual violently aggressive and drunken fashion. He was deeply unhappy with our chaperoning Zach and certainly made his feelings clear, but this time we ignored his hostility in the hope that the band would come together once they were on stage. Between the five of them, they were able to run through their set. We struggled to instil in Zach the belief that something good might come out of the evening, but it was difficult to see how, especially when Tosh decided to return home for something he had 'forgotten in the rush'. Who knew what this was? We thought probably a large bottle, 100 per cent proof, although it is just as likely that it was some kind of narcotic. This pressurised the guys more, and Zach especially, even though they had become accustomed to Tosh's disappearing acts. This was an extra anxiety that everyone involved could have done without.

Looking back, I wonder why we ever felt that they could pull it off and didn't cancel the whole shebang beforehand. But the opportunity was something we believed would not present itself again and so we all became caught up in this fantastic reverie. Shortly before they were scheduled to go on stage, and with the band wondering what had happened to him, Tosh reappeared, still drunk and even more offensively insulting. In her naivety, Beth asked him why he had to come back like this. Why did he have to drink so much, why couldn't he just behave normally, respect everyone else, especially tonight? He knew that this gig was their most important and that Zach had been ill. His response was typical. He rounded on her, spitting venom. 'Shut up, you fucking bitch!' he yelled, shoving her away from him. 'Get out of my fucking way. You don't know what you're fucking talking about!' It was as if he too was possessed, his face a mask of hatred. He made her cry and instilled in me a wish to punch him.

I left the club and sat outside at one of the abandoned wooden benches. It was drizzling sporadically. I lamented my fate, feeling abnormally sorry for myself at that moment. Camden on a cold November night is not a wholly alluring place. Drunks paraded the streets and the homeless and drug dealers proliferated along the canal. One or other of us had accompanied Zach outside every time he'd wanted a cigarette or a break and by this time we wished the evening was over with. We had been hanging around the pub for hours, watching rehearsals and playing babysitter. We were haggard with nervous anxiety and irritation. I felt as if I would never be clean again. I went back inside. The venue stank of beer, smoke and takeaways. The floors were awash with spilled drinks, cigarette ends and other debris. Bodies now lined the bar, calling out for refills, and the din of the support act, together with the noise of laughter and shouting, was wearing. The place was packed, crowded with bigwigs from the record companies and their staff, as well as journalists, promoters, fans, friends and families. We recognised the reporters who had followed their every move and written about them copiously. We noted the loyal fans who had been with them from the beginning and the guys who ran fanzines throughout the country. The promoter who wanted them for the tour of Ireland was there. He loved them. 'It's arranged,' he yelled at us through the din. 'Every university!' But the atmosphere was palpably uneasy. The other act finished their set, collected their equipment and left the arena.

Everyone filed into the main space, sweaty faces glistening in the light of the overhead spots. Then Zach and the boys came out and there was a roar of anticipation. Even though Sam and I were just weary from the sheer anxiety of the whole ghastly event, the adrenalin flowed. They gathered their instruments and launched into the set. The first five numbers were amazing and they blew everyone away. Almost everybody knew the songs and sang along with them. We watched the crowd, enjoyment written vividly on their faces. The entire audience was at one, moving to the music, arms and legs pounding to the beat. Fabulously hot, we were crowded together in one sweaty mass, visibly moved.

We generally disliked Tosh's voice, which was on the whole tuneless, but Zach's playing was inspiring and uplifting. The sound was tremendous and the band as an ensemble looked great, with Zach on guitar, Tommy on bass, Jack on keyboards and Bone crashing away on the drums. Then Zach broke a guitar string. Nothing new – he was quite capable of changing guitars mid-song. But Tosh's reaction made no sense. He started screaming at Zach and then, even more bewilderingly, stopped singing. The band played on. I shuddered. 'Another of Tosh's characteristic self-centred tantrums?' I asked myself. Yes, it would appear so. Self-centred to the extreme. Throwing himself around in a frenzy, the spotlight still shining on his uncontrollable actions, he unleashed a blistering attack on one particular record company that had wanted to sign the band, working himself up into a rage against it and its employees, using the most profoundly insulting language in order to make it plain to them that he, Tosh, would never sign to them! His skinny body convulsed, his face contorted in a paroxysm of fury. 'This is our last gig!' he yelled. 'The band's breaking up tonight! You can all go fuck off!'

Baffled. Beads of perspiration laced themselves across my forehead. My heart palpitated. I stood there mesmerised. Where was this coming from? What the hell was he doing? The rest of the band continued playing without the singer, trying to keep it together. But it was impossible. Having killed the performance, Tosh kicked off an orgy of destruction. Aiming his steel toe-capped boots at the amps, he kicked time and again into the soft belly of black webbing, until they collapsed onto the back of the stage. The microphone he flung into the air, spitefully bringing it down onto the wooden struts and stamping on it until it too was destroyed. The stand he hurled into the crowd, causing everyone to scatter out of its trajectory. All the while, he continued to scream epithets at the record-company personnel and everyone in the audience.

At first, people looked at each other in bemusement. Was this a part of the act? After that, bewilderment set in and then anger. Boos and hisses greeted Tosh's performance. The diehard fans were practically catatonic in their grief at this exploit. The journalists had seen it all before. Another talented bunch of kids imploding. Drugs, booze, insanity – who cared? Then they began to leave. The Irish promoter looked over at us. Drawing his fingers across his throat in a pantomime of suicide, he smiled a rueful smile and departed with his entourage. At this juncture, as if hypnotised by Tosh, the normally sedate Jack interjected his own venomous curses. Zach and the other band members stood around the stage, looking at one another in disbelief. Jack's parents, having attended each and every live performance, looked at me, shocked. 'What's Jack doing?' they asked. Who knew? Who could understand this? For reasons that only he understood, Tosh ripped the band apart. For weeks, while Sam and I had maintained a vigil over Zach's mind, Tosh's answer to this control, compassion, succour had been coalescing into a tumultuous explosion of pent-up psychopathic rage against everyone and everything and, because it was primarily Zach's band, Zach above all. We were told by the management, 'They'll never play here again.'

* * *

26th November

Morning. Zach didn't sleep last night. He came down into the kitchen very early. He made himself some breakfast then he had a long, long shower. He's very, very talkative. Presumably what they call 'pressured speech'.[7] *But it's all rubbish. None of it makes any sense or is articulate, coherent. What's it all about? The latest symptom in the long line of weird actions is that he now demonstrates some kind of obsessive–compulsive behaviour. He tightly hangs on to his diary and keeps referring to it constantly. So odd, he generally doesn't even use one. Keeps on making lists of things he has to do. Wants to 'organise'. Talks about the band in the past tense, says he 'doesn't care'. Doesn't blame Tosh. Says it was 'time'. Disagrees when I say that Tosh deliberately destroyed everything that they had worked so relentlessly for.*

He needs constant reassurance and has to be told what to do all the time. Now he speaks in song lyrics. Something he started doing earlier this week – mostly his idols, Suede, Morrissey. This is so eerie. He had a pill at 9.00 a.m. We took Max for a walk together but he was unable to walk fast. Going up the road seemed mountainous to him. He broke down a number of times, sobbing. Says he knows he's ill but doesn't know how to deal with it. He's up and down. Goes around in circles of moods. He's manic and psychotic and then calm for a few hours afterwards and then it begins again. Agrees that he needs the medication. I really and honestly believe that he should go into hospital. I've been told to increase the dosage tomorrow – which really scares me. He dictated to me how to give him the pills. He's still talking in riddles, numbers and lyrics and appears to be getting worse, not better. He needs to sleep for many hours but how do I make him? How can we tell him how fractured he is and how emotionally vulnerable he is? He can't concentrate. Has a very short-term memory span. Repeats himself and his actions. Wants approbation. Desperately wants to be loved and nurtured. Says he needs to see Sam. He can't read or concentrate on books but will insist on reading stuff out loud.

Night. He woke up. Thought it was still daytime and that he had slept the entire night. He took yet another shower and washed his hair again. He wanted to go out. We said it wasn't safe. That he wasn't well. He should stay at home. Then he just lost all control. He ran into the hall, yelling and kicking out at us. He punched the walls, shattering the glass in the school photographs. Shards flew in all directions, littering the corridor. We remonstrated with him. We were terrified that he would slash his arms or sever an artery but he yelled at us that he was 'impervious to pain'. He refused to be still and darted from room to room, swearing, shouting and crying. If one of us came near to him he lashed out, shoving furniture in our way or throwing objects in our path. We tried to stop him but he repelled us violently, running down the stairs to the kitchen, throwing open the back door and sprinting towards the back of the garden where he threw his never-worn-before-tonight reading glasses to the ground, fracturing them. He pulled off his shoes and socks and threw them up into the trees, wildly gesticulating, yelling and crying.

The night resounded with the uncanny shrieks and howls and at this stage I was frightened that the neighbours would call the police. We persuaded him back into the house but once inside he bolted up the stairs to his bedroom. With us behind him, trying to make a grab for him, he managed to shove on more layers of clothes then clambered across his bed, saying he was going to jump from his bedroom window if we didn't let him out. He was like liquid mercury, utterly slippery and, although he's slight and thin, incredibly powerful. All the time he was shrieking hysterically and Sam was shouting at him. They had both lost control. I tried to calm them but Zach clambered onto the windowsill and he was halfway out before we physically heaved him back in, shrieking and swearing at us. It was horrifying and frightening. Who is this? Then, when Sam and I paused for breath, he bolted downstairs again and made for the kitchen door, thrusting his arm through the glass, shattering that too. Again there was glass everywhere and Sam was an emotional casualty, crying that he was no longer able to deal with him.

Once more we hauled him back into the house and this time he was restrained by Sam physically sitting on him! If it were not so horrific, it would have been funny! Beth was upstairs, under the bedclothes, and the poor dog was whimpering outside her door, terrified at these events. Sam shouted to me to call the police. To tell them that we couldn't control Zach. That someone has to help us! I shook so much that I found it almost impossible to press the digits but I managed to call and explained to them that my eighteen-year-old son had totally lost control of his senses and was attacking us. They arrived incredibly quickly and were brilliant. It appeared that the two who visited us were versed in dealing with these situations. When Zach saw them he quietened down, curiously hiding his clothing under the cushions on the settee. He played a 'role' for them. They spent ages talking to him, persuading him to calm down and to listen to us. He said he would. Then they left and his mood changed again and he recommenced the verbal assault, uncontrollably spewing the most venomous vitriol and abuse. Sam collapsed, weeping hysterically. Hesitantly, Beth appeared and attempted to console him. Noting this, Zach laughed in a maniacal high pitch, sneering scathingly that Sam was 'suffering a nervous breakdown'. Is this what they call 'transference'?

6

A Section Experience

27 NOVEMBER 1997

Somehow, I pulled myself out of bed and lugged my worn-out body into the bathroom, where I sat on the edge of the bath, too drained to lean over the basin and brush my teeth. Sam slept on. The house was silent, dead. There was life outside but I felt as though I were cocooned, as if there were layers of lagging between my emotions and reality. Every action took an age to fulfil. I ached with weariness. Everything was in slow motion. Finally showered and dressed, I crept down the stairs to the landing that led to Zach's and Beth's bedrooms. Beth's door was shut tight. Zach's was halfway open. I peered in and saw him lying in a heap across the duvet, his arms above his head, his mouth slightly open, his breathing laboured. The room was a mess. The window was open and the wind blew the curtains askew. I was frightened to make any sort of noise, wishing him to remain comatose, wanting him to sleep for as long as possible. I crept out, only to step on some broken glass that had been overlooked in the torrid night's aftermath.

Inching my way down to the kitchen, I resolutely dialled Dr Goode's emergency number. It was too early even for him, so I left a long, meandering message in the desperate hope that he would call as soon as he arrived at the office and that his dedicated secretary would impart to him the hopelessness in my voice. I fed the dog and let him out into the garden, all the time trying to avoid the glass surrounding his paws and my feet. I tried to make myself some breakfast but my appetite disappeared. All I was capable of swallowing was strong black coffee.

Within an hour, Dr Goode returned my call. Sam was up. So was Zach. The doctor advised me to bring Zach to the Griffin, a private psychiatric hospital. 'We'll assess him there,' he reassured me. 'That way we'll know how best to treat him.'

How were we going to do that? I asked myself. 'There's no way he's going to be compliant and come to hospital,' I told the doctor despondently. 'He still insists that he won't seek any medical help. What will happen when we bring him in?'

There was silence at the other end. 'You'll have to get him here somehow,' Dr Goode replied. 'I can't do anything at your home or in my office. It has to be in a hospital situation.'

I listened to him disbelievingly. Did he understand what I had just told him?

'If we are to section him,' he continued, 'then he has to be seen by two independent doctors and a social worker. We can do it from the Griffin, although quite honestly it's not totally the best way around it. But you have to get him here somehow.'[8] He breathed deeply. 'You get him here and everything will be set up for you. Let me know what happens. Be strong.'

Fine for him to tell us to be strong, I remember thinking. We were going to need more than strength. We were going to need guile and, eventually, lies and more lies. Looking back, I was (I think understandably) frustrated with the situation. No doubt we were no different to the parents of any of his other patients and, ultimately, all he could do in any case was to give advice and medication.

Zach's mood hadn't changed. He was still manic, still confused, fractured and irritable. His eyes were preternaturally bright, huge and glassy in his thin, unshaven face. He was dressed in an odd assortment of clothing. He had packed a bag.

'I'm off,' he told us.

'Off where?' we asked.

'South America, Thailand, anywhere.'

'How do you expect to get there?' we asked. 'You don't have any money. You've gone through everything you had. You've been buying everyone drinks for the last six months!'

He glared at us. I realised that I was going to have to be devious and had to think quickly. 'If you're going travelling,' I explained to him, trying not to be antagonistic, 'then you'll need to see Dr Goode before you go and have a check-up.'

Was he going to believe this transparent lie? I examined his face. Watched him considering. There was a flicker of suspicion and distrust but also of vulnerability. 'All right,' he agreed reluctantly, 'but it has to be today.'

I said that I would make the appointment with Dr Goode and made a pretence of calling him from the study before returning to Zach's bedroom, where Sam kept a vigil. 'It's OK,' I told him, looking over at Sam, whose expression was disingenuous. 'He has a space this morning. Only it has to be at the Griffin because he's working out of there all day.' An attempt at levity: 'You're not the only nutter he sees!' He laughed at that but it was a cheerless, humourless laugh.

I believed this was a dreadful piece of psychological manoeuvring but neither Sam nor I could come up with another ruse, or indeed something less deceitful. Although he made further protestations, Zach got into the car with us.

'Why do you both need to come with me to see Dr Goode? Why isn't Dad going to work?' He asked endless questions of us, irritatingly opening and closing the car windows, restlessly jiggling his legs and tapping on the seat in front of him. He insisted on taking his bag; he was going on a journey. I was terrified that he might make a bolt for it at any time. My heartbeat accelerated, my palms were sweaty and I had a lump in my stomach. The trip seemed endless, although the hospital was not very far away. Traffic clogged the streets and pedestrians appeared intent on throwing themselves under the wheels of the car. We made inane conversation, anything to steer our minds away from what was about to happen, although we had no clear idea as to what indeed was to happen. We only knew that something had to be done with Zach. He had to be held in a secure environment so that events like those of last night would not be repeated. When we arrived at the hospital, we hustled him in, fearing his violence and anger, but he allowed himself to be guided into the lobby and Dr Goode appeared and took him away from us.

Unlike at the Central Middlesex, there was no human waste embellishing these walls. Instead there were single rooms, each containing a narrow bed, a side table with a jug of water and a small en suite bathroom. It was pure luxury by comparison. There were even Laura Ashley printed curtains at the windows. The barred windows. We were shown to a room close to the nurses' station and requested to wait there while Zach was being assessed. There was nothing to do *but* wait. We paced up and down, making small talk, attempting to mask our anxiety.

Eventually, after about two hours, Zach was brought in. He was furious with us and very agitated. 'Where were you?' he demanded. 'Why are they keeping me here like this?' He strode over to the bed and, gathering his backpack and loading it onto his shoulders, he headed toward the door. 'I'm going travelling and you can't fucking stop me!' Sam made a grab for him but he rushed out of the room, down the corridor towards the exit. Two middle-aged men dressed in blue uniforms similar to those worn by security guards scuttled out of the nurses' station towards him. Seeing them, he made an about-turn and bolted in the other direction. We scurried out of the room, staggered that he was behaving so uncontrollably here.

The guards sprinted towards him shouting, 'Zach, come back here! Don't be ridiculous! Come on, lad!' There was only one exit from the ward and that was where the nurses' station was situated. As the ward itself was a U-shape with individual rooms leading off it, there was no other way out. Whichever way he ran, Zach could only end up at the same place. He continued running, down the corridor, in and out of rooms, becoming more out of control the faster he ran, the longer he managed to evade the guards. Other patients came out of their rooms to see what all the commotion was about and support staff called for them not to become involved. The guards shouted for us to go into Zach's room, wait there, that they would manage the situation, that it was best if we were not a party to it. Reluctantly, we did, but not before we saw them finally catch up with Zach and, with no degree of sensitivity, manhandle him to the floor. One of them drew out a syringe and roughly injected him in his rear. Section 3 – up to six months' hospitalisation.

* * *

The sun shone on frosty days, or it was grey and cloudy. Sometimes it rained. Life went on. People worked, they dined out, they saw movies. The hype of Christmas reached its apotheosis and we, too, were caught up in it. Sam travelled, visiting clients, Beth toiled on her various projects. I walked the dog, managed the housework, saw friends and continued my assignments, taking myself off to the library to try to do my research or write up my notes, but my heart wasn't in it. It snowed. We went out to parties, feigning enjoyment, while all the time my stomach was knotted, my appetite reduced, my heart hurting, heavy. It was an awful time. I couldn't believe that it was happening to us. I remember one evening Sam and I visited Zach in hospital before going on to a Christmas party. Turning up in our black-tie finery, we made a quite surreal addition to the comings and goings on Zach's psychiatric ward. He noticed nothing, totally and compellingly involved as he was in his own horror film. The sadness of it enveloped us all when we should have been looking forward to Christmas – delicious food, the unwrapping of presents and the joy of being together.

We visited Zach regularly and his mood veered wildly. There were times when he appeared pleased to see us, others when he was maniacally resentful. His demands increased, for cola, for sandwiches, for any food that was not prepared at the Griffin. Sweet stuff, cigarettes, croissants, burgers, chips. His medication was increased, a nasty, hefty dosage of antipsychotic haloperidol doled out to him every night. He loathed it. It gave him the shakes, made him shuffle like an old man, his nose ran, he drooled and exhibited Parkinsonian facial tics. He coughed incessantly, wiping the sputum away from his lips with the back of his hand. He hated the remedy and so did we. They told us that it was the best for bringing him down from the florid mania that he was experiencing. He wanted his guitar, so we took it in to him; he wanted music, so a small stereo system made its way to his room. But for the next few weeks, it was rare that he bothered with either.

He wandered around the wards, going from room to room, restlessly talking to whoever was about. There was a mix of patients. He was on a locked ward and there were several like him, many young people with varying psychiatric disorders whose fees were met by their private health companies. There were also others who, because of the lack of NHS facilities, were deposited in the Griffin at immense cost to local authorities. Most suffered a range of mental-health problems; some were chronically ill and, were it not for their having been picked up by the police, would have been sleeping rough on the streets, abandoned and alone. George, Zach's Glaswegian charge nurse, a short, tough, no-nonsense Celt with a heart of gold, tried to paint him a picture of how it would be for him if he didn't look after himself and stop taking drugs. 'You're no gonnae like it on an NHS ward, Zach, when there's some old geezer pukin' his guts out in the next bed to yours or someone else stealin' your bits. You're no likely to have your own bathroom there. They're no gonnae look after ye like I do! Be a good wee boy and do as your mama says!' How likely was that?

The weeks passed while Zach remained in hospital, the winter having arrived with an Arctic chill. Pedestrians walked with their heads down, coats buttoned up, scarves, gloves, breath forming white clouds that glistened in the murk. Slushy, dirty piles of ice and gritty snow were scraped by the side of the streets, mixed together with salt and sand, staining leather, spraying jeans. Beth and I collected Zach from the Griffin for an afternoon out. 'Lunch?' I asked him. He gave me an imperceptible nod. 'Where to?' I queried again.

He was apathetic. 'Wherever you like,' he responded. 'It doesn't matter.' Beth and I looked at one another. This was going to be difficult. We decided to go into Café Rouge. It stank of musty cigarettes and chips, and the wooden floor was slimy from wet shoes and umbrellas, but it was hot inside and we sat ourselves at a table by the window overlooking the High Street.

Zach had difficulty removing his jacket. His fingers shook so much they were unable to gain leverage over the buttons but he refused help. The waitress appeared and we ordered. Zach fumbled with cigarette papers and loose tobacco. It seemed to take an age for him to roll a short, thin, battered fag. We attempted conversation. Beth was as uncomfortable and anxious as me. Zach was quite uninterested in discussing anything to do with either the outside world or his inner journey, or anything to do with the hospital. Perspiration dotted his forehead and his eyes were lacklustre. There was a tremor in his legs and his knees jerked up and down uncontrollably. While he ate, he continued to smoke the cigarette, picking it up between bites of burger. He wasn't interested in the food. He stared at the table, showing no joy in having time out. He pushed the plate away from him. None of us had any appetite. Cheerful lives went on at tables surrounding us; we were in a vacuum of grey despondency, compassion and guilt.

'Is there anything else you'd like to do now?' I asked after Beth and I too had pushed our food away, half finished.

'No. Just take me back.'

So back we went to the hospital and I was glad to take him there.

It was so hard to be with him, to have to face him, to bear his pain. To watch him suffering – and he *was* suffering. I felt so bad: I had betrayed him so shoddily but I had no idea what else I could have done. No one had given any of us directions. No one had explained to us what his condition was, what we could expect, how he might react to the medications, to his hospitalisation. Sam and I felt as though we were alone in the world having to deal with Zach's illness. In a despondent moment, I toured the local bookshop and purchased a book about mental disorders, but we still had no firm diagnosis (the doctors had advised us that they had to see how Zach responded to the medication he was being given) and reading these case histories appalled me. I was aghast at the horror of it all. None of it made sense. How could it be happening to us? Was it possible that he was schizophrenic? Could he be bipolar? Was there a cure?

We had many a spat with him during his sojourn in hospital. There were days when we arrived to visit him laden with goodies in order to placate our feelings of remorse and he was unable to control his anger and hostility toward us, kicking doors, petulantly breaking things. After twenty minutes or so of venomous invective and ugly threats, we would leave, exhausted and emotionally ravaged. He refused to join in with group therapy or go to the various remedial and art classes that were held. He refused to talk about himself to the doctors or support staff. He was increasingly difficult to reach. However, in spite of his bitterness, animosity and resentment, Zach did write to us while in the Griffin. It's a very touching letter. He's still high but it's before he slips down towards the flip-side of mania and during one of those spells when some insight cracks through:

Dear Mum and Dad:
I am genuinely sorry for the undue stress that I have put on you over the last 6 weeks/4 years.

I am deeply gratified by the extremes you have taken to ensure my well-being and speedy recovery. Believe it or not, I feel that these last few days at the Griffin have most definitely been beneficial to my gradual recovery. As it goes, at this particular moment I have 'never felt better' and am looking forward to sleeping in my own bed (eventually) and seeing Max.

I solemnly promise NOT to indulge in any dangerous narcotic substances EVER again.[9]

I have started to feel properly normal again (as I have most definitely caught up with my sleeping problem). My recovery seems to have gone hand in hand with the general reduction of pills . . . yesterday you saw me at my very worst . . . but from now on 'things can only get better'. Ever since I took the meds last night I have felt warm and relaxed and in perfect condition to come home.

Love you lots, Zach xxx

ps Thanks for the chocolates and goodies . . . you must be the greatest parents in the world.

pps I worked out that I am still worth over £400.

The reason that MOST people like it here is because it is preferable to home.

However, I would feel far more comfortable with my own familiar surroundings.

7

An Interlude

July 1998

Andalucía was magical. Sam and I had rented a small car and driven from parador to parador. I adored the heat, the amazing colours of the skies, the shimmering edifices rising out of distant hills. White towns, white heat, azure pools and quiescence. It was as if the last year had faded into a distant fugue. I suppose it was a denial, a pretence that it had never happened. It was easy enough to do. We ate, drank, shopped and sunbathed. We endeavoured to sleep away some of the fears and anxieties that had remained dormant within us. We were staying in Ronda with our friends Carlos and Luisa, when, in the midst of an eight-course tasting menu, Sam's mobile rang. It was Molly's mother, Olivia. 'I'm so sorry to speak to you now and to have to tell you this,' she explained, 'but Molly called. She's very upset. Zach's been arrested in Greece and he's in a jail on an island somewhere. Looks like he's ill again.'

* * *

The Griffin had discharged Zach after Christmas. He wasn't cured and he wasn't well but, they explained, there was no reason for him to remain there. Evidently the psychiatrists reckoned that he was no longer a danger to himself. The elation had abated. Indeed, his condition was the polar opposite. For the next four to five months, he experienced the most acute misery. This was the reverse of mania: suicidal depression, an utterly grotesque, debilitating disease. The break-up of the band had clearly had a severely detrimental effect on his fragile psyche but he was unwilling to talk about it. He blamed himself for that night. He refused to apportion blame to Tosh and, apart from Tommy, none of the group had visited him or spoken with him.

Tommy and Dominic were practically the only ones among his friends who made the effort to visit him during the time he stayed in the clinic. Zach was wary of talking to anyone about anything remotely to do with how he was actually feeling, other than to complain bitterly about how our actions had resulted in his being admitted to hospital and sectioned. He blamed me entirely for his incarceration. None of it was his fault. He held me responsible for having deceived him into going to hospital and then having been a party to the section. I am a few months older than Sam and legally judged to be Zach's principal carer. I doubt he saw it like that. It was extremely difficult to deal with Zach's denial of responsibility as well as with the guilt I did indeed experience. It was horrendous to have to be a signatory to one's son being locked up and forcibly prescribed mind-numbing chemical straitjackets. I could not remember a time during his childhood or adolescence when he had experienced such acute melancholia and again he hurled his accusations towards me. 'I've never been depressed until now!' he ranted. 'It's all these fucking pills you've made me take – that horrific haloperidol . . .' Was the despair the result of the psychological trauma that had emanated from the break-up of the band or was it the organic volte-face of manic depression?

This debilitated Zach had turned into a reclusive depressive who found it practically impossible to leave his bed. He had to force himself to get up, otherwise the likelihood was that he could remain there for days on end. If I did not take him food to eat, he would not bother to go down to the kitchen to fix anything. Proper meals remained uneaten. He simply tolerated junk food and a never-ending supply of Coca-Cola. Washing himself and wearing clean clothes were not part of his agenda. When he did get up, it was to shamble around the house, switching the television on and off, playing music half-heartedly or going in and out of the garden to smoke his roll-ups. He was unable to focus on any one thing, even to read the sports section or listen to the football scores. He occasionally requested that I drive him over to Molly's, where he would sit, head down on her bed, dejectedly mumbling inanities. They had reignited their relationship in a somewhat desultory way and she tried hard to help, spending hours with him so that he would not feel that she too had abandoned him.

Where once he would have had a social life and gone out with the boys to the pub, to gigs or band practice, none of this was now possible. Inexplicably, he persisted in maintaining his relationship with Tosh. However, on the nights that they got together, Zach would invariably arrive home in a bitter temper, worse for the drink that Tosh manoeuvred him into swigging, despondent and morose. On the whole, apart from Dominic, his closer friends had melted away. Dominic remained there for him, uncritical and caring. He would turn up at the house and coerce Zach out of his room, ignoring his feeble excuses that he had no energy, desire or motivation to see him. But he was alone in his efforts. If Zach was in shock and denial, then it was hardly surprising that the mostly immature and unreliable young men surrounding him would prefer not to have to face him. They had earlier been unable to deal with his mania. How were they possibly going to cope with his depression?

Our meetings with Dr Goode were consistently frustrating and, by and large, unproductive. The three of us would go along together or Sam and I would go alone. Dr Goode varied the medications, trying a bit of this, adding a bit of that, but nothing changed Zach's mood. He remained dulled, his world grey, and by all appearances, despondency was the most prevalent emotion he experienced. He existed in an all-pervading numbness. When Molly was around, he tried harder but inevitably there would be words of some sort between them and tears at the end of her visit. The only thing that did appear to give him some solace was the thought of travelling – getting away somewhere, anywhere, so that these walls were not a constant reminder of his nothingness.

I perceived his fixation on all things Egyptian to be wholly inappropriate, a part of his illness, but he was desperate to go there. 'Why don't you take him there, then?' queried Goode. For once, it was as if a beam of light had illuminated the obvious. Why not indeed? It was not entirely out of the question. Sam could take a week's holiday and there was nothing, apart perhaps from his debilitated mental health, to stop Zach from travelling. We discussed it. Sam made enquiries. We both believed that Sam should be the one to go with him, that their relationship needed a fillip, that maybe some father–son bonding would be advantageous to them both. Beth needed me at home and I needed a break from Zach. So, in spite of the recent wave of atrocities in Egypt, during which Islamic terrorists had murdered a number of Western tourists, a booking was made and they went off together.

Sprawling Cairo, the pyramids, the Great Mosque and the Egyptian Museum were all to be stops on their journey. Zach took pleasure in the trip along the Nile to see the son et lumière performance at Giza and smoked his first hubble-bubble. He actually laughed at the surreal juxtaposition of the Pizza Hut franchise opposite the Sphinx and was enthralled at the enormity of the Valley of the Kings at Luxor. Both Sam and he described feeling a frisson of curiosity mixed with fear at having to be escorted by a bevy of armed guards to Aswan, their convoy of jeeps enjoying the accompaniment of heavily armed soldiers hanging out of the back doors and smoking cheroots. The camels en route, their back legs hobbled and tied to stakes in the ground, stared moodily at them or yawned, their great teeth chomping with cartoon clarity. They stayed at near-empty hotels, ate in deserted dining rooms and swam in huge art deco swimming pools. The food was wonderful, the weather bright and sultry, and their guides lavished time and attention on them: they were practically the only tourists in the land. Halcyon days.

In photos taken by Sam against all the classic backdrops, Zach looks more human, staring out towards the camera, eyes half shut against the glare, his sunglasses perched on top of his head, his shoulders slumped. He remained thin, his jeans hanging down low on his belly, his belt straining to keep them up. On the whole, his mood stayed subdued. He became angry during a boat trip one night when the sand was up and the wind gusted dirt and dust into gritty eyes. He berated Sam about our having connived to get him into hospital on false pretences. But this was the first and only time during the entire trip that he referred to his condition. They flew back to Cairo for one more night near the City of the Dead and then returned home.

The break was beneficial to Zach. The absent, haunted look was not entirely gone but he became more positive about life. He appreciated the trip to Egypt and did, it would appear, respect that we wanted to help him. Although unable to motivate himself entirely, he tried harder to converse with us. His mood remained quite low during the spring but Molly and he saw more of each other and decided that in the summer they wanted to go to the Greek islands and spend some time away together. Would we underwrite his costs?

It was a difficult choice to make. How much should we help? We pondered this and decided that for this year, while he was recuperating, we would pay for the flight, so long as he made an effort to find some work in the meantime. An opening for an assistant in a friend's office was offered to Zach and he just about coped with this, even though he was reluctant to get up in the morning and disliked being given tasks by a rather officious young trainee. He had always considered himself to be above all that; his arrogance never died away.

The days grew longer. Dour spring turned into dazzling summer. Then Zach began to see his old acquaintances and go out to his old haunts: the pubs, clubs and games of football in the park. His medication was decreased and visits to Dr Goode became less frequent. Drugs appeared again, after a hiatus. The furtive concealments continued in spite of our heavy rebukes.

'It's *only* draw. It helps me sleep.'

I wouldn't accept that. 'It's not "only draw",' I remonstrated with him. 'You don't know what it does to you, what effect it has on your brain. You shouldn't take anything, especially while you're taking medication!'

How much he used, I have no idea. He never appeared to have any money. 'I'm saving. Saving for *my* holiday!' Perhaps we should have said no then. No to any more money, holidays, indulgence. In the light of his refusal to commit himself to stop the drugs, we should have been heavier, more consistent. It's all very well after the event. At that time, we believed we were doing the right thing. Beth was away at summer camp and Sam and I had organised our trip to Andalucía. I guess we wanted to escape, give Zach his head and, hopefully, enough rope to make his mistakes but not to hang himself.

As Zach and Molly's departure date drew closer, I noticed that his mood had lifted considerably, so much so that I began to be concerned, although I was reluctant to discuss this with anyone, in the belief that maybe I was simply exaggerating what was a normal pattern in youthful behaviour. I told myself that we all have mood swings of some kind or other. It is not unusual to experience highs and lows throughout one's life, although, of course, these highs and lows are relative. I too was in classic denial.

The day before they were due to leave, Zach and I went to a local Italian restaurant for pizza. I noticed that his eyes were exceptionally bright again, that he spoke forcibly and quickly and that a lot of what he said was childish nonsense. I was also embarrassed in the restaurant at what I thought was his inappropriate behaviour. He was very flippant, playing around with the drinking straws and laughing and joking in an adolescent way. He thought he was very funny. I got the impression from the waiter that he was humouring us and that once we had left he would discuss us with his workmates and maybe laugh at Zach's rather infantile conduct.

Early the following morning, as arranged, I gave Zach and Molly a lift to Heathrow. They were both very chirpy, giggling and laughing the entire journey to the airport, obviously happy to be on their way. In addition to his backpack, Zach carried his guitar. I noticed that inside his guitar case he had stowed an antique walking stick given to him as a birthday present by old friends of ours. At the time, I thought it very odd that he would take it with him but kept the information to myself. I wondered what else he had secreted on him but I was pleased to see him off. The pressure of the last few months had, it seems, eroded my good sense. But it encouraged me to see him happy and this effectively prevented me from asking questions. I did not want the answers or the behaviour that would, predictably, ensue. Zach and Molly shrugged their belongings onto their shoulders and strode off to the departure lounge. I waved goodbye and drove back to London. These were the days before we were all so attached to email, so, apart from a call to say that they had arrived on an island off the coast of Turkey, we heard nothing further until the telephone call in Ronda.

8

An Athenian Tragedy

The eight-course meal did not remain a part of me. I returned to the table to find Sam in deep discussion with our friends. He looked towards me. 'Olivia said she'd call again when she has some more news. She told Molly to call her as soon as she knows something. Probably later this evening.' Sam placed his mobile in front of him. 'It's so unusual,' he said to Carlos. 'I never leave my phone on when I'm out. We seem to be fated.' My feelings were disjointed. I felt disappointed, angry and almost humiliated. I really had no wish to share our intimate family problems with others. Sam explained to our friends what had happened. The breakdown. The band. The stay in hospital. The drugs. The story so far. I apologised for having ruined their evening. Both Carlos and Luisa remonstrated that we had nothing to apologise for, that they would help in any way that they could. 'I have to go there,' I said to Sam. 'I have to go to Athens, tomorrow.'

Sam agreed that I should go, although neither of us knew exactly how I could help. He would return home with our suitcases. The problem was how to get to Athens from Ronda. There was no direct flight from either Malaga or Seville. Within an hour, Olivia called back again. 'Molly rang. She said that Zach was picked up yesterday by the local police. His behaviour had been deteriorating over the last few days, culminating in his pretty much destroying their hotel room. I think there were some punches too. She didn't say too much. They're keeping him in a prison. She's pretty upset.' Olivia paused for breath. 'Apparently they met up with a television company and had been working with them all hours. They had a row and he lost it. I'm sure there's more to the story.'

The following morning, suitcases packed, Sam waited and made telephone calls while Carlos and I sprinted around Ronda arranging my flight, or flights. We eventually found a hugely expensive way of travelling to Athens via Zurich on a one-way ticket. I had no idea how long I would be there or even what I would do when I got there. I only knew that I had to go to Greece and *save* Zach. Sam made contact with our health-insurance company so that they could begin his repatriation or at least get Zach out of jail and into a hospital. Anything, I thought, had to be better than a jail cell.

I left Spain later that afternoon. One small black bag was all I took with me. Sam's mobile, some dollars and various credit cards were stashed in my jeans pockets. I'd never travelled so light. It was emancipating, although having to change planes and wait around for hours at Zurich airport, overlooking snow-capped mountains, made the journey seem endless. It wasn't the first time that I had travelled alone but hitherto there had always been the thought that I would know someone when I arrived at my destination. I hadn't done the backpacker route. I hadn't travelled to far-off lands with a spirit of adventure. I was at a loss here and felt extremely vulnerable, even though I was only going to nearby Greece.

Someone from the television company was supposed to be meeting me on arrival. Someone who, Olivia had informed Sam, had helped Molly when Zach was arrested. Someone who spoke Greek, who knew Greece intimately and whose local knowledge would be indispensable. When eventually I did arrive, it was late at night; the sky was pitch black and the terminal mostly emptied of its day-trippers. There was no one waiting for me, no signs bearing my name, no one looking curiously at the travellers exiting the baggage hall. I had eaten nothing but two or three small packets of aeroplane crackers the entire day and had drunk only a few small plastic cups of water. I was tired, hungry and anxious. Still no one turned up to meet me. I continually called the number I had been given but no one answered. No one else was going to be involved. I was on my own.

After half an hour of waiting and walking around and around the small, basic terminal searching for the invisible someone, I made my way to the information desk and asked them to appeal for whoever was supposed to greet me to make themselves known. This request was refused. It was explained to me that unless I had the name of the person collecting me, they could not broadcast the message. It was against airport policy. I hadn't been given a name. I had no clue as to who was supposed to be there, even whether it was a man or a woman. No one called me. I waited another hour in the desperate hope that maybe they were just late or even on another flight. I became more and more anxious. I had Sam's mobile and he was still in transit. There was no one I could ask for advice or aid. I had to do it myself. 'Come on,' I said to myself. 'You can do it. Pull yourself together. That's why you're here.'

I needed somewhere to stay, somewhere close to the airport, but I didn't have a clue how to organise this. Then salvation. Hidden behind a screen in a secluded spot at the back of the concourse was a sign proclaiming 'Accommodations'. I headed towards it. A small booth stood alone, decorated with posters of the delights of Athens: the Parthenon, the Acropolis. Two young women in navy uniforms manned the desk. 'I need a hotel,' I informed one of the girls, 'somewhere safe, somewhere near the airport. Somewhere not too expensive.'

She looked at me, weighing me up, and then she consulted a list written in Greek. 'I have somewhere very close by.' She smiled at me. 'It's safe. It's got a lovely pool and is very pleasant.' She looked behind me. 'Is it just for you?'

I nodded. 'My son's ill in hospital. I've come to help him get back home.'

Her look was curious but also sympathetic. She picked up the phone and dialled a number. Speaking rapidly, she was apparently making a reservation for me. 'How many nights?' she enquired.

'I don't know,' I replied. 'Maybe three or four. I've no idea how long these things take. Could be more or less.'

She spoke again, replaced the receiver and wrote something on a piece of paper. She pointed to a section in front of the terminal. 'Give this to the taxi driver outside. He'll take you there. Pay the price on the meter. No more.'

I thanked her and walked out towards the line of waiting taxis.

Was the hotel in close proximity to the airport? Oh, absolutely. In fact, it positively overlooked the runway! For the next four days, acute anxiety giving way to hysterical mirth, I was surrounded by a legion of plane-spotters, watching the take-offs and landings of the world's major airlines. I became a plane-spotter extraordinaire, joining the anorak brigade, armed with their catalogues and notepads, in their forays to the roof of the adjoining hotel. It was my only source of pleasure during the time I spent in Athens, a somewhat surreal addendum to my late-summer vacation. The hotel was small and sweet, probably three-star, although possibly one of those stars may have been stolen from a grander establishment. A small swimming pool was ensconced between two concrete columns complete with plastic vines and metalwork window boxes full to their brims with bougainvillea. Miniature olive trees represented an attempt to enhance the surroundings and create a more Byzantine atmosphere. The late-night accordion player with his never-ending renditions of 'Zorba the Greek' was certainly no improvement.

The guests were a mixture of British and German plane-spotters and working-class Greeks spending two or three days taking in the sights of Athens while awaiting ferries to all points east and south. Their time was spent sunning themselves by the small pool and eating endless kebabs, downing the local retsina while their children ran about in among the chairs, laughing and screaming in enjoyment. I had no desire to spend any time in their company. I felt too detached from their world and the very last thing I wished to do was to give explanations as to why I was spending my summer holiday on my own. I preferred my own company and my own four walls. My room was on the third floor, reached via a narrow, claustrophobic lift. It contained a double bed, a bathroom and a small kitchen. A blue plastic table and two white plastic chairs were placed on the balcony in such a position that the voyeur would be able to see the planes landing without having to crane his neck too painfully. I ordered room service and ate Greek salad for four days. There was no television and, apart from the daily performances on the runway, there was no entertainment. The waiters must have thought I was very odd indeed.

For the first twenty-four hours, I had no idea where Zach was being held. I had been in contact with the British Embassy and was told off in no uncertain terms by a soulless female voice at the end of the telephone. 'Your son broke into and smashed up a hotel room,' she told me curtly. 'He was uncontrollable. The police are deciding whether to press charges.' I had always thought that the British Embassy was there to help but this woman seemed less than sympathetic. She repeated what the Greek police on the island had told her: 'They said he was drunk and got into a fight and the doors were destroyed.' She continued scathingly, 'There's been too much of this sort of thing going on with young English drunks.'

I reiterated that Zach didn't drink. 'My son is not a drunk,' I explained to her. 'My son is ill.' She seemed indifferent. I persisted, 'He suffers from a mental illness. There's no way that he would have got into a fight. He's passive.'

It wasn't enough to convince her to change her mind. She, of course, had no idea of Zach's history. 'That's not what I heard,' she retorted.

I slept restlessly that first night, waiting for news, unable to unwind between take-offs and landings. The following morning a telephone call from our health-insurance company's European office in Paris woke me up; it was followed by another one from Molly, who had finally managed to find a telephone that worked. Molly had left the television company and was on her way to my hotel with Zach's bags. Olivia and Sam had made contact, so someone at least knew where I was.

The insurance company offered a lifeline. They were onto the case. 'It's Erik here,' a young Swedish-accented voice announced at the end of the line. 'I've been passed your file. What a horrible thing to happen. The British Embassy has told me that Zach was very drunk and got into a fight and smashed up a hotel room. I understand he's been arrested.'

I was so angry at this lie. 'That's not true!' I interrupted him. 'Zach's ill. He has a mental-health problem and it looks as though he's been having some kind of manic episode. His girlfriend is coming to me here and she has all the information. He wasn't drunk. He was psychotic.'

Erik mulled this over. 'Let me make some calls and I'll get back to you. I'll try to find out where he is exactly and then see if we can send a doctor over to examine him. If he is ill and it's not a criminal matter, then we should be able to at least get him over to the mainland and then go on from there. Don't worry,' he reassured me, 'I've had harder cases!'

My relief was palpable. 'My mobile is stuck to my hand,' I laughed. 'You can reach me *anywhere*!'

When she eventually arrived with Zach's almost empty backpack, Molly filled me in to some extent on what had happened on the island. It was not the version spouted by our valiant Foreign Office. Things were entirely different. There was no drunken behaviour, only mania and confusion and fear. There were attacks by wild dogs and angry motorcycle rental agents and hotel staff. Zach had tried to wash his passport in the Aegean and, once again, discarded his clothes. He was very ill and totally out of it. I tried not to let my mind dwell on what could be happening to him in a Greek jail on a small island, raving.

Molly sat with me on the balcony. We had moved the chairs and table around so that we could face one another. I had ordered room service and we picked at the salads and bread and cheeses. I opened a bottle of dry white wine and poured out two glasses. We settled back into the chairs, enjoying the gentle breeze, the all-encompassing warmth. Now, as the sun was lowering itself in the evening sky and with the planes arriving more reluctantly, she told me her story.

'He hadn't been taking drugs or smoking dope or drinking,' she related. 'The first island we went to was absolutely gorgeous. We did all the usual stuff: eating, swimming, acting like tourists. Things were fine. We stayed there a few days and then decided to take the ferry to Santorini. We stayed in a tiny, beautiful hotel but I could tell that Zach was beginning to act erratically, so much so that the woman who ran the hotel threatened to kick us out if Zach couldn't behave himself. He lost his temper a number of times and broke things, like ashtrays and glasses. It wasn't that he was crazy, more that it was a kind of *drunken* thing, even though he didn't drink. It was more like antisocial behaviour, that kind of thing.

'One day, on the way to the bus stop, a dog tried to bite his trouser leg. The dog was just having fun but Zach was beginning to get paranoid. He thought the dog had rabies and tried to run away from it. Strange, really, because he loves dogs. You know he adores Max. Then he started to spend huge amounts of money. He wanted to buy me presents all the time, sunglasses and stuff, but because we couldn't make up our minds which pair to buy, he'd want to buy all the glasses in the shop! We went out for fancy meals and he was constantly buying things for his "mystical treasure hunt", so we ran out of funds.

'Then he was convinced that the island had bad vibes. He said they were affecting his mood, so we decided to return to the first island. When we got there we happened to run into some friends from home who were making a low-budget film and, as we were practically out of money because he had been spending so much, I asked if we could do some work for them – any sort of work. So they employed us as runners for a week. I thought that being busy and having a structured day would help Zach. It seemed a good idea at the time, being in a community, but he kept on renting mopeds and crashing them and then having to reimburse the cycle shops and it all came to a head one day when, in the middle of a take on the other side of the island, Zach started shouting and the director went ballistic. He told Zach to shut up and get off the set, so Zach grabbed me and forced me onto yet another moped and we rushed off only to crash it within moments.

'I realised that this was not just going to go away, this craziness. I tried to think of a way around it. I knew by now that we had to get back to London. I thought maybe I could tell the travel agent that Zach's father was ill and that this was why he was in this altered state. Maybe then the insurance company would pay to take us home. I went back to the hotel to try to do something about it but the door handle had been removed for some reason and I couldn't find Zach. Our room was on the ground floor, overlooking the gardens. I walked around the side. Zach had smashed the window. Slivers of glass were on the ground and he had made geometric patterns from them. I looked into the room and I could see that there were all sorts of weirdly wrapped packages on the bed. They were covered in twisted pieces of paper inscribed with his writing. He'd written stuff across the bedroom walls and his tarot cards were littered about the place. He always took his tarot cards around with him. They were wrapped up in a silk scarf. He was really good at reading them. When the hotel manageress saw the state of the room, she was absolutely furious and started shouting at me. It was a small hotel and everybody in the street came out to see what was happening. They all had something to say. Some of them were tapping their heads and saying "crazy". Others said that they had seen him taking pills but I didn't believe that. I hadn't seen him taking any pills.

'There was no sign of Zach or the moped and by this time I was pretty hysterical. I ran into the town to try and find him. I looked around for him for ages and then, in the distance, I noticed a small chapel set back off a square. I went inside. It was dark. Zach was inside. He had bought a knife. I saw that he was stabbing at an icon of Jesus. It was horrific. But he didn't seem surprised to see me there and explained that he thought that the icon was "trapping Jesus" and he was "setting him free". Then he turned the knife towards me. I had no idea what he was going to do next, what he was really thinking or quite how paranoid he was. He was behaving so abnormally, being so horrifyingly strange, but I never believed that he would actually be violent towards me. He'd always hurt himself, never others, not deliberately, but then he cackled almost demonically and the pupils of his eyes were tiny and weird and he said, "Don't worry, I wouldn't do anything *to you* . . ."'

Molly stopped. We both took a breather. She finished her glass of wine and went into the kitchen, opening the small fridge to remove a bottle of fizzy water. I cleared up the plates and put them back onto the tray. It was becoming quieter now and I watched while two or three planes landed at the end of the runway. It was all so surreal. The sun had set and the sky was an amalgam of blacks and blues, interspersed with distant, bright stars. It was still hot and sultry but the breeze had diminished. The buzz of the night-time insects increased, and mosquitoes began to appear around the table. I noticed that the hotel had had the foresight to distribute citronella candles about the balcony, so I joined Molly in the kitchen to look for matches. I found some and returned outside. I lit the candles and the somewhat chemical lemony scent wafted over us, along with the smell of aeroplane diesel. Lit up by the kind flame and the waxing moon, Molly resumed her story.

'I don't know how I did it,' she continued, 'but I used all my persuasion to get Zach to leave the chapel and go along with me to the travel agent. I don't know what I told him but he can be manipulated at times. The only thing was that once we got there, he simply couldn't calm down or behave normally. There were travel leaflets and brochures dotted around the walls on racks. He went over to them, gathered them up by handfuls and tried to stuff them into his bag. I asked him to stop it but he wouldn't. He just kept collecting the stuff and shoving it into his bag, his pockets, anywhere. The travel agents could see that there was something seriously wrong with him and told us to leave. I wanted to quieten him down. He just couldn't. After they shouted at us to get out, he yelled at them that he wasn't going to stay in there anyway and he "had to be somewhere to do things". Then he ran off again.

'I was in tears. I just didn't know what else to do. I was exhausted by it all. I went to look for Sean, a friend of ours from the film crew. I'd spoken to him about Zach before all this and he said that if I needed any help, then he would be there for me. He was an actor and had told me that he had a cousin who suffered from mental illness. He and his girlfriend were in their room when I got back to the hotel and they agreed to come and help me find Zach again and get him to a hospital. It was a wild goose chase. Fortunately, there weren't that many places he could go and eventually we found him. Sean persuaded him to go with him to the local clinic. Sometimes Zach's easier to deal with when strangers or people he knows only slightly are involved. I knew what medication he took when he was ill. When we got to the hospital, we saw a doctor and I asked him to prescribe the right medication. The doctor refused. He told us that unless the police arrested Zach because he was considered to be a danger, he was unable to prescribe antipsychotic medication. Sean said that he would stay with Zach while one of the assistant producers, a girl who spoke Greek, came with me to the police to explain the situation. The police agreed to go and take Zach into custody. The girl told me to wait at the police station while they went to arrest him. Apparently, it was pretty awful, because they found him on the beach, naked, surrounded by a pack of feral dogs.

'The island was so tiny and the hospital so small that they couldn't care for him there. They simply didn't have the resources. When I went back to the clinic to see what was happening, a policeman was stationed outside his room, even though Zach had been sedated. I went out again to get him some cigarettes and something to drink and when I got back, about forty minutes later, the policeman said that they were going to take him over to a jail on another, larger island and I wasn't allowed to see him again. It was just awful. I felt so guilty. I said to the policeman that they should be taking him to a larger hospital, not a prison. But what could I do? I was in such a state by this time.'

Molly stayed with me overnight. The following day, we managed to get her a flight back to London. She was overjoyed to be going home but felt terrible about having left Zach in jail. It was an impossible situation for her. He was so lucky to have had Molly and the guys from the production company. They had been incredibly altruistic, giving up their time to accompany him to the hospital and wait with him and try to ensure that he was safe. Again and again during Zach's various episodes, many, many strangers have come forward to help him. He has never made any conscious effort to show appreciation.

Within another twenty-four hours, Erik had managed to work a small miracle. 'I've got the police to release him,' he informed me. 'I don't know why he was still in a jail. He's a kid, after all.' He sounded wound up. 'We're arranging for a plane to take him to Athens and then to a private psychiatric hospital. They weren't happy about this but we persuaded them that as he is a young man with a history of problems, they should release him into our care. Or something like that.'

I listened intently. Erik went on to say that he was surprised by how unhelpful he had found the British Embassy staff to be. I too had been bewildered by their seeming lack of support. Surely this was not the first time that such an incident had occurred on a Greek island?

'I think the police are probably happy to see the back of him,' I said to Erik, glad that there had been some movement.

'I don't know what the place is like where they are keeping him,' Erik murmured, 'and I doubt that they can really look after someone who is mentally ill.'

I simply did not want to think what it could be like. *Midnight Express* came to mind.[10] 'Do you remember Section 13, the psychiatric ward in the Turkish prison where Billy Hayes was held?' I asked Erik. 'He was reduced to a babbling mess. Can Greek jails be any better, especially if you're sick?'

We discussed the film and he remembered the story. 'This is different,' he contended. 'Zach wasn't smuggling – he's ill. And anyway, it's Greece, not Turkey. Try not to imagine too much. I'll be in touch and let you know when he arrives at hospital, hopefully later today.'

* * *

It took the taxi about forty minutes to drive across Athens to the suburb where the hospital was situated. There, a squat white construction was spread across perhaps an acre of prime real estate. Darkened windows looked out over a jam-packed highway. Tall, spiked metal gates opened onto an overgrown path strewn with parched grass and wild flowers. The front door was a barred mahogany affair with three bells, one for each department. Regardless of its modernity, it looked forbidding. I had no idea what to expect. I rang the bell. I could hear shuffling and muttering behind the door. An elderly Greek woman opened it and gestured for me to follow her along a wide corridor. The place stank of rancid cooking oil and unwashed, sweaty bodies.

A cacophony of noise accompanied us. People were everywhere, in and out of offices and rooms leading off the corridor, on the stairs going up and down. Everywhere people were shouting – at each other, at doctors, into telephones. Others were running in and out of the back of the building, where I could see a large area of trees and scrubby grass, ending in a rough version of a football pitch. All the while, people were yelling at one another. Were they unable to speak in normal voices or walk about silently? Was this a vision of Bedlam? There was no semblance of normality here. Just chaos.

The elderly woman pulled at my shirt and I was directed into a small room off the corridor. It housed a desk, two chairs and an extremely harassed-looking doctor. Various certificates adorned the walls. An unfinished, dried-up cake lay mouldering on a paper plate; two glasses of sooty coffee stood sentinel at each end of the desk. While I prepared my first sentence, at least four people barged into the room demanding the doctor's attention. I tried to make myself heard above their yells. 'I'm looking for my son, Zach, an English boy who was flown over yesterday from an island!' The doctor looked over towards me and wearily got up. He appeared inordinately worn out. He smiled a half-hearted smile that somehow made his appearance less tired and held out his hand. I shook it.

'How are you?' he asked.

'I'm bewildered,' I replied. 'Is it always like this here?'

Before he had a chance to answer, another voice raised itself above our limited conversation. He took a breath inwards. 'Zach is upstairs.' He gestured out of the room, pointing upwards. I was relieved that he spoke English. I had been afraid that no one would. 'The third floor,' he continued. 'He's in a private room. Please, you'll find it easily. The third floor.' He then turned in the direction of the other voice, which was now quivering with exasperation.

In spite of the anarchy, the smells and the noise, it was cool inside the clinic. Long windows graced the entire back of the main building but they were mainly darkened so that the outside glare was diminished into a series of shadows playing over the corridors.

Dust motes glinted in the intermittent brightness, then faded and died on a breath. The walls held various notices but most were stained while others were torn. There were no flowers in vases or compassionate plants to enliven the dour environment. The floors were of brown stone inlaid with green and blue mosaic. They were badly stained, either from wear and tear or by the ubiquitous cups of coffee that were placed on every surface. The doors were made of heavy metal, each one having a large padlock to the exterior. The staircase was grey cement surrounded by an iron handrail and my footsteps reverberated as I made my way upstairs. On each floor was assembled a confused collection of humanity, all of whom were shouting at each other, even the nurses in their drab uniforms. I continued making my way higher up the building. Eventually, the staircase tapered off towards a darkened area. This was the 'private room'. My heart beat wildly. To the left of the shadowy grey area, a small door was ajar. I could see a sliver of light. I went towards it. The door gave way to a gentle push.

Daylight hit me. I ventured into the room. It was enormous. The whole of the top floor of the clinic devoted to one patient – utterly inappropriate to meet the needs of one psychiatric casualty. On my right, a narrow antediluvian iron bedstead appeared to contain an inert body. To my left, I saw a nurse sitting in a large armchair, knitting. She got up when she saw me and pointed at the bed. I went over as Zach turned towards me. He saw me and tried to rouse himself. He attempted a grin but then collapsed onto the cushions. 'Mum,' he was barely able to mumble. 'Mum, you're here.' He pulled at the bedclothes and gestured towards his feet. 'Look what they've done to me.' I looked down at the end of the bed. Two skinny legs protruded, one of which was encased in a leather shackle around the ankle. The shackle was locked and a longer piece of leather was attached to the bed. He was physically imprisoned, unable to move without difficulty, tethered like a mad dog.

9

Repatriation

My mouth was dry with shock. I felt as if I was going to vomit. Where *was* I? I was so angry. I had never felt such rage. I rounded on the nurse. 'What have you done to him?' I shouted at her. She responded in Greek and broken English and hand movements. From what I understood, they were afraid that he would fall out of bed because of all the medication they had given him. I stared at her, bewildered. This made no sense. Shackled because of too much medication? What perverse judgement was this? I went back to him. 'Zach, can you move?' I tried to rouse him again. He was almost comatose. I shook him violently. He babbled at me, saliva dribbling from the side of his mouth onto his dirty, soggy T-shirt. He was terribly thin. His chin stuck out of his wasted face, which had a sweaty, shiny pallor. His nose was blocked, so he took deep, lumbering breaths through his gaping mouth. Dark-red circles shadowed his eyes and there were the remains of bloody cuts around his neck and forehead. I moved the covers down and saw that his entire torso was covered in weals and sores and scratches, as were his feet and legs. The shackle had caused inflamed gashes where it had rubbed at his skin. These wounds were turning yellow with pus. He was skeletal.

There was nothing I could do with the nurse. She looked baffled at my reaction. I shook Zach again. He mumbled, unable to piece words together. 'I'm going to speak to the doctors,' I told him, replacing the creased, grubby sheet around him. 'Now. I'm going to get you out of this. I've never seen anything so barbaric.' I walked quickly to the door. 'I'll be back as soon as I can.' He muttered something but it was unintelligible.

I scrambled as fast as I could down the stairs towards the office where I had initially met the psychiatrist. My fury showed no signs of abating. I was breathless with ire. While I ran down the stairs, I attempted to call Sam on the mobile. Tears of anger clouded my eyes. I was unable to see the numbers. I had to stop myself and take deep breaths before I could speak to him. 'Sam!' I managed through clenched teeth. 'Sam! They've shackled Zach to his bed!'

I could hear a sharp intake of breath. 'What d'you mean they've shackled him? How?'

I was almost crying. I tried to explain coherently. 'He's shackled to his bed with a leather strap and it's got a key in it and the only way he can get out of bed is if they actually unlock it. It's medieval. I'm going down now to the doctors to get them to take it off him. He can't even talk to me. He's completely doped up, like a zombie. He's covered in cuts and bruises. He looks terrible. I can't believe it's him.'

I shoved the bodies barring the door out of my way and barged into the office, oblivious to everyone. The harassed doctor, in the middle of a meeting with two relatives as confused as me, looked up, startled. 'Take it off him now!' I shouted at him. 'He's shackled to a bed! How could you possibly do something like this? How could you do such a thing?' He got up from his desk and came towards me. 'He's actually shackled to a bed!' I reiterated, my usual eloquence having been reduced to repetition.

'It's the way we do things here,' he responded, with utter fatigue. 'We were afraid that he would collapse if he got out of bed.' He bent down and rummaged around in a drawer, then, lifting the receiver of the telephone, he spoke quietly into it. Within moments, a young woman made her way into his room. He gave her a small bunch of keys. 'She will remove the restraint.'

He sat down again resignedly. There appeared to be no other doctors in the vicinity and I felt guilty at having shouted at him. 'I'm going to get Zach out of here as soon as I can,' I explained to him, this time more lucidly. 'I'm going to get him back to London. This is no place for him.'

The doctor sat back in his chair and once again shook his head. 'Your son is very sick,' he reiterated. 'He will need months in hospital. Wherever he is. We are just doing what we can for him. It may not be the way you are used to.' He seemed young, probably thirty or thirty-five, but his hair was greying and his eyes were bloodshot and heavy. The responsibility appeared to weigh him down. He took a sip from one of the glasses of coffee and then replaced it onto a stained exercise book that rested on a pile of patients' notes. He looked down at his hands and picked at the skin of one of his nails. 'Zach has been heavily sedated. I understand how you must feel but it was the only way to treat him. He was too violent to be allowed to mix with the other patients.'

I rounded on him. 'Is that why he's so comatose? What about the other patients? Aren't they equally ill?'

The doctor again smiled his weary smile. 'You know,' he acknowledged, 'we have little room here for new patients. We are understaffed. I am the only psychiatrist on call here today. I understand your frustration. I am sorry that this is how it is. Is it any better in England?'

I stopped and considered this question. 'I can see how overwhelmed you are,' I responded. 'But I've yet to see anyone literally shackled to a bed so that he didn't collapse and kill himself in that way. Maybe you should ask yourself just why you need to dole out quite so much medication.'

I turned out of the office and followed the young woman up the stairs, pushing at anyone who dared to be in my way. I was far too agitated to care about being in the least understanding of anyone else's insanity. Once again in the room on the third floor, I watched while the woman inserted the key into the sweaty lock and removed the restraint. Zach was still far too numb to notice. She left after having gestured to me that I should expect Zach to collapse were he to get up. The idea that he might be able to attempt to stand up was laughable. Was she unable to appreciate how much damage the drugs had done to him? I stayed with him for another hour or two, until suppertime. Although he managed to awaken slightly, there was no point in my staying with him. The nurses changed. Another woman sat in the armchair, this time armed with the Greek version of *Hello!* magazine. I was scared to leave him there alone and go back to the hotel. What more might they do to him? But by this time I was mentally drained and wanted to get away from there so that I could have some time on my own to absorb what had happened to my family. 'Zach,' I said, trying to resuscitate him, 'Zach, I'm leaving now. I'll be back in the morning.' He moved slightly then continued snoring. I pushed the hair away from his face and wiped it with a wet flannel that I had found by the sink. I made an effort to give him some water but there were no straws nearby so it trickled out of his mouth onto the grimy sheet. What was the point of having a nurse in here, I wondered. Was she going to watch him slowly expire? I pulled at the sheet so that it covered him and moved the pillow so that he could breathe more easily. It was beyond me to do anything else at that time.

I wearily left the room and descended into the wild cacophony below to confront the doctor once again. I knocked on his door and poked my head around it. Another glass of coffee graced the desk, this time accompanied by the cigarette smoke that was a feature of the hospital. 'I'm going now,' I told him, 'but I'll be back again tomorrow. You need to do something about his ankle and all the other cuts and bruises.'

The doctor came out of his office and accompanied me to the door of the clinic. 'I'm trying my best,' he remonstrated with me. 'But you can see I'm swamped.'

It was a private clinic in an exclusive area of Athens. I hated to think what their general psychiatric hospitals were like.

During the following three days, I got to know Athens. Taxis were about as common as beached whales on the banks of the Thames but I needed to get to and from the clinic. Unless the hotel managed to order a taxi for me, I could wait up to an hour in the baking sun before I saw one and then, invariably, the car was already occupied. The second day I was more clued in. Waving hysterically when a taxi eventually appeared, steaming along outside the clinic, I almost ran into the road to stop it. The driver showed no surprise when I shouted at him in English that I wanted to go back to my hotel. It was of no consequence that it was already occupied. You shared taxis in the same way that you shared trains and buses. I had a few interesting journeys to and from the clinic. The Athenians were unfailingly courteous and polite. Whenever the question of why I was taking a taxi from one side of the city to the other arose, I skirted the truth by explaining that my son had been taken ill and that I was here to help him return home. This appeared to suffice. However, my feelings of anxiety and despondency were not alleviated. I was continually on to the insurance company, which was my only lifeline. Although I spoke to Sam regularly, there was nothing he could effectively do to help us.

At the hotel, life continued at the pool, in the restaurant and on the roofs nearby. I saw the anoraks greeting one another and leaving early on, armed with their notepads and bottles of water. It surprised me just how many of them were women. Maybe they had come for the pool, sunshine and retsina. They certainly spent enough time imbibing the latter and their shiny, leathery copper skin was tribute to their adoration of the rays. But most of them left the hotel arm in arm with their partners, only to return later in the afternoon, having spent a fun day recording the numbers of the aeroplanes passing overhead and landing on the glistening tarmac of Athens airport. They were certainly deriving far more enjoyment from their sojourn in Greece than I was.

On that second day, I decided that if I left the hotel by midday, Zach would hopefully have slept off some of the previous night's medication. Then I would stay with him until the early evening. He reluctantly got up when I arrived, gingerly manoeuvring his fragile torso from the flimsy metal bed while holding on to the almost rusted bedstead. Invariably, the profound dizziness he experienced on getting up meant that he had to sit down almost immediately. In his weakened state, he shuffled around the room like a decrepit old man. He needed assistance to go to the toilet and to dress himself but I left the first part to the nurse, feeling that perhaps his sense of pride would not allow me to help him there. Dressing was not such a terrible issue; apart from a pair of boxer shorts, he insisted on wearing the same disgusting T-shirt the entire time. He stooped and his skinny arms stuck out at funny angles as he tugged at his mucky hair or scratched at one of the weeping sores around his ankles or the weals on his legs.

The nursing staff had not bothered to deal with Zach's cuts and bruises, so I took in plasters and antibiotic cream and sterilised wipes from the chemist facing the clinic, alarmed that the superficial injuries might become infected. He had one pair of scuffed trainers with him but his toenails were jagged and bloodied. They had removed the laces and he had no socks. He had no real appetite, which, perhaps, was fortunate because the food in the clinic was largely inedible. Each day, a slovenly porter would bring up a plate of swill masquerading as mashed potatoes or pasta of some unidentifiable type, mixed together with a grim, grey mass. This, presumably, was meat. I could not envisage that it could possibly have derived from anything having four legs. One look was enough to cause anyone to have a breakdown.

Zach's mental condition remained bleak. In spite of my being there and watching like a hawk the amount of medication they prescribed in ever-larger doses, he remained severely ill. His moods were all over the place, at once irritable and volatile, conciliatory and depressed. On one level, I could tell that he appreciated my having flown to be with him and get him back to London. On another level, his mental disturbance meant that he profoundly resented my presence. Although constrained by the chemicals, he continued to vilify me personally as if it were my fault that he found himself in a psychiatric clinic once again, and at times I was fearful of his rancour. His wild eyes and facial tics and grimaces were frightening and, notwithstanding his feeble state, I knew what physical power he could have over me were he to use his strength. I had to employ all of my cunning to keep him as calm as possible. It was excruciatingly arduous.

Even in the grip of his bitterness towards me, Zach insisted on my accompanying him wherever he staggered around the clinic and it was harrowing to see the way in which he attempted to interact with the other patients. On one occasion, he ventured into the gardens and, having seen that other guys were playing basketball, he removed his trainers and his T-shirt and would have removed his boxers had one of the older men not prevented him from so doing. Despite their various degrees of mental disturbance, the players recognised the incongruity of his actions and gesticulated and laughed at him. I felt immensely humiliated on his behalf. However, I told myself that, as he had no insight into his condition, he was not concerned by his own strange behaviour.

My conversations with Erik in Paris followed identical lines, with him repeatedly relaying the difficulties he was encountering with the different authorities. 'I've had a far easier time getting a man out of Uzbekistan,' he told me plaintively. 'He'd broken his leg but within twenty-four hours I managed to get a private plane and air tickets from Moscow. This is a mission!' I queried whether they had had to repatriate others with mental-health problems. 'Yes,' he replied, 'but it's always a problem with young men who have had trouble with police. Because of his instability, it's a question of who will accompany him back. Whether it's enough that you are with him or if someone from the clinic needs to be there.' This only added to my anxiety. There was no possible way that I would be able to manage Zach on my own.

Negotiations became more convoluted and intense, and as each hour passed I became more despondent. How were we ever going to get back? Were we going to be incarcerated here for months? Zach sensed my anxiety and as a consequence his mania accelerated. Although the manacles from which he had been released had been replaced by medication that was akin to a physical restraint, the drugs did not contain his psychotic instability. He was unable to comprehend why he was still in a hospital in Greece and expected, in fact demanded vociferously, that he be released so that he could 'continue his holiday'.

Three, four times a day I called Paris. Each time I spoke to him, Erik expressed his annoyance and frustration with the way in which we were being treated. He assured me that he was doing all he could to move things along but said that neither the British Embassy nor the Greek authorities were helping, indeed he believed both were demonstrably hindering the repatriation process. Then, late on the third day, he called with good news: the green light on repatriation. 'Thank God!' he exclaimed. 'The Greek authorities have finally made a decision. He can leave so long as a doctor and a nurse accompany him – preferably psychiatric. I've spoken to the Griffin. It's arranged. They're going to fly out a doctor and a nurse first thing tomorrow morning and then you'll all fly back tomorrow night.'

I let out a huge sigh of relief. At last! I told Zach that I was going back to the hotel to check out. Having done this and paid my bill, I returned to the clinic to spend the last night there. Zach was in a terrible state when I arrived back. Each day, I had told him that we were on the way home and he continually nagged at me, asking endlessly: When? Now? How much longer? Why do I have to stay here? When can we leave? Why is it taking so long? Now at least I could tell him that the cavalry was on its way. All we had to do was wait for the moment we would hear the galloping horses.

* * *

Zach's bedroom window overlooked the grounds to the back of the building. Here, a rough patch of brown stubble was home to approximations of a football pitch and a basketball court. Overgrown trees created shady bowers in which the patients could lie about, talking, smoking and waiting until the time came for the next dose of medication. I had looked down at this vista each day that I had been at the hospital. Now I paced up and down Zach's room, continually looking out of the window in the vain hope that maybe the doctor and nurse would arrive across the scarred lawn. Zach had not slept the previous night. He had got up and out of bed several times, restlessly wandering in and out of the bedroom and up and down the stairs. He had refused to take his medication and because the medical staff knew that he was about to leave, they did not force it upon him this time. His mood reflected this. He had traipsed in and out of the bathroom, drinking copious cups of water and wiping his mouth with the back of his hand. I tried to get him to wash himself and don his only decent T-shirt, which I had found in his filthy backpack and washed in the hotel room. He refused, all the while picking at himself and at his crusty scars and relentlessly and repetitively enquiring of me when they were going to be here.

The previous night, I had made my way over to the clinic full of hope and expectation. Now it was way past morning and there was no sight nor sound of the cavalry, only the continual noises that made their way up the staircase to what I now perceived to be my own prison. I attempted to reassure Zach that they were on their way, patronisingly explaining that things took time and that 'at any minute' they would be here, but my heart beat wildly and I felt sweaty with anxiety. The flight was supposed to have left London at five in the morning. If they were on it and everything was on time, then they should have been here by midday at the latest. It was now past three. Again I rang the Griffin and again I was told by the ward clerk that they were on their way and that I had no reason to fear. I irritably explained to her that it was easy for her to mouth these words; she was not incarcerated in a psychiatric clinic with an increasingly manic young man.

Then, suddenly, I heard voices, English voices, coming up the stairs. Two large men appeared in the room, carrying small backpacks. My saviours! I recognised them from the Griffin. Dr Cooper had previously treated Zach. The nurse, Duncan, I also knew. It was as if all the cares had left my shoulders; I experienced a most wonderful feeling that someone else could take away some of the burden.

'What happened to you?' I asked them.

'Unbelievable,' replied Duncan, in his broad Ulster accent. 'We've been taken on a complete wild goose chase around Athens, for hours. The taxi driver couldn't find the clinic. We'd been given the wrong address!'

I remembered spelling out letter by letter to Erik the name of the clinic and the road and the area. I guess it wasn't his fault but, boy, was I angry!

Dr Cooper walked over to Zach, who gave him his widest grin. 'How're you doing, Zach?' Zach hugged him and Dr Cooper looked over at me. 'He's terribly thin, isn't he?'

I nodded. 'He's hardly eaten anything since we've been here. The food's been disgusting and he's really not well.'

The doctor opened his bag and took out various medical instruments. 'I'd like to do a quick examination before we leave. We've got time – that's if we can order a taxi.'

I made towards the door. 'I'll go downstairs and ask them to book one now. Hopefully by the time we're ready to leave, it'll be here.'

Dr Cooper's cursory examination revealed that, among other

things, Zach was severely malnourished and dehydrated. The doctor was angered by the state of his other injuries, the sores and bruises and his ankles, which were now ulcerated. His blood pressure was low and he was running a fever. There was not too much that Dr Cooper could do for him at that moment. He gave Zach painkillers for the fever and cleaned up his external lesions as best he could. It was decided that we should leave and make our way home.

I was delighted to bid farewell to the clinic. The complicated paperwork finished with, we piled into an aged taxi driven by a coughing, gasping driver in whose mouth was clamped a foul-smelling cheroot. From time to time, lurching across lanes and into the face of oncoming traffic, the driver would wind down his window and, taking huge, deep breaths, cough up great gobs of sputum. I thought this a fitting end to my stay. I just wanted it to be over with and to be on the plane back to what I believed would be some kind of normality.

When we arrived at Athens airport, however, nothing went smoothly. Although Dr Cooper had administered various tranquillisers, Zach was unable to remain calm or conduct himself in a manner akin to the usual holidaymaker. His appearance and behaviour meant that he attracted attention. He insisted on insinuating himself into other travellers' conversations and resisted our endeavours to hinder his more manic actions. He needed the toilet. He wanted a drink. He was *famished*. He wanted duty-free.

'You have to wait until we've gone through passport control,' I told him.

'But I need cigarettes now!' he hissed at me.

'I'll buy you a pack,' I said, succumbing to his manipulations. 'You stay with Duncan,' I pleaded.

Another nightmare. Now that he was released from the virtual prison of the clinic, he wanted his freedom – to wander, to run around like a headstrong toddler. We three had to babysit him, otherwise it was likely that the airline would refuse to have him on board. In fact, the representative at the check-in desk already seemed doubtful. 'I don't know whether he can fly in this condition,' she informed me.

'What do you mean?' I responded testily. 'He's got three people watching him. Nothing's going to happen.' It was only because Dr Cooper used all his psychological wiles and charm that she agreed to allow us to fly home and it was almost the moment we boarded before we knew for definite that we could.

I had climbed Everest. Every bone ached. My head pounded. The three of us thrust Zach bodily onto the plane, attracting curious glances from passengers and staff alike. We sat him down and told him to be quiet until take-off. His beaming smile demonstrated his joy of deliverance. A collective sigh. Kisses for Erik. He'd managed to fly us back business class. Champagne all round!

10

Fast Forward, Rewind

The ambulance met us at the airport. Zach refused to be transferred to it by wheelchair, even though he had hardly slept and Dr Cooper's best efforts to keep him immobile had been rebuffed. During the flight, Duncan and Dr Cooper would take Zach into the tiny toilet area and administer various jabs to his bruised, skinny posterior, each time returning with shocked expressions. The doctor was barely able to express his dismay at the extent of Zach's external injuries. 'Poor kid. How could he have been left like this?' he asked. 'Why didn't they do anything about his injuries?' It was apparent that Zach had been badly beaten, presumably in the Greek jail. Evidently, he had not yielded to their orders for calm quickly enough and they had clapped him in handcuffs and leg irons. Arguably unaware of his mental-health status, they seem to have had no understanding as to why he was behaving in such an aggressive manner. They therefore fulfilled their duties of containment: tie him up and beat him down. Dr Cooper also voiced deep concern regarding Zach's continuing mania. He anticipated, however, that once Zach was back at home he would eventually calm down, get back to normal and join the dots.

So here we were, back in sunny London. Once more, Zach was deposited at the Griffin. A room was arranged and ready for his sojourn and he set about making it his own. Our medical insurers had paid the larger part of the claim but we were out of pocket big time. It being August, Dr Goode was absent on his annual leave and a Dr Sinclair was filling in for him, a semi-retired, ebullient grandfatherly type of psychiatrist with years of experience. We liked him very much, although Zach displayed his usual suspicion, which was not surprising considering his recent history.

While Zach had been incarcerated in Athens and during my jaunt there, we had lied to Beth, spinning her the line that everything was fine. 'I *knew* something was going on,' she would complain later. More guilt, deception and misrepresentations. Back to Heathrow and another weary plane ride as I flew off to Connecticut, where Beth was attending camp, to explain to her what had been going on. To her immense distress, I filled her in on the news: Zach was back but he had somehow left part of his mind on a Greek beach.

Our lives had changed dramatically. We had been a close family but we now led disparate lives, each of us bearing this new reality in the way we were able. For Beth, this meant that she sealed herself off from Zach. Only three years separated them and they had always been the greatest of friends. They had had a deep, loving bond, a similar sense of humour and musical tastes. Now these ties were wrenched apart and Beth was utterly traumatised, so much so that she too had to seek psychological help, counselling and medication. Her good relationship with Zach was one she would attempt to rekindle after each and every breakdown but one that became more and more tenuous as time elapsed. Zach was oblivious to this and only recently, after a lengthy series of family therapy sessions, has he been made aware of the impact that his illness, and his denial of his illness, has had on us as a family.

Repatriated from Greece, he remained manic. The medication was altered substantially. He continually went walkabout in the hospital, roaming from room to room, floor to floor, attempting to create relationships with all and sundry. Although the staff were used to an informal atmosphere, this behaviour began to annoy them. It was a busy time for madness. The long days, the heat and the freedom of summer are a perfect breeding ground for mania and there was an ever-growing number of new patients. The days were long and hot. The skies may well have been bright and clear but Zach's mind was nothing of the kind. He considered the clinic his 'home from home'. His room now resembled his bedroom at our house: his clothes were strewn across the bed, the chair and table; countless paper cups half-filled with water teetered on all surfaces; and his guitar was at the ready for the incessant strumming. He would continually call his friends and family – indeed anyone he could get hold of who would listen to his frantic sentences – manipulating them and making demands. Molly came in most days and, allowed out with her as a minder, Zach would go with whatever whim took him, to the extent of dyeing his hair blue and cutting it into a Mohican. Unfortunately, he carried out this artistic process in the hospital, leaving entire walls filled with his azure handprints. Dr Sinclair attempted a hollow laugh. 'I think that maybe Zach should be given an army-issue brush to remove the offending petrograms,' he said, motioning to the wall outside his office, newly decorated, 'especially those that surround the buttons on the lift.' Zach had no insight into how others viewed these juvenile and frustrating actions. He persistently denied he had an illness that required him to take some kind of proactive role and absolved himself of all responsibility. Furthermore, he refused to participate with other patients in group activities and resented any form of psychotherapeutic counselling.

However, the good news, if you could call it that, was that there was a diagnosis. After a lengthy assessment, Dr Sinclair prescribed lithium, the so-called 'wonder drug'.[11] 'I believe that Zach has bipolar disorder,' he informed me, 'previously known as manic depression. Lithium works for many, many people. I think that he is a good candidate. Let's try it.' So another new medication was added to the growing list and Zach duly succumbed to the sweet revenge of lithium: the mind-numbing, cotton-wool-cloying, distance-inducing, sweat-provoking, jittery jiving salt cellar.

The hospital respite ceased. We collected him and all his recent acquisitions – lithium, sleeping tablets, tranquillisers and antipsychotics – and, together with the highly attractive blue hair, we made the journey north to dog and newly refurbished bedroom. Zach was clearly happy to have everyone at his beck and call. Within days, Beth returned and rejoined us, greeting Zach tremulously, hoping that perhaps he would be able to respond to her as an equal. He was having none of that, though, his compulsively manic energy manifesting itself in immature and frenetic behaviour. Whether this was the result of the illness, a reaction to medication or even the fallout from the drugs he had used and, to some extent, still indulged in, we had no idea. In any event, he drove us nuts.

It was arduous spending any time with him. He was up early and increasingly late going to bed. The very same noises as before emanated from his room. The volume of his voice and his music increased. The stamping on the stairs, the crashing of doors, the crumbs, the dirty glasses. The idiotic demands. The Reading Festival was upon us. Could he go? He requested. He insisted. Another quandary. More soul-searching. What do we do? Do we let him go on his own? With friends? Do we take him? He was meant to be an adult. Not that he behaved like one. How could we constantly monitor him? Yet we understood that we had no other option. It was all too dangerous – for him, for others. We entreated poor Beth to go with him to the festival to give us a break for a day, a whole Sunday. It was as if we were stuck with an unruly child. 'Just go with him, Beth,' we pleaded. 'We'll pay. Just make sure he doesn't slip away from you.' So, with a great lack of enthusiasm, she agreed to accompany him. That night, when we collected them from Paddington Station, she looked worn out, fed up and angry. 'Oh, there were times when he was all right,' she told us. 'But at others he was just talking crap. He was fidgety and jumpy. I made sure he took his meds but I'm sure he took too many. There was no major drama but he wasn't right. He wasn't well at all.'

Time elapsed. Medication coursed its way around Zach's body. The mania abated to some degree and it was back to the guys and another band. Even though he hated what the lithium was doing to him, he insisted, maturely in this instance, that he was not going to let it stymie his musical ambitions. Back to songwriting, the search for 'adequate' musicians, rehearsals, toxic Tosh. This time, I refused to be involved in any of the arrangements, to have anything to do with a band. I didn't want to have Tosh anywhere near me, to be subjected to his malign influence, his rancour. Zach, however, rejected my uncertainties and fears and was determined to give him another chance. So this damaged ghoul stayed away from us, focusing his toxic energy on Zach's defenceless soul, while all the time being swept along to his own perdition. There was a gig in Camden, some more reviews, but nothing concrete would come of it. Ultimately, the necessary resolve was absent. Zach was left at the crossroads of his adolescence, from where he was propelled into attempting the university route that had been mapped out for him at an earlier, happier moment in time.

11

Wayward Moods

With no great enthusiasm, Zach set in motion his new career, which included the cerebral challenge of lectures and seminars, alongside the crucial student existence of pool, football and the pub. Nonetheless, he was not a typical student. He made some friends but they were on the whole an unsavoury bunch whose intellectual insight was more or less limited to knowing where the best 'kif' was to be had, where the next anti-globalisation demonstration was taking place and where the best squats were situated. His moods continued to veer wildly up and down, and, even though he was in general comparatively 'down', his hyper-elation showed no real signs of slowing. It was a wonder how he functioned at all.

We weathered the days. We tried to keep tabs on Zach, to see what he was up to, where he was going, who he was seeing. It was an impossible task. He tried to beat the moods, took the meds, wrote some essays – but the drugs were always in attendance. We just didn't know which ones. In the New Year, Sam, Zach and Beth took a skiing trip while I stayed at home with the dog, trying to get my own life in order. There had been no major upsets during the holiday but on the return flight, unable to sleep, Zach consumed far too many Valium, together with an endless supply of airline vodka. He wound up and aggravated the other passengers to the extent that the captain radioed ahead for instructions. When the air steward informed Sam that this was airline policy, an incandescent Sam responded that this was par for the course with his son, that Zach should not be arrested on arrival in London and that Beth and he would take control. Zach eventually passed out in the aisle, to be jostled back into his seat by Sam and Beth, a spent force. When I met them in the airport crush, it was obvious that things had taken a turn for the worse. I was cursed with having to drive home, unable to escape the black vitriol that Sam vented at Zach: 'I will *never* fly with you again! I will *never* go anywhere with you again!' This was meant as a show of force but we knew what he meant: it was all too *tedious*.

Then the bleak forces of depression ventured forth. That flat, hollow melancholia, tiresome to those around you, so aptly described by Kay Redfield Jamison in her memoir *An Unquiet Mind*:

> *People cannot abide being around you when you are depressed. They might think that they ought to, and they might even try, but you know and they know that you are tedious beyond belief: you're irritable and paranoid and humorless and lifeless and critical and demanding and no reassurance is ever enough. You're frightened, and you're frightening, and 'you're not at all like yourself but will be soon,' but you know you won't.*[12]

Absolutely.

That winter, Zach was tearful, depressed, low and unsure about how he was going to spend the rest of his life. He had little appetite and was uninterested in everything. 'What's the point?' he would ask. He was unable to shower, wash his hair or brush his teeth unless pushed. He had no real interest in travel any more and had an all-encompassing fear of loneliness. And he *was* lonely. All his friends were doing their own things. Again, Dominic was around or spending hours on the phone to Zach in his best endeavours to drive away his inertia and suicidal thoughts. But Zach had lost interest in his comparative religion course at university and was unable to do anything independently for himself.

No humour, no joy, simply listless. He took no care of his appearance and wore the same clothes day in and day out. He maintained that he wanted others to believe in him and he was distressed that the family bond was severed. He would have loved things to revert to how they had been before but was simply unable to talk to anyone about how he was really feeling. It took all my stamina to stay around for Zach at this time. It was an almost impossibly draining experience. Then, having succumbed to those yawning depths, suddenly the ascent began, the bitter March doldrums leading to a luminous May.

Against his better judgement, and because of Zach's incessant nagging, I had coerced Sam into buying a Piaggio motor scooter so that Zach could take himself off to university. The campus was situated no more than three or four miles from us, on a straight run, and I thought that it would give Zach a sense of responsibility to get there on his own. He had previously shown no inclination to learn to drive and to this day he has a simply colossal hole where a sense of direction should be situated, even though he manages very well to find Everest Base Camp or his way around Bangladesh! We are all capable of making some terrible decisions. This was not one of my smartest. Why couldn't he take the Tube like everyone else? The scooter would save him money, he maintained. He would be able to get to friends without recourse to trains or taxis. Ultimately, it would save *us* money, he insisted.

One Saturday morning, we watched while he manoeuvred the bike out of the showroom and set off gingerly along Camden Road. He weaved slightly to the left and right, folding in behind the traffic, and right again on the circuit north. My heart was in my mouth but I kept telling myself, 'He's nineteen, for God's sake.' Other nineteen year olds were driving. They were away at university or even, though it's pretty rare these days, had careers. Why couldn't mine navigate a Piaggio?

Zach managed to find the route home without incident but subsequently, within days, the first of many 'little' accidents happened:

a contretemps with a bus on the Finchley Road dislodged the front bumper. Another momentary lapse resulted in the dismantling of the rear light. Not much later, he discarded the bike in the deepest shadows of Seven Sisters, and Sam was the one who arranged for its return. Consequently, many times I lay awake at night, ears pinned back, antennae twitching in anticipation of hearing him draw closer to home, the pop-pop of the engine corroborating his existence. What a fool I was. Zach's disastrous experiences with motorbikes of one sort or another have been an attendant theme to his moments of madness. These 'glitches' were just a precursor of worse problems, as were the moped crashes in Greece.

I continued to write down my observations. I needed some control, some clarity. Following the first episode, I had sought out and attended various meetings; otherwise I felt that I existed in a vacuum, alone. Even before the diagnosis of bipolar affective disorder, I had contacted the Manic Depression Fellowship (now MDF The Bipolar Organisation) and gone along to some of their meetings; for the drugs issue, I attended Narcotics Anonymous. Another society encompassed all types of mental illness. Sometimes it helped. Often I wondered why I was there and for what purpose. Listening to others discuss their lives and those of their friends and relatives, with all the attendant symptoms, you needed emotions of stone not to be moved but, moreover, you could become depressed and despondent. How many times could we go over the same ground? None of the psychiatric or pharmaceutical treatment Zach received seemed to make any meaningful difference to his condition and we felt desperately alone and helpless. Various friends would ring and ask how things were going but there was only so long that I could discuss it before I curtailed the conversations. 'It's enough,' I would interject. 'This is getting boring!' My background as a historian convinced me that keeping a record of events would help my understanding of them, but whether writing notes did in fact help me at the time is arguable. Now, obviously, they provide an invaluable account of his moods, his life:

May 1999

The week beginning the 3rd. Zach's started acting bizarrely again, with the usual ridiculous exaggerations. He slept seventeen hours one day – not much the other. Voluntarily took Procycledine [used to treat the Parkinsonian side effects that can result from antipsychotic drugs] one day and then one Resperidol [antipsychotic]. Over the weekend he wasn't too bad but on Monday began to lose the plot. I spoke to Dr Goode, who advised more medication, so he took two Resperidol in the morning but I didn't see him again until 2 p.m. on Tuesday, when he was very elated. He'd left his bike in Seven Sisters because he felt he was unable to drive it. He's been spending money quite extravagantly and is presenting the usual strange behavioural mannerisms: smoking loads, pressurised talking, gathering rubbish, rituals, fears. He's very thin again and has bad asthma. He realises he's ill, so he's now taking three Resperidol twice a day, plus one Ativan [antipsychotic] three times daily, plus yesterday took 10 mg Diazepam [tranquilliser] and an extra Ativan. He must be rattling.

25th May

Now he's mostly down again. It's been an intensive two weeks. The medication is maintenance lithium plus all the other stuff. We went to see Dr Goode yesterday, who thought he was 'OK', but he's unbearable to live with while he's manic like this. It's awful and he started criticising and threatening Molly. I don't think that she will tolerate it again. She's had enough. He shouted at her violently and was vitriolic and malicious. I think he should go. Move out. Take responsibility for himself and his moods. It would be far better for him.

The problem with all the medications was that they disorientated him and made him forgetful. In addition, he became increasingly restless, yet dopey; he was unable to concentrate or sleep beneficially, and theoretically he was meant to be embarking on exams. Not a good mixture. As an addendum, he unrelentingly smoked weed, while spending nights drinking mescal. 'Even the worm,' added his friend Dylan incredulously. Looking back at the curve, it is obvious that he was also seeking out and using ketamine again. Why he should want to remains unfathomable for those of us who have never been subject to the insidious stealth of an addiction. The knowledge that it could send him over the edge was insufficient reason to stop. Even the thought of another hospital stay was not enough to deter him from taking these highly dangerous risks.

Drugs were very much part and parcel of the overall illness, and we felt that Dr Goode was the best person to challenge Zach about the issue. We had presented the doctor with chapter and verse regarding ketamine. He agreed that drugs were a problem and that they compounded the difficulties he had in treating Zach's illness but it seemed to me that he shied away from dealing with this facet proactively. He might, of course, have raised the issue with Zach in their private meetings. There is a tendency for psychiatrists to avoid this line of enquiry, especially since it is difficult to obtain an accurate history regarding addictive behaviours from individual patients. It is the proverbial chicken and egg situation: what came first? Our profound belief was that drugs stalked Zach's every waking move. Even if he was not physically addicted at that time, he was psychologically so.

In the years to come, it would become clear that Zach was suffering from a 'dual diagnosis'. Various studies have concluded that bipolar disorder and drug/alcohol abuse go hand in hand.[13] As both manic depression and substance abuse create a disturbance in mood, there is a major common characteristic that they share: psychosis. This is presumably why, at the very outset, the psychiatrist at the Central Middlesex recognised in Zach the telltale signs of mental illness. Difficulties in making a definitive diagnosis of bipolar disorder can be aggravated because the underlying mental illness is masked by the existence of drug-induced paranoia. The primary illness is itself often precipitated by drug abuse, after which there is no way back. Then there is the added problem of genetic predisposition. Studies have mostly focused on the correlation between families suffering a history of alcohol and bipolar disorder. There is less data regarding bipolar disorder, drug abuse and the genetic link, so it is difficult to state categorically that such a link exists, at least until further research is undertaken.[14]

What we were able to ascertain was that Zach used drugs as a form of self-medication. Arguably, suffering as he did the most profound depressions, which invariably led to the most awful manias, it is not surprising that he would attempt, perhaps subconsciously, to subsume these exquisite tortures. Surely, he would reason to himself, it would be sensible to take something that would elevate his mood? Conversely, why not then take something else that would depress it? Thus a stimulant such as cocaine is often the bipolar patient's drug of choice to elevate his mood, while heroin, an opiate and therefore a natural depressant, is used to sedate. It is also the case that once his mood is elevated through self-medication, the patient is likely to take more stimulants, increasing the energy he experiences, so that mania often ensues while all senses are discarded. Zach's indiscriminate use of drugs certainly demonstrated this proposition.

He had only a few exams to take that spring but I was unable to envisage how he could possibly write something that would even be sensible. He no longer had the pop-pop bike. Having been bent and battered, lost lights and bits of plastic, it now lay belly up in a friend's garage like a poor beached dolphin, waiting for the mechanic to take it in hand once more or for the verdict of its final demise. So, the ever-idiotic mother that I was, I drove Zach to university and deposited him near the gates of the library. I thought that at least that way he would get there, take part in the exam ritual and thus be able to pretend to himself that he was part of the student fraternity, irrespective of whether he could write convincingly. He came back home after one of them, excitedly recounting how he had written the 'most brilliant' essay. However, as far as I could gather, it had absolutely nothing to do with the topic and far more to do with his state of mind: *The Illuminatus! Trilogy* rewritten.[15] I imagine that the lecturer marking the paper must have scratched his head in bewilderment: 'Did we study this topic this year?' Obviously, Zach failed. Maybe it *was* a brilliant essay. Maybe it simply went over the head of the baffled don. It was remarkable that he passed any of his exams. He was told that he would have to resit in order to come back in October. A letter written by Dr Goode to the local education authority notes that Zach was unable to finish his course because he 'had a manic episode during part of the last year and was unable to work and do his examinations effectively'. At least this way he could continue to receive his student loan.

And then it was off to Glastonbury again and the particular fallout that was about to ensue. Another stifling June day and Molly, Zach and Jeremy, Molly's brother, were going to take the bus westwards. I had profound misgivings. I explained to Molly that Zach was spiralling. She knew just what I meant but believed it would be disloyal to remain at home. 'I told him I'd go with him,' she said. 'I know he's not good but I thought that if Jeremy came along, then maybe he'd calm down a bit. You know, with us both there and some more of my friends are going too . . .' I pointed out to her that it was dangerous, the mood he was in. She understood. 'I'll keep an eye on him. Make sure he doesn't do anything he shouldn't.' I was doubtful that anyone was going to have any influence over him now and he was furious with me for daring to discuss his condition with her.

As it was, all one needed to do was glance at him to know that something was horribly amiss. He looked seriously weird. His sleep patterns had changed for the worse. He had stayed up nights, relentlessly banging around. Food was just a stopgap, to be consumed rapidly with no sense of decorum or manners, half-chewed sandwiches shoved down his throat, followed by tumblers of orange juice or fizzy water. He was oblivious to how he looked. Food stains created grimy patterns on his shirts and jeans, and bits of sandwich caked his teeth. He sniffed continually and noisily cleared his throat, hoarse from the never-ending cigarettes. For days, he had been in an absolutely foul mood, culminating in his displaying a violently aggressive volatility.

Beth had kept out of his way. Sam made sure there was enough work to keep him in the office. There was little I could do. He was there. I had to be around him. 'You shouldn't go. You're ill.' Wasted breath.

I called Dr Goode. 'Tell him to take his meds,' was all he could offer me.

'He needs to go into hospital,' I told him.

'There's nothing I can do,' was his response, 'not unless he volunteers to come in.'

As if. Zach's mood was black, blacker than it had been for ages: the legacy of sleepless nights, hunger, lithium and, presumably, ketamine. Scruffy, sweaty, grubby, he had tied the usual detritus to his belt: Swiss Army knife, money pouch and sunglasses. These items seemed to me to be ill omens.

'Don't go,' I again requested.

'Fuck off,' was his response.

12

Rehab

Two and a half days later, they were back. Monday afternoon. In the midst of a tranquil, shiny summer's day the telephone rang. Ominously. It was Zach. 'We're back and we're at the station. We don't have any money.' He sounded edgy. What was I supposed to do? I asked him. 'Come and fucking pick us up!' A request such as this was not going to elicit a positive response from me. I refused this demand and received a mouthful of invective from him.

'Are Molly and Jeremy still with you?' I asked.

'Who the *fuck* d'you think would be with me?' was his retort.

I yielded, yet again. 'Then take a taxi,' I said, wearily dreading his return, 'and I'll pay for it. You can owe me.' Some hopes.

Within half an hour, a black taxi turned up outside the house. I retrieved my wallet from my bag and walked over to the cab. The driver looked at me curiously. What did I have to do with this peculiar kid? Inside the cab, I could see that Zach was shouting at Molly, out of control, seemingly unable to restrain his vituperative, nauseating temper. She looked overwhelmed by it all and miserably distressed. Jeremy appeared disorientated, a baffled, rueful expression on his face. Zach got out of the cab, slammed the door behind him and shoved me to one side. Again, he yelled at Molly but he was unintelligible. Without another word, he hoisted his backpack onto his shoulders and strode across the road with not a backward look or a greeting for me.

I was utterly humiliated by his foul behaviour. The taxi driver scowled at me as if I were the one who ought to have borne the brunt of Zach's performance, not him and Molly and Jeremy. How could I blame him? Who knows what Zach had been yelling at Molly the entire journey back? From experience, I knew it would not have been dulcet words of endearment. I fumbled in my wallet and gave Molly enough so that the driver could drop them back home. 'I'm so sorry, Molly,' I said to her. I was out of words. The taxi driver sat there in his cab, the engine running, while Molly tried to give a quick explanation of what had happened during the last three days.

Although they had gone to Glastonbury together with a bunch of her friends, they split up on arrival. Tickets were far too expensive, so they walked around the perimeter fence until they found one of the more entrepreneurial festival-goers, who stamped their hands for £10 and then smuggled them inside. Once in, they made for the Stone Circle, set up their tents and Zach disappeared. This was Friday. On Sunday night, late, he turned up at the tent, his clothing covered in mud, in a jittery, abusive state. Molly realised that he must have been smoking ketamine, although it was more than likely that additionally he had taken anything or everything on offer. Jeremy was also sharing Molly's tent. His had been stolen. This calmed the situation somewhat. In the morning, they had to use all sorts of persuasion to get Zach back onto a bus heading for London. Alexei, a good friend and a member of one of Zach's previous bands, was there with his girlfriend, and the five of them sat at a table at the front of the coach.

For the entire journey, Zach was uncontrollably, threateningly aggressive towards Molly and everyone else on the bus. He was so loud that the other passengers tried to move away from him. No doubt they were all suffering from post-festival hangovers and his psychotic behaviour was hugely detrimental to their tranquillity.

All they wanted to do was rest and sleep and dream of warm food and clean sheets and showers. All Zach could do was yell abuse and blame Molly for everything that had gone wrong in his life. By the time they arrived outside our house, Molly had had five hours of unrelenting threats and insults. She had had enough.

During the following days, Zach's unpredictable and disturbing behaviour was almost unbearable. His irritability and restlessness drove us to distraction. He became increasingly erratic. Whatever I tried to do for him left him cold. I endeavoured to get him to eat but he refused nourishing food and would eat only soggy pizza. He had practically stopped sleeping and came in and out of the house at all hours, having spent God knows how long doing God knows what God knows where. When he saw any one of us, he would start talking non-stop drivel, believing it was the most intellectually challenging discourse. If we attempted to make the point that what he was saying was utter hogwash, he became frighteningly hostile, so we tried to keep away from him as much as we could. I was constantly on the phone to Dr Goode, but his only advice at this point was to keep on increasing the medication.

Zach refused to follow any routine and eventually stopped taking the lithium. Barbiturates he would swallow: diazepam, lorazepam, any barbiturate would do. He took abundant amounts but there was no positive response. Antipsychotics were thrown back in my face. He desperately needed to take them but how could we make him? Subterfuge. Surreptitiously, deceitfully, I ground them into tiny talcum-powder specks and whisked them into glasses of orange juice, which I thrust upon him. This too made little difference. He remained highly strung, wired, agitated and agitating. He wanted money but I refused to give him any, so he taunted me with the threat that he would take his guitar and go and busk in the High Street.

'How ridiculous you are!' I yelled at him. The thought of anyone recognising him *begging* was hugely embarrassing. I was at the end of my patience.

'I'm a brilliant guitarist,' he reminded me grandiosely. 'I'll make hundreds in no time!'

Panic-stricken, I called Dr Goode. 'Zach says he's going to busk, in the High Street!'

He laughed. 'What can I do?'

I had no clue what he could do but I wanted someone to *help* me. 'I don't know what you can do. How can he go and busk?'

He too was beginning to sound exasperated – probably with me, though. 'What do you think will happen?' he questioned me. 'Let him go.'

So Zach went off, guitar on his back, in his filthy, torn jeans, with his grotty blue hair and wild eyes. Within fifteen minutes, he was back. 'They came out of Sainsbury's and told me to move on.'

It was a war of attrition and I was the one being crushed. He had no insight, no idea how his behaviour affected me. He was uncontrollable. Each day, each hour, we shouted and screamed at each other. It was just so repetitive, so monotonous. His behaviour would have been infuriating even in a child, from whom childishness is expected. We had been through all this thirteen years ago. When it comes from a six-foot adult, it is simply too much to endure. The situation was impossible. 'You have to go into hospital!' I shouted at him. 'We can't live like this!'

I rang Dr Goode again. 'We have to do something about this. I can't go on.'

The doctor, always at the end of the phone, listened once more. 'See if he'll come in to see me.'

I knew that there was no possible way I was going to be able to coerce Zach into the car. But I had had an idea, something that I had been mulling over in my mind for the past few days. Possibly the last resort. 'What do you think about rehab?' I asked the psychiatrist.

No answer but I could hear him scrabbling around in a drawer. 'It's possible but he'll have to calm down, be less manic, agree to go.' I could hear the shuffling of paper. 'There's a place near Brighton that I've sent patients to in the past.' He slowly read out the blurb.

It sounded nice. Too nice. Too *normal*. We were clutching at straws. 'Do you think they'll take him?' I appealed to Dr Goode. 'Do you think he'll go?'

I went up to Zach's room. The door was shut. Music blared out. I entered. He was rambling into the telephone, just for a change. I stood and waited for him to finish. He waved me away as if he was in the middle of a crucial conversation; obviously I was disturbing him and he wanted me out. I gestured that I needed to speak to him. He continued to shout into the receiver, all the while tramping around the room, picking up and discarding stuff from the floor and drinking out of various glasses that contained congealing traces of squash or juice. I stood my ground. I made as if to cut him off and he angrily slammed down the receiver.

'*What* do you want?' he barked at me.

It took all my willpower not to hit him, not to walk away. 'Dad and I have decided that you can't stay here like this. You either go into hospital or rehab.'

He looked at me curiously. 'Rehab? Where?' He managed to take a break from insanity for a moment or two.

'In the country,' I answered him. 'Near Brighton.' I decided to try cajoling him. 'You can go to the beach if you like, and there are horses and a pool room.' It was like persuading a kid to go to the dentist.

'And if I don't go?'

I glared at him, my anger bubbling up. 'If you don't go, we'll make sure that you go into hospital. Any way necessary!' This was an idle threat and I knew it. Unless he was a danger to himself or anyone else, there was no way we could get him into hospital unless he volunteered.

He knew it too. He was playing. 'Maybe.'

Once again to Dr Goode. 'I think he's agreed to go.' The insurance company and the rehab centre both agreed that Zach could be a candidate 'so long as he wasn't manic'. What a joke. Dr Goode suggested once again that we up the antipsychotics. Zach hadn't been taking them – what good would they do now? In my heart of hearts, I knew this was a long shot. I climbed the stairs. Maybe the lure of unknown female talent would entice him away to try something new. Pool was always an encouragement. Probably the thought of another echelon of dealers and junkies was far more attractive. Whatever . . . he had to get away from here, deal with some aspects of the illness, even if it meant only one of the symptoms would be alleviated. All I could do was use persuasion – and probably lies again. How low could I get? Horrible. 'There's a place for you on their programme,' I told him, 'but you have to agree to take the right meds to calm down before you go. And, more importantly, agree not to use while you're there.'

The whole thing was probably a pointless exercise, as Zach's mental illness meant that he was way beyond the reach of the Twelve Steps. Looking back, I can't help but wonder whether Dr Goode agreed to sign simply to appease me. Zach remained elated. He packed his bags and insisted that Molly accompany us. He was insufferable the entire journey. It was purgatory. He refused or was unable to stay still. Another blistering, sweaty summer's day and we were packed into a car going on a journey that none of us wished to take. We had to stop endless times so that Zach could run into corner shops and buy drinks. He seemed to have an incessant, boundless thirst. Molly tried talking, stroking, holding him, anything to calm him down, to no avail. Driving through the unremittingly tedious south London suburbs, Sam became increasingly aggravated with him. I entreated him not to respond to Zach's madness, to ignore him, to just *drive*, but his exasperation boiled over. He turned around numerous times to shout at him: 'Shut up! Sit still and be quiet!' We had regressed. We now had a four year old in the back. Horrific.

Leaving London behind us, we drove towards the coast. The traffic was lighter but we saw streams of cars piled up with bags heading towards the ferries. I wished we were among them – anything to escape this torture. The sun retained its fierce heat and even though the car's air-conditioning system belted out stale cold wafts towards us, we were all hot, sticky, peevish and fractious. To some degree, Zach quietened down but he continued to burble mostly inane comments. He knew he was unwell and he knew, obviously, that there was no way that he would observe the rules and regulations at the centre. I think that, as far as he was concerned, he was in control and we were just along for the ride. We left the motorway and Sam consulted his map. This was right. The treatment centre was only a few miles away. I felt the usual dreaded anxiety: dry mouth, palpitations. What now? Hills loomed up in the distance and then we saw a small signpost directing us to a narrow lane on the left. A large Victorian edifice appeared to the right of us and we moved forwards along the broad, oak-lined gravel driveway.

The scene was one of beautifully laid out grounds full of mature shrubs and flowers. The air smelled of lavender and honeysuckle, and I could see beehives dotted in a field beyond. The place was designed to be enticing enough to persuade the junkies and alcoholics and addicted personalities to put their lives on hold for a few weeks or months – so long, of course, as someone else was footing the bill. It looked like a spacious, upmarket country hotel. What addict would not wish to come here to get clean? Only one, of course, who was non compos mentis or so far gone that it didn't matter to him where he was if he couldn't get his next hit. There were a few people scattered around the lawn, standing in small groups or going into the centre through a lush, clematis-strewn bower. It was so pastoral, rustic. Marooned in the midst of the countryside, quiet, miles away from anywhere: an idyllic bolthole. I was envious of Zach; I wanted a bolthole from him. We all got out of the car. I looked towards Zach. He seemed bemused. Taking Molly's hand, he entered through a heavy wooden door. We followed.

Malcolm Green came towards us. He must have been about six

foot three, ramrod straight, with a military moustache. His greying hair was short on top and brushed back off his forehead, yet he wore it long and tied into a ponytail at the back, a rather strange mixture of metaphors. His country attire consisted of grey cords with a tweed jacket and a tie. Not what I'd expected of a detoxifier. He looked us over and smiled. 'You must be Zach!' he cried jovially, wrapping an arm around his shoulders. 'We've been waiting for you.'

Zach stepped back, away from him. 'This is my girlfriend, Molly,' he replied, edging her forward. 'She's come to see me settle in.'

Malcolm laughed. 'That's right,' he said, 'anything to help the settling-in process. Is that your stuff? Your room is ready. Come on up and I'll show you around.'

Zach and Molly followed him up an elegant staircase. Within minutes, they were back down. Molly came over to me. She looked perturbed. 'It's really nice,' she said, very quietly, 'but I don't think Zach's going to do what they want.' I had my own misgivings.

Zach had followed on her heels, pushing towards me. 'They're going through my things!' he shouted angrily. 'Why are they going through my things?'

Sam's ire resurfaced. 'Why d'you think they're going through your things? This is rehab! Who knows what shit you've brought with you!'

Malcolm took control and, taking Zach by the arm, manoeuvred us out of the hall and into a smaller room furnished as an office. 'Sit down for a moment, Zach. All this paperwork needs to be done.' Malcolm guided Zach to a large leather armchair. He sat down and Molly perched on an arm. Forms were filled out, awaiting our signature. 'It's policy,' Malcolm explained, 'that Zach doesn't contact you until after detox, and you'll probably not be able to see him for the first month. This includes Molly.'

Zach was not happy with this arrangement. He looked suspiciously around him and got out of the chair. 'I don't like this place. I don't think I'm going to stay.' He made as if to leave.

'Oh, yes you are!' I responded testily. 'Oh, yes! We've bloody brought you down here to detox. There's no way we're taking you back.' I held him by the arm. 'It's here or back to hospital.'

Persuaded by Malcolm and compelled by our scheming and cajoling, Zach grudgingly agreed to stay but he became more jittery and confrontational the longer we remained there. Sam and I made eye contact, inclining our heads towards the exit. 'We should go,' I said.

Malcolm agreed. 'Don't worry. We'll call and give you updates.' Zach knew that there was nothing further to discuss. Taking another look around, he went over to Molly, hugged her gently and kissed her. 'See you. Call me.' He refused to look at me or say goodbye to us. I was upset but I was past compassion. I wanted to see the back of him. I needed some respite from him and if this gave us some time to regain our strength, all well and good. I wanted him better but I knew that this was not the place for it. We were all pretending. Sam left some money with Malcolm for cigarettes and phone calls, and we left, soberly.

We travelled back to London in silence, passing through the sunburned countryside, past the very same shops we had stopped at earlier, held up by traffic in the grubby, littered suburbs, back to our side of the river. The car was now peaceful and quiet, and each of us was using the time to mull over the day's events. My dominant emotion was an all-encompassing guilt. It was all so appalling. Zach was ill and there seemed to be no recourse to a cure, no way of really dealing with his symptoms. We were at a loss to know what to do and the only advice we were given by the so-called experts was confused and jumbled. Perhaps it was time to get a second opinion – but from whom? We knew that the drugs contributed substantially to his wider problems but by sending him to detox were we addressing the issues the right way round? Had we done the right thing today? we wondered aloud. Within two days, we had our answer.

The wretched phone call. Sam sounded despondent. 'Malcolm Green just called me.'

My heart pounded momentarily. 'What's the problem?' I asked.

'Depends what you would call a problem,' he responded, with a worn-out laugh. 'They want him to leave.'

I supposed this was pretty much what I had expected. 'Why? What's he done?'

Sam laughed again. 'It's what he hasn't done. It's what he can't do. Malcolm says he's too manic and won't do anything they ask of him. Basically, he said he's too ill to be there and that it's a waste of time and money.'

I sat down, cradling the phone in my hands. God. To have to go through it all again. 'When do they want us to pick him up? Not yet, surely!'

Sam was in no mood for long-drawn-out explanations. 'Today,' he replied tetchily. 'I have to go and pick him up today. I am so fucking sick of this! I've spoken to the Griffin. They've agreed to have him back.'

The phone went dead.

13

Sticky Particles

FEBRUARY 2000

I drew patterns on the windows. The temperature plummeted and we became colder and colder the longer we waited. Three breathy discharges fogged up the windows, causing a steady erosion of light from the street, and a nervous compulsion to do something made me create endless circles and spires on the clammy, hazy screen. Two hours. By this time, the street lights were throwing evil shadows across the road. I opened and closed the windows and the bitter air penetrated the car. We three were all now in the same predicament; before we could participate in the final act, we had to see movement. Zach was in his bedsit, across the road from us, incontrovertibly and uncontrollably going mad.

* * *

We had made our best endeavours yet. But nothing had changed. Last summer and a further hospital release into the cold grey light of day. An alternative array of medications, further conditions placed on Zach by us, more promises that things would improve, that he would make an effort to lead a regular life once the meds had kicked in. More discussions, prescriptions, hollow vows. Zach no longer made daily or weekly appointments with Dr Goode. They now met once a month, when the doctor would write out Zach's prescriptions in his alchemist's script and they would spend a chatty twenty minutes discussing Zach's current frame of mind but not the reason for the fluctuating moods nor their probable recurrence. He took the lithium. Had the blood tests. Saw a therapist, unwillingly. Occasionally, Sam or I would speak with the psychiatrist but to us it seemed that he still didn't have a handle on the drugs issues and didn't show any great desire to involve himself in supporting us or forcing Zach to take any kind of proactive stance.

It was evident that Zach had to do something with his life. This led to a heated debate, resulting in an agreement of sorts. He would go back to university in the autumn. Maybe if he retook the first year he would have a basis to continue on to better things – a future, perhaps. But it was not to be. He revisited the guys in the squats, the drugs, late nights and old friends. Tosh swaggered around in his elevated shoes, his face menacing, sneering and snarling, but I wouldn't allow him back into the house. My enmity towards his very existence was unrelenting. Then October crept up and, pregnant with malice, November led on to depression and mania. This time the depression was all-pervading and was still with him through the entire Christmas period. We dealt with it as best we could, airing the usual platitudes. It was a desperate and gruelling juggling act that took all my emotional strength and resources. We teetered on the edge, riding the storm between the moods, infected by them, never grasping how best to contain Zach. Beth busied herself, absenting herself from us, powerless to bear the misery of depression and then the despair of mania, the pure fury she felt towards her brother, his betrayal. His metamorphosis.

He couldn't live with us. It was an impossible situation. It wasn't a question of evicting him; we simply had to remove him from our orbit so that we could all breathe more freely. Be less anxious. Give him some space. A friend had a studio that was empty. 'Could Zach live here?' I asked Clara, once I had seen it and decided that it was a chance for him. 'Can we rent the room?' She agreed. So we moved as much as we could. The belongings that he needed with him: books, CDs, musical equipment. It was a bitterly cold winter but the studio was bright, if not terribly warm. We hoped that he would make the best of it. Be responsible. Come to terms with who he was. And we left him there. After two months and endless complaints from neighbours about noise and late-night pranks by Zach's inebriated or high acquaintances, with Christmas having passed in a haze, my friends Jon and Will and I were killing time outside the flat, waiting for the local NHS mental-health crisis team – waiting to have him put away, again.

I guess I'd lost it this time. Zach had disappeared from sight. I was pretty much on my own. Sam was away on business. I held back from involving Beth. Over the preceding few weeks, I had watched while Zach had become thinner and thinner, his face a skeletal mask, his cheekbones jutting out, his eyes sinking further back into his skull. His clothes hung off his emaciated frame. His behaviour became wilder and wilder. I'd contacted those friends with whom he had re-established ties; they had lost sight of him. Dominic too. He was running with a crowd I didn't know. If he came home to me, it was to borrow money, maybe eat a quick sandwich, make a few telephone calls. We would have the standard conversation. 'Are you using?' His response: 'Is it *your* business?' It was my business, I maintained, if he was coming to me to borrow money. 'I'll give it back,' he promised. 'You know I will – eventually.'

I was more concerned now about how thin he was, how unhealthy he looked. I went out and bought him a weight-gain powder. Another insanity. 'It's chocolate flavoured,' I advised him.

'That's nice,' he said, gathering up the canister, opening it and, taking a large spoon from the drawer, inserting it into the drum. He brought out an enormous heap of the concentrate and, spilling great mounds of powdery particles over table and clothing, dumped it into a glass of milk. He swigged it down. 'That's great,' he mumbled. 'I'll take it home with me. I'll put on weight in no time.' He left, brown residue trailing behind his ghostly figure.

Now he was lost. No one had seen him for days and he hadn't turned up for his meeting with Dr Goode. Hours before I had appealed to Will and Jon for help, I had decided that I had to find Zach. The not unexpected phone call from Dr Goode had precipitated my new journey. 'Is Zach with you?' he asked me. 'He hasn't turned up.'

He knew that Zach no longer lived with us. 'Zach's not here,' I answered him. 'Haven't you heard from him? Hasn't he called you?' It was the first time that Zach had missed a Sunday meeting.

'No,' he responded. 'He should have been here an hour ago.'

The debilitating anxiety returned. 'I don't know where he is,' I told Dr Goode, heated breath, dry mouth. 'I saw him briefly last week but he was manic again. I didn't ask him about your meeting.' Anger and disappointment boiling up. Stupid, *stupid* me. 'I'll go and see if he's in his flat.'

Dr Goode attempted reassurance. 'I doubt there's anything terrible to worry about,' he informed me. 'Just let me know when you find him.'

I promised I would do that. 'He's probably going to need to have to go back to hospital,' I told him, 'and I think he's using again.'

A semblance of a chuckle. 'I've no doubt about it . . .'

I went up to Beth's room. She was asleep. Max slept beside her, on the mat next to her bed. 'Beth,' I whispered, guilty about waking her but knowing that this was precisely what I had to do. 'Beth, Zach seems to have disappeared. I'm going over to the flat to see if he's there. He hasn't shown up for his meeting with Dr Goode.'

Beth turned over and pulled herself up on one arm. She rubbed at her face. 'He's not shown up?' she mumbled. 'Where is he?'

I bent down to her to rub her back. 'I don't know. I'll let you know when I get there.'

She took her glass of water off the bedside table and swallowed a mouthful. 'Does Dad know?'

I shook my head at her. 'Too early. He'll be asleep and there's no point in worrying him. What can he do anyway?' Lucky Sam. No reason to call him. 'He'll only worry unnecessarily.'

She nodded at me. 'I'll take Max out. Let me know what happens.'

I took the spare keys and drove over to Zach's flat. It was quiet, still too early for the neighbours to be about. Perhaps it had been too ambitious to have expected Zach to attend a rendezvous with his psychiatrist at nine on a Sunday morning. It was an additional appointment, made earlier in the week in the abject realisation that he was breaking up, relapsing. I should have known, been aware, that unless I physically accompanied him to the consulting rooms, there was no way that he would make it. Now I was reaping the benefits of wisdom retarded. Thuds. Perspiration. Where *is* he? I parked the car outside the block of flats and walked along the path to the front door.

Free newspapers littered the doormat, along with empty milk bottles and cigarette ends. I peered around me and tried to see through into the flat. I rang the doorbell. No response. I knocked. Nothing. I put the key in the lock and opened the door. It was freezing cold inside but a strange smell assailed my nostrils, chemical, burning. There was no one there but the lights were on, those that hadn't burned out. The place was a tip. In the corner lay a tower of unopened mail. I picked up some of the flyers and envelopes. They were addressed to previous tenants – so many different names. Dozens of pizza-delivery adverts, Indian takeaway menus, 'Let us iron for you!', old news, all jumbled together. The weird smell was all-pervading. I walked over to the kitchen area and saw to my horror that in his demented state, oblivious to the flat and his responsibilities, Zach had flown the coop in a complete daze. He hadn't switched off the lights; he hadn't turned off the stove. God knows what he had been cooking but a trail of brown powder gave me a clue. One of his saucepans remained on the hob, burned out, black and stinking.

Sticky Particles

The pan was scorching hot. I tried to lift it off but it was almost welded to the cooker. I looked around for an oven glove but nothing except for a filthy kitchen towel was available to me. Some time back, it had been brand spanking new and spotlessly clean. Now it was stained brown and rancid, as were the dishcloths suspended haphazardly on hooks. A grubby pile of plates and cutlery and pots and pans had collected around the sink and on the draining board. Nothing had been washed for weeks, it would appear. The saucepan was beyond repair. I looked into the cupboards and the tiny fridge. No food. The microwave was encrusted with sticky particles. These I recognised. I opened it. The inside, too, was swathed in the stuff. The glass plate was tacky, covered in the residue of some ghastly substance. I took a whiff. The strange, pervasive metallic smell hit me. Jolly old ketamine again.

The animal tranquilliser, the immobiliser. Ketamine or 'Special K' or 'Vitamin K', or any of those nomenclatures that the aficionados append to that most delightful of all noxious substances. How much he had been using, I had no idea. It must have been substantial. You'd think that he would have learned. Not Zach. 'I'm in control,' he would boast. A short time ago, I met a guy, an addict, who had only once tried ketamine. He was aghast that I had even heard of the drug. 'That stuff's fucking awful. Disgusting,' he told me. 'Someone gave it to me at a club. I thought it was ecstasy. About fifteen minutes after I swallowed it, I went into a "K-hole". I thought I was going to die. I felt as if I was going down and down into a vortex. I was paralysed. I couldn't do anything to help myself. I had to call my best mate and the only way I could come back to earth was for him to talk me out of it and then fill me up with jugs of orange juice. It was vile. The most grotesque experience I've ever had. I've used everything but this stuff was the worst.' I constantly ask myself the same question: why would anyone desire this stuff? I still have no idea what Zach found so enticing about it.

The walls of the flat seemed to close in on me. A cold draught crept from under the door. There was no semblance of 'home' here. Just a place to rest a body. I continued looking around. I wanted to find a clue as to where he could possibly be, where he could have gone. The pattern was recurring. Once again, he'd taken out the lyric sheets from his CDs, opened them and arranged them, so that they were stuck indiscriminately over the walls. Books and videos were in the usual disarray. What clothes he had were rolled up on the bed. I sat down and, pulling pairs of jeans over towards me, I rifled through the pockets. They were mostly filled with dirty bits of tissue or the scraps of tobacco. Then I came across a tattered piece of paper that contained names and numbers. Aha! I didn't recognise any of them. Maybe there was someone here who could help me? They were probably all dealers but it was worth a try. I took out my phone and started dialling.

* * *

The car zigzagged across the road. Another lapse of concentration. I hauled the steering wheel back around and regained control. The *A–Z* lay flat in my lap. I pulled over towards the pavement and tried to find the turning. Somewhere in the maze of Dalston lay a small council estate. In this council estate was situated a flat. It was there that I was heading but I had no idea where it was and the *A–Z* was of no help. From what I could make out, there should have been a tiny turning off the main road on the left but, of course, this being London, none of the streets displayed names. If they did, they appeared at the very beginning and the very end of the road and nowhere else in between. Typical. I retraced my journey along the map. Tim had told me where to turn. I thought it was the next left. All I could do was make use of my sense of direction. I *hoped* this was where he'd said. A series of buildings held together by walkways appeared towards the bottom of the road, an emblematic 1960s construction of discoloured grey concrete interspersed with mottled red balustrades. It was neither ugly nor imposing. Just utilitarian. Three storeys at the most. No trees, only bedraggled, nondescript bushes. Litter bins overflowing, various antique cars lacking windscreens, or in some cases engines. A perfect locale for a disappearance.

I parked the car outside Block D and locked it, looking around as I did so. Who knew who could be lurking nearby? If I had come looking for a junkie, it stood to reason that dealers and other junkies would be in the vicinity. I had no intention of being mugged. I looked up. Flat 16 was on the top level. Why was I doing this? Objectively, it made no sense. I should really be leaving well enough alone. Leaving Zach to make his own bloody mistakes. Not involving myself. Allowing him to fall as far as possible. But I told myself, naively, that this illness had to be cured. I climbed the stairs, which smelled sweetly of urine and sick. Nice. I found number 16 and knocked.

I continued to knock. There was no reply. I could have kicked myself. Then I heard a shuffling and the door opened slightly. 'Yes?' said a muffled voice.

'Hi, we spoke earlier,' I called through the gap. 'It's Zach's mother.'

The door opened. Behind it stood a tall blond man, cradling a very fluffy black cat. He wore jeans but nothing on top. 'Sorry,' he told me, as he replaced the cat on the carpet. 'I was just having a shower. Come in while I put on some more clothes.' I walked in. The place was remarkably clean and tidy. He went into another room and then came out, this time wearing a white T-shirt with an animal motif. 'I'm Tim,' he said, extending a hand. 'Thanks for coming but I'm afraid you're too late. Zach's gone.'

I gulped air and sat down on a sofa. 'I don't believe it!' I groaned, head down, neck aching.

'I tried to keep him here,' Tim explained, 'but he was just too far gone. Wasn't listening. I told him that you were going to give him a lift home but he really didn't have a clue what I was on about.'

I looked at Tim. He had a sweet, open face. He didn't look like a junkie or even as if he'd smoked a spliff in his entire life. 'What was he doing here?' I asked him. I had found the phone number on the piece of paper in Zach's jeans and called it in the hope that maybe whoever answered would actually know him. It was pure chance that Zach had been here over the weekend.

Tim sat down opposite me. 'You know, he'd brought this powder stuff with him. Brown, sticky stuff in a tub. It got everywhere.' He laughed apologetically. 'I got the impression that he thought it was some new kind of drug!'

I joined in with his laughter. The irony of it. 'It's supposed to help you put on weight,' I offered feebly. 'Zach's so thin.'

Tim offered me tea, which I refused, and a precis of the events of the weekend. It seemed that Zach had turned up, chocolate powder in hand, quite out of his head. He'd stayed overnight and Tim and the other guys who shared the flat had tried to care for him, to get him to eat and sleep, but they realised that it wasn't simply the drugs that were problematic here. Zach was unbelievably manic. They didn't know him that well. They were friends of friends of friends and somehow Zach had a phone number and an address for them. They hadn't met him when he was well and so had nothing to compare his current condition with. They just knew that his behaviour was out of the bounds of their experience. When I had called, the others had still been asleep. Tim, altruistically, had stayed with Zach overnight in the faint hope that nothing terrible could happen to him if there was someone keeping an eye on him.

'He didn't stop talking or moving the entire time he was here,' Tim reported. 'It was shattering. I don't know where he got the energy from.'

I did. I'd seen it too often. 'Manic energy, Tim,' I explained. 'Could you understand any of it?'

Tim laughed again. 'No, it was all drivel. He thought he was Jesus.'

The settee was deep and comforting. I wanted to go to sleep. Forget the rest of the day. Forget why I was here. Tim looked at me expectantly. I had anticipated that the flat would be a junkie's den but it was nothing of the sort. Evidently, they were all good, clean-living, working guys. What on earth had Zach been doing *here*, then? It was all very strange. I looked around me at the ordered books, the china teacups set out on a wooden tray, milk in a jug, a teapot at the ready. So clean, so tidy – so middle class.

I started to move. 'Is there anything more I can do to help?' Tim enquired.

'No,' I said, standing up. 'Thanks. He's gone. Thanks for trying.'

I pulled at my sweater, straightened my jeans. Now what? Then my phone rang.

'Hi.' That foreign accent. 'It's Alexei here. Zach's gone back to his flat. He just called me.'

I looked over at Tim. 'Zach's turned up,' I mouthed towards him. 'Thanks, Alexei,' I said, turning back to my phone. 'I'll come straight back. Could you go over? Can you keep him there?'

* * *

Alexei walked across the road towards the car. I rolled down the window. Jon, Will and I looked at him in anticipation. 'What's happening?' I asked. He looked grey, drawn, frazzled. His fraying sweater, baggy jeans and punk hair belied his maturity: he had taken on the supervision of one highly loopy individual with equanimity. He looked worn away with the anxiety of metaphorically hanging on to Zach and physically restraining him from making a bolt for it.

'I can't do this,' he said wearily. 'I don't know what else to say to him, what else to do. I don't know if he believes me.' He rubbed at his chin, scratched his head. 'I've never seen him like this before,' he continued. 'He's really disturbed. He's muttering all the time. Shouting . . . at nothing. He keeps on taking the CDs out of their sleeves and mixing them all up, because he's on a "mission" of some sort.' Alexei stopped talking to take out a cigarette. He bent down and put his head through the window. 'Can I have a light? Zach's used up all my matches. I'll have to go and buy some otherwise.' I started the engine and gave him the car lighter. The red glow lit up his troubled, sleepy green eyes. I felt guilty that he had volunteered to do this. He took a deep drag, leaving the cigarette dangling on his lower lip. 'How much longer?' I looked down at my hands. I didn't know how long the crisis team would be. He removed the cigarette with shaky fingers. 'I can't understand what he's on about. He's completely crazy.'

Will motioned to Alexei to come closer to him. 'Do you think you can take another half an hour?'

Alexei shrugged. 'I don't know. I told him I was going out to buy something to eat. You have to help me here.'

I watched while Alexei retraced his steps across the road. We looked at one another. How much longer? The night had drawn in around us. There was little activity in the street but who knew who was watching us from behind drawn curtains? We sat there in silence. None of us had the heart to listen to the radio or to music. Will and Jon were old friends who had often offered help, advice. They both volunteered for the Samaritans and had some insight into the psychologically wounded. I'd called them early afternoon and they'd dropped everything to meet me here. For once, I felt that I couldn't do it on my own. We waited in the dank cold, fidgeting, coughing. Then a car pulled into the street as if looking for an address. Headlights pointed towards us, included us in the glare. It stopped across the road, outside the flat. Three people got out of the car. 'They're here,' I said, clambering out and walking towards them. 'Crisis team?' I asked.

A short, bearded man with rimless glasses smiled at me. 'Yes, it's us,' the doctor said. 'I'm sorry it's taken so long. It's been a busy day.'

I grimaced. Merely another busy day, another set of symptoms, maladies. All in the line of duty, just a hard day's work. Could they understand my predicament? The other two were women, who peered at me, trying to work out the relationship. Another doctor and a social worker, out in the dark on this biting Sunday afternoon in order to make up the legally defined crisis team.

'What's been happening here?' the bearded doctor asked. I explained as best I could. This was the first time that the NHS had been called, the first of many more to come. It was clear that Zach desperately needed to be hospitalised and we had realised that involving the local authority crisis team was the most straightforward way to ensure he was sectioned and received care as soon as possible. There was a new file to be completed, filled out with illegible notes. 'We've called for an ambulance,' the doctor told me. 'It depends on Zach, though, on how ill he is, whether or not the police will also have to be called.'

I breathed deeply. Not again. 'He's pretty bad,' I explained. 'I don't think he's going to go in without a fight.'

How much Zach knew about what was going on, I had no real idea but I didn't want him to see me. I didn't want him to condemn me once again for calling for help and securing a hospital bed. This time, I believed, it wouldn't be a nice private room but the local hospital. The locum psychiatrist crossed the road with his entourage, with me at the back of the procession. 'This is it,' I pointed to the entrance. The doctor looked around him, at the crisp brown leaves gathered around the steps and the evergreen bushes in the front garden. Madness knows no boundaries. Next door lived a world-famous actor, upstairs a renowned cellist. The medical fraternity gathered themselves. The doctor knocked at the door. The sound reverberated in the silence of the night. Alexei came out. He looked crestfallen, guilty and sad.

'I'll wait out here, then,' I said.

'We'll be out to let you know what's happening,' said the doctor. 'Hopefully, it shouldn't take too long.'

The three of them stepped over the threshold and closed the door behind them.

Jon and Will had joined me when they saw Alexei coming out of the flat. 'What now?' asked Jon.

'Another wait, guys,' I answered. 'I'm sorry.'

We stood at the door in a huddled group beneath a single light bulb. I rubbed at my hands to warm them up. Will pulled up the collar of his jacket, tucking in a woolly scarf. 'So cold,' he said. Alexei lit up again. I could see that he was desperate to be free of this. He had had enough. Time for him to get his life back to normal. 'Thanks so much, Alexei,' I said to him. 'You've been absolutely fantastic. I don't know what we would have done without you.'

He smiled at me. 'Not to worry. Can I do anything else? Do you need anything?'

What more could I ask him to do? 'No,' I replied sadly, disconsolately. 'You've done more than you needed to. I'll call and let you know what happens. I guess they'll get him into hospital. At least I hope so.' He came towards me and, putting his arms out, hugged me to him. He was trembling. 'It was so good of you to help like this,' I said quietly to him. 'Go and get some sleep.' He shook hands with the guys and left us.

An ambulance made its way along the street and stopped outside the flat. Two paramedics, a man and a woman, descended from it and walked towards me.

'Any movement?' asked the guy.

'I don't think it'll be much longer now,' I replied.

'We've got to wait for the police, though,' the woman, younger and broader, told me. 'We can't take him if he's likely to be violent.'

This amazed me. Then why did they come?

'What do you mean, you can't take him if he's likely to be violent?' asked Will.

'Health and safety,' replied the man. 'Too many of us have been attacked in the past. We can't take mental patients if they're violent.'

Great. Another hour passed before the police turned up – Arsenal were playing at home. The voyeurs in the street must have had an eyeful: the police car stationed outside in case of a health-and-safety disaster; the crisis team members and Zach coming out of the flat. He was in a maniacally calm stage but looked decidedly peculiar. From the shadows he spied Will. He went round the police cordon, going over to pump his hand. 'Hi, Will! What're you doing here?' I looked at Will, whose expression was a mixture of surprise, compassion and shock. I could see why. Zach, for some reason known only to him, had taken scissors and cut his shirt into shreds. It fluttered about his shoulders in kite tails. He had slit his jeans repeatedly from ankle to thigh, creating ribbons of denim. What kind of sartorial decision was this? They didn't cover his knees, flapping around his legs as he walked. He carried his anorak under his arm. His belt held the usual idiosyncratic accoutrements but hardly fulfilled its role. The jeans just about held together. It was beyond belief that he was unconscious of both the cold and his bizarre appearance. I tried to keep out of his way but when he caught sight of me, he turned towards me angrily. 'I should've known *you'd* be here,' he snarled, coming towards me aggressively. Then the police took him to the ambulance and he left us.

14

'That's It'

This time it was a write-off. Complete. Utter. 'Nice one, this,' said the young guy collecting the remains. He shifted the deflated undercarriage with his Doc Martens. 'Salvage? Insurance?' He grinned at me. 'One half too many? Girlfriend trouble?' He chortled, easing his hands into goalkeeper-sized gloves. From the back of the van issued a ramp with various pulleys and ropes and metal brackets. He bent over to straighten it up, his rump rising out of his greasy overalls, a patchwork of flags and roses. I tried not to look, mesmerised by the Chelsea flowers, 'Mum' in gothic script. Within seconds, he had wrestled the bike onto the platform, tying it down, making sure it wasn't going anywhere ever again. Although we had had it repaired and the bike had spent months in a garage awaiting Zach's good health, it had now irrevocably met its demise. Two grand down the tubes. An expensive lesson in how not to bring up kids, especially mad ones. He closed the back of the van, giving the door a hefty shove with his right foot. 'That's done, then,' he said to me, taking out a pen from his back pocket. He leaned over into the driver's seat and brought out a sheaf of paper. 'Here you go, sign your moniker on the right.' I took the pen and paper and added my signature, pleased to see the back of the both of them. He tipped an imaginary cap and climbed in. 'See you later.' No, you won't, I thought. No, you bloody well won't.

* * *

Two days. Within two days of the section, Zach was out of the NHS hospital and driven across London to the Griffin. Reprise. Why we took him out, I don't remember. Maybe we thought it would help his recovery. Another locked ward and another large male psychiatric nurse shadowing his every movement. Sam returned. He had been updated on the situation while in the back of a taxi on Sixth Avenue. By the time he reached his meeting near the Port Authority, he was close to meltdown.

'Did you think this was unexpected?' I asked him.

'Not unexpected,' he replied tersely, 'just bloody unwanted. I thought maybe something would have changed.'

I understood but what could I do about it? He came back from New York and our accustomed visits began again. Same attitude: 'It's not my fault.' Same resentment: 'Trust you to interfere.' Same denial: 'I'm not sick.' The circles continued. More meds, arguments, appeals. A twenty-first birthday spent on a locked ward in the Griffin. Not everyone's dream celebration. Three years of this awful illness. No party, no friends, just us sitting on a single bed covered with a flowery eiderdown. Some memories are simply too painful. The hospital smells permeated the room. A clammy heat clung to us. The windows were locked fast and there was no way to open them so that something of the outside world could penetrate the despondency. A shop-bought birthday cake. Smoked salmon sandwiches, cans of Coke and a bottle of fizzy pop. Photographs that depict a sick, confused young man. No wonder the depression bit.

Section 3. The idea behind it is that six months' treatment on a psychiatric ward will lead to a happy release. But it's rare that someone actually sees out half a year in hospital. For that to happen, the patient usually has to be incurable or have nowhere else to go. After eight weeks, Zach was transferred to a halfway house. He spent another two months wasting time, was discharged and forwarded back to us. The summer hiatus. He found employment and for once, I think, he enjoyed the occasional jobs, liked the idea of earning money. There were new friends and other activities. We insisted that he attend Narcotics Anonymous meetings and visit a drug counsellor. The private health-insurance company wanted to get shot of us. A letter was sent informing us that they considered Zach a 'chronic' case. They would no longer cover him for inpatient care. So that was that. He was now at the mercy of the NHS. No more of our relenting and removing him from its jurisdiction to a pretty private institution. Outpatient care the insurance would cover, for the time being. Our futile meetings with Dr Goode were included. The drug counsellor was not. So we stumped up the money to pay for these sessions, while Zach continued to sniff, smoke, cook, drink and chew whatever was available to him.

Summer wove its heady fragrance around Zach. He held down the jobs he took but without any notion of trying to develop them into something with more of a future. His life was permanently on hold, as if he thought something better was going to come along. What he was expecting, I had no clue. Sam and I tried every tactic to instil some kind of ambition in him. How he had changed! As a child, he had wanted to do everything. Now his only aspiration was to make enough money to buy cigarettes and, maybe, to travel. The break from Molly was permanent. Understandably. It was a wrench but it did not prevent him from meeting girls and having relationships. His innate charm, good humour and intelligence surfaced once again – as they always do during the summer months. He absorbs the daylight, reflects the sun, as is the case with so many manic-depressives. It is only with the onset of the autumn and winter months that the lack of serotonin hits, as it was about to do once more.

Late October. Dr Goode dispensed his advice at various clinics throughout London and its suburbs, and Zach and I were on our way to one that seemed to be the furthest away. The journey took us past an endless stream of roads, bridges, walkways and warehouses. I put my foot down fully on the throttle. I felt frustrated and helpless. I had said I would accompany him and so here I was, in the driving seat yet again, trying to assert control. Zach was next to me in body. Not in mind. He fumbled and muttered but resisted my requests that he shut up. He was no longer hearing me. A steady stream of medications flowed through him but they were no longer having the desired effects on his brain. Those neurotransmitters were battling in overdrive. His mood had been escalating and tumbling repeatedly over the past few weeks. Initially, he had listened to us and increased the meds, seen the doc. But his continuing use of mind-altering substances had played havoc with his good intentions. Fallout. Explosive black moods. Arguments.

The bike sat peacefully in the driveway. Zach insisted on driving it. I had hidden the keys. He was pretty much unable to catch a bus or take the Tube, the mood and state he was in. How could he ride a bike? We fought this point the entire journey.

'It's mine,' he informed me. 'I'll do what I like.'

I gripped the steering wheel. 'You should *not* be riding a bike,' I rejoined. 'You're a danger. You don't know what you're doing. You could kill someone.'

He shifted around in the passenger seat, his head nearing mine, spitting bile. 'You can't tell me what to do! I'll drive the fucking bike if I want to!'

I clenched my teeth and kept driving, desperately trying to keep my temper. I was out of options. 'Even Dr Goode will tell you that you can't drive it,' I responded witheringly, clutching at straws.

'Yeah?' he challenged me. 'Yeah, let's ask Dr Goode. He'll know what to do.'

I parked the car and walked over towards the clinic. Zach lit a cigarette. I waited for him to join me.

'I'm not going in.'

I looked at him. 'What?'

He kicked at the gravel. 'I'm not going in again. I'm not volunteering. I'm not getting sectioned. Don't you put your oar in.'

I stopped outside the doors. It was pitch black. Few lights shone round about. The clinic, an old '30s block on an unpaved street, was blank and unwelcoming. Dr Goode's name was one of a number engraved on a discoloured bronze plate. My resolve weakened. 'That's not why I brought you here,' I explained. 'It's another regular meeting with the doctor. You know that. It's just to go over your meds and stuff.'

He shuffled over, stubbing out the cigarette. 'I'm only here to ask him about the bike. That's all.'

Whatever. This was soul-destroying. 'Go in, then,' I said to him. 'Do your worst.'

I sat in the waiting room while Zach saw the doctor. I attempted a read of the evening newspaper but put it down again, unable to concentrate on anything. I went over to the water dispenser and struggled to extract one of the plastic cups. A feeling of hopelessness rose up within me. What now? Within twenty minutes, Zach reappeared, grinning. The cat had got the cream.

'Dr Goode says I can ride my bike.'

I jerked my head towards the doctor. 'He says what?'

Zach laughed. 'You see? You don't know everything after all!' He walked past me. 'I'm going out for a fag.'

Dr Goode came out of his office and stood beside a tall vase, whilst Zach exited. 'I've increased his medication and told him to come back next week,' he said to me, extending a hand containing yet another prescription.

I refused it. 'How can you say that he's able to drive the bike? He's completely nuts! He doesn't know what day it is!'

Dr Goode grimaced. 'I can't stop him. I can only tell him to take care.'

What was going on? 'He's manic,' I persisted. 'He's on all that medication.'

The doctor told me, 'He just has to be careful.'

I was astounded and felt even more paralysed by helplessness. Who had he been speaking with for the past twenty minutes? Did this have something to do with patient confidentiality? Was he trying to protect Zach in some way? Who could stop Zach from destroying himself? Was everyone, his parents, his psychiatrist, really this powerless?

Zach came back inside. 'OK? Can we go?'

I repeated my question, irrespective of Zach's sensitivities. I was worried about him living long enough to take the increased medication and even more concerned that he could kill someone else. 'How can you say that Zach can drive a motorcycle when he's ill like this? Surely he's a danger to himself? What about other people?'

Dr Goode went over to Zach and took him by the hand. 'Here, Zach, here's the prescription. I can't stop you from driving. But be careful.'

Zach retrieved the script and put it in his jeans pocket. 'Yeah, thanks. I will. I'll be *very* careful.'

* * *

My phone vibrated in my pocket. I answered it. Five minutes earlier, Sam and I had left home. I had deposited Zach back at the house, exhorting him to stay in and rest. He wanted to go out again, insisted that I tell him where the keys to the bike were.

'Stay in,' I implored him. 'You shouldn't go anywhere. You're ill.'

He laughed in my face. 'You heard him. You heard Dr Goode. He didn't tell me not to ride it.'

I took a deep breath and tried to think what the doctor would have said to a son of his own if he had been in our situation. What more could I do? Say? There comes a time when you simply give up. Sam and I were unable to restrain him physically, apply cuffs, irons. The doctor could not, it seemed, ban him from driving and we couldn't forcibly keep him in the house. I put the keys back in their usual place. We watched Zach don his helmet, start the engine and teeter off down the driveway into the gloomy street. Such foreboding. I felt at a loss. I couldn't stay in. 'Let's go and get something to eat,' I said to Sam. 'Let's switch off for an hour, have a drink. Stop thinking about it.' Now the phone was ringing. Fifteen minutes later. A strange number appeared in the display.

'Hello?' I asked.

'You don't know me,' answered a woman, 'but I've been asked to call you. There's been an accident. Your son has been involved in an accident.'

We turned around and headed back. The traffic was light. It had been drizzling and the pavements threw up the disjointed images of passing buses and taxis. What pedestrians there were hurried along, their umbrellas unfurled, towards the Tube or the various bus stops dotted along the road. The supermarket remained open and I noticed that the *Big Issue* seller was still offering his goods to weary shoppers, his dog lying under an old tarpaulin. We came to a halt at the traffic light, waited for it to change colour and then headed up the hill towards the ambulance. Its lights reflected conflicting patterns of red and blue onto the leafy autumnal tarmac. The paramedics went in and out of the rear doors. Zach's bike rested in a lifeless heap at the side of the road, finally defeated in all its workings, its tail lights smashed, the front wheel at right angles to the body. An old-model Peugeot was parked in the middle of the street. A front wheel had come off and the car was lying on its axle, a huge dent adorning the front panel, its windscreen shattered. The right-hand door was spreadeagled open and the contents of a plastic bag spilled onto the street – cans, crisp packets and bottles. A young couple stood nearby, clinging to each other, shocked.

With a mighty sigh, Sam pulled over and parked the car. We alighted and walked towards the coloured lights. I didn't know what to make of the situation. Sam was incensed. Zach leaned by the side of the ambulance, wiping at his head. His leather jacket was torn at the shoulder, exposing a skinny arm. He was pale but perspiration glimmered along his brow. He grimaced when he saw us coming towards him and moved slightly away from the vehicle, no doubt anticipating an imminent confrontation.

'What the hell happened?' demanded Sam. 'We've only just left you!'

One of the paramedics came towards us. 'There's been an accident,' she said, attempting an explanation.

'I can *see* there's been an accident!' Sam snapped, furious and blind to the possibility that someone had been injured. He rounded on Zach. 'Didn't we tell you not to drive tonight?'

I went over to Sam. 'Don't make it worse,' I appealed, sotto voce. 'Don't lose it.'

He brushed me off. 'What the fuck did you do this time, Zach?'

The paramedic urged restraint. 'I don't think he's hurt too badly,' she said to me. 'But he refuses to come to the hospital to be checked out.'

I understood that point only too well. I took Zach by the elbow, looking up at his face. 'Are you all right?' I asked him. 'Are you injured?'

He rubbed at his head again and then, with trembling fingers, took out a packet of cigarettes. He lit up, his whole body now quivering. 'I'm all right . . . I don't need to go into hospital. I'm just a bit shaky.'

The paramedic stroked his shoulder comfortingly. He attempted a smile. I realised that he was desperately trying to hold it all together. The last place he wanted to be right now was hospital, although, of course, the best place for him would have been a secure bed. I didn't know whether to hug him in relief that he was not badly hurt or shake him in irritation, so I left him and went back across the road. The car was a complete write-off, resting forlornly across a speed hump. What could Zach have been thinking of? Was it the other driver's fault? I doubted it.

There had been no traffic on this stretch, Ian, the Peugeot's driver, informed me. He and his partner, Judy, were on their way home from work. They were tired but looking forward to spending an evening together, eating a takeaway, watching telly. The street was dimly lit. Suddenly, from nowhere, a single penetrating light came upon them, on their side of the road. No way to avoid a collision. Zach was driving on the wrong side, as if he were riding his Piaggio on a single-track lane in rural Italy. He hit them with such force that he demolished both his bike and their car. Although their vehicle was in its dotage, the only reason for its demise was the full-frontal assault of a scooter going at forty miles per hour. The bike skidded from under him onto its side. Zach was thrown head first onto the bonnet. His body then pitched upwards. He bounced off the roof of the car and landed in the centre of the damp, dirty road, into the path of oncoming traffic. Only he was lucky: there was none. Arguably, because he was so doped up, so full of uppers and downers, he was like a cat, no fear, his muscles relaxed, his brain unengaged. Another one of his lives used up. Someone somewhere was looking after him. Another person would have been killed instantly. He suffered bruises, cuts and abrasions but nothing else. Was he shocked? Who could tell? It was a small miracle.

Miracles do happen. The luckless succumb to their destiny. But Zach was lucky. Obviously, his destiny was not to die under the wheels of an oncoming vehicle that night. However, the accident should never have happened. Zach should not have been driving anything bigger than a Tonka car. On the packaging of tranquillisers, antipsychotics and even antihistamines, consumers are urged to refrain from driving while taking the medication. Those words of advice are presumably intended to prevent this type of incident. Within two hours of Zach having seen his doctor, and despite words of caution and our futile attempts to stop him driving, he was involved in what could have turned out to be a fatal accident. He was lucky to escape with his life. He demolished the motorcycle as well as a car. Two innocents were caught up in Zach's personal chaos. He could have killed them. Luckily, they were unhurt, albeit shaken and angry. Fortunately, they were covered by insurance.

While the ambulance discharged carbon monoxide, we made

arrangements with Judy and Ian. Their car was scraped up off the road onto the back of a recovery vehicle. The bike was abandoned, a sad heap of metal, thrust onto its side, awaiting its end. Nothing could persuade Zach to go to hospital, even to have his obvious injuries checked out. The paramedic shrugged. 'Shall we go now?'

I nodded. 'No point trying to force him,' I said to her. She was unaware of his mental-health problems and thought that his strange reaction, behaviour, tics were the result of the accident. My head informed me that I had to tell her but, curiously, my heart wasn't in it. Could she have shown more insight? I doubt it. Our meal forsaken, we pushed our son into the car, no one saying a word, even Zach, nursing his wounded head. We got him back home.

We were in a dilemma: what should we do with him? Sam and I debated all the questions. There were no answers. Zach was in no state to take responsibility for himself and refused any further medication or to take our advice. I called the local-authority crisis team. It was late. There was no one there to speak to me. I left my number on the answerphone. No one called back. I called one of the local hospitals. Again no one was available. So frustrating. It was as if there was a conspiracy of silence. No one would take responsibility for one very sick young man. What kind of system was this? Call back, I was told. So for the next two days, I rang continuously, speaking to myriad individuals. It was as if the onus was on us because we were the carers. It was surreal. We were within touching distance of someone suffering a potentially fatal illness and no one seemed willing to offer help.

Finally, at last, I was put in touch with a consultant who deigned to answer the phone, but I felt that he was reluctant to take a history over the phone or make a house call to see Zach. 'Bring him in,' he said. 'Bring him to the hospital.' I told him that Zach refused to go anywhere near a hospital. I described the situation, explaining that we were no longer covered by private health insurance and that to date Zach had not been interviewed by a National Health psychiatrist. This member of the medical profession was our only recourse but he seemed to distance himself and sounded annoyed with me. He said he would call back, maybe arrange a home visit, see what his agenda was like, how busy he was. He called me back the following day, catching me frantic once more. Zach had stayed out most of the night. We didn't know where he was. The consultant informed me that he would visit us with a psychiatric nurse. 'See *how* bad things are,' he told me. 'See what we *can* do.'

They arrived late. It was already night. I showed them into the house. Zach had turned up earlier on, disinclined to explain his absence other than to refer to his having been mugged by someone carrying 'a machete', who had stolen his mobile phone. We presumed that in fact he had sold it for K or dope. He was now in his room, rummaging around. I told him that the crisis team were on their way to assess him, see if they could help. He came downstairs when they appeared, showered and cleanly dressed. Obviously, he was making an effort to appear conventional, acceptable. The psychiatrist introduced himself and shook Zach by the hand. We moved into the sitting room and sat down. They looked around, taking in our background, our situation, but I felt that they had little interest in being there. What I had to say seemed to be irrelevant. My belief was that they were solely on the side of 'Zach the victim' and that we were the enemy here – for some inexplicable reason, we wanted to have him locked up. Their initial approach made me feel as if they didn't believe there was anything wrong with him. Although it was the first time they had met Zach, they did not consult the sheaf of notes I presented them with. They seemed uninterested in his history and I felt there was little analysis in their questioning and nothing they said implied any depth or intelligence.

Yet again, I explained what had happened. How often Zach had been 'mugged' (when he wanted money); how his daydreams were now part and parcel of his ordinary consciousness; how he generally no longer ate or slept or washed or had restraint over his actions. But, of course, Zach played his part well. He spoke clearly and calmly. He maintained his equilibrium; he even came across as confident and charming. It was quite a starry performance. It is often the case that manic-depressives manage to hold it together and convince professionals that there is little wrong with them. It was beyond my comprehension that these same professionals might be taken in by the act. The latest manifestations of our inept health service probably spent no more than half an hour with Zach. I explained about the accident. Not within their remit, they said. What were we supposed to do with him? I asked. Irrespective of his recent history, they were not going to set in motion the procedures necessary to section him this time or ask him to enter hospital voluntarily. To me, it was as if they were saying they were not prepared to take responsibility for him, to stop him from killing himself. Zach grinned at me again. 'See?' the implication was. 'It doesn't matter what you do.'

The meeting ended, leaving us maddened and exasperated. Zach went straight out and spent another fraught, nihilistic black night miles away from our home. He threw himself off a low bridge and, injured, made his way to the nearest hospital. In his severely manic state, he avoided their security and made his way to an operating theatre, disrupting all the medical staff. There was a scuffle and his uncontrollable actions led to his being arrested once more. It was a heartbreaking repetition of past behaviours when others had had to be roped in to rein him in and manipulate him so that no more damage could be done. The ambulance deposited him in a new sickbay and he was sectioned in an NHS hospital – the very same establishment that I had called so many times just hours before. On seeing Zach, the consultant and nurse showed no surprise. It seemed to me as if they had never met Zach or interviewed us. So life continued in its giddy track. Two months in hospital, full of anger, bile and despair. Christmas Day and New Year's Eve on the crazy ward, a victim of the thundering television and the rank hospital meal. An ineffectual psychiatrist for whom Zach had no respect and to whose advice he therefore gave no credence. He was on day release and more street drugs were smuggled in. We chucked him out.

15

A Cold, Dark Time

My last few years could've been more interesting, well here's a summary:

Three Mental health Sections
Three Near Death experiences
The occasional spontaneous street performance and a job to boot.
Special branch, Wombles, Activists, Revolution?

I'd like to die knowing I'd really achieved something, only got about 11 years left (if my calculations are correct). So far, well probably achieved more than most of my age; an almost successful band . . . shit loads of pointless dead end jobs, failed romance, lost lots of really good friends . . . did you know last Christmas Day was spent trying to ponce some free food . . . I had so pissed off my parents that they fucked off to the Caribbean and left me alone in London and wouldn't give me the fucking house keys . . . and I don't even blame them . . .[16]

The suitcases lay on the bed. I had almost finished packing. It was a Sunday afternoon in late December. We were leaving the next day for a last-minute holiday in the sun, away from grim, grey, cold London. Away from the visits to the soulless psychiatric ward and away from the constant discussions about what was to be done. Away from Zach. He stood there, looking out of the bedroom window. The conversation trailed around in circles, doubling back on itself.

I told him again that he was no longer welcome to live with us, no longer able to share our home. If he was unwilling to attempt some kind of rehabilitation, then we had gone as far as we could. We were throwing him out. We had come to the very end of our forbearance. The charity had stopped. It was now up to him to do something. Whatever it was.

He turned back to me. On the chest of drawers lay a sheaf of estate agents' brochures. The last weeks had been spent searching for alternative accommodation – not for him but for us. Sam and I had had to make another horrendous decision: we were going to move house. Our parameters had narrowed. Viewings were confined to flats that had space for just the three of us – Sam, Beth and me – and a garden for Max. We needed somewhere considerably smaller than where we were then living, somewhere Zach would, due to the lack of space, be unable to share with us. The daily problems we encountered with him were too manifold to contend with. The family was on the verge of a break-up. Our belief was that in order to maintain some kind of sanity, we had to split up. We had no intention of not seeing Zach, helping him or maintaining the family thread; we simply felt that we could no longer live under the same roof. I continually told myself that we *had* to do this, that there was no alternative. It was final. I was giving up the garden that I had spent years nurturing, so that each summer we could enjoy intense colour and fragrance; my huge, bespoke kitchen with its French double oven and granite tops; my study; Zach's bedroom. His home.

I looked at him, utterly dejected. There was no joy in moving or going away. The darkness and cold of the outside world had seeped through into my heart. I was unable to find the words, yet again. I had explained time and again to him what our decision was, what choices we had made. He continued to stand in the middle of the room with an air of bewilderment. He was no longer manic or drugged, yet he was seemingly bereft of any considered response. I tried to keep explanations short and simple. Maybe that way he would absorb the gravity of the situation and of his condition. I propelled him towards the bed. He sat down. I stood beside him.

'I'm terribly sorry, Zach,' I said, my voice unsteady.

'Why are you sorry?' he asked.

'I'm sorry,' I replied, 'because I've told you this already. I've explained it to you a hundred times. You can't live with us any more.'

He looked at his shoes, reaching down to fiddle with the laces. 'Where shall I go? I've got nowhere to go.'

Tears pricked my eyes. My head felt hot. 'How many times have we told you to find somewhere?' I asked him in exasperation.

'I know,' he answered me, 'but I don't know what to do.'

I sat down next to him, taking him by the hand. 'Zach, you've got to take control of your life. You've got to do something with it. For the last three years, you've done nothing but pass the time between episodes and sections . . .'

We sat there, saying nothing. He got up and went over to where one of the cases was balanced precariously on the duvet. 'What time are you leaving tomorrow?'

I wasn't entirely sure. It was some time in the late morning. 'At lunchtime, I think.'

He opened then closed the suitcase. 'Are you going somewhere hot?'

I pulled myself up. 'I've told you where we're going!'

He laughed quietly to himself. 'I know. So you really want me to go, then?'

How many more times could I do this? How else could I explain to him? 'I've told you. You can't live with us. You have to go. Anywhere. Wherever you can find a bed.'

He walked towards the door. 'OK, I've got your message. I'm going.'

I went over and hugged him. Tall, thin, slightly sweaty, he still smelled like my son. Still smelled like the little boy whom I loved to distraction, whom I still adored but who was breaking my heart.

He hugged me back. 'See you later,' he said. I watched him leave, walk down the stairs. A few moments later, the front door slammed. He was gone. The tears that had stung my eyes now coursed down my cheeks. I tried to check my sobs so that no one would hear, my shoulders heaving. There is nothing worse than evicting your child from his home. I wailed to myself, pressing my fists into my eyes to clear away the burning tears. The waste-paper basket filled with used tissues. My face was streaked, red, swollen. My breath shuddered. I was bereft.

* * *

Sam and I returned to London rested somewhat but dripping with guilt and discovered that Zach had found accommodation: a homeless hostel housing all sorts of strays, alcoholics and the mentally ill and the discarded. There was no solace here. I hoped that maybe in falling so low he would be taught a salutary lesson, that in order not to have to share a room with a smelly stranger he would forgo the drugs scene and take whatever meds he needed to keep him sound. I hoped he might make something happen, realise the ghastliness that his life was becoming. These sentiments were not evident in him but his mood *was* more up. 'I don't want to sleep on the streets,' he told me. 'I've found a bedsit nearby. Will you help? I can go and find work and pay you back.' We agreed.

In recent years Zach has admitted that he understands why we did it, why we moved, why we threw him out, but he still resents us for our actions and he resents Beth – she was allowed to stay. He still refers to his expulsion from our home with sadness and I understand him. It seems such a cruel and callous decision to take. But in spite of the emotional trauma that such an extreme action has on a family, it can be recommended. The strain on resources when dealing with someone with acute psychological troubles is such that everyone's attention is inevitably focused on that person. No one else exists. A vortex is created that sucks the life out of the carer and the extended family. The result is that energy and motivation fizzle out and everyone suffers. So often, carers hang on, frightened to let go. By letting go, one loses control. If it is the case that the patient is a close family member, a son or daughter, then one's first motivation is to care for him or her. But in some cases, one is no longer caring but controlling. The sufferer is stymied, unable to grow as a mature adult, to make his own mistakes or make the best of his responsibilities.

We bankrolled Zach once more. We paid the rent, helped him find work, bought him clean clothes, made sure that he ate. He visited us. We gave him keys to our new flat. He formed new relationships. He saved money from the various jobs he secured and headed for Guatemala, intending to spend three months in Central and South America, to change the focus of his life. In the summer of 2001, I drove him to Heathrow on a hot July morning recalling the day he and Molly had left for Greece. I watched while he made his way across the frenetic concourse to his flight. His guitar case bumped against him as he lugged his backpack onto his shoulders once again. He looked well, happy. He turned around and waved at me. I waved back and blew him a kiss.

Part Two

16

Travels

It was a Sunday morning in October 2001. My hair was frizzled, damp against my head. Max thumped his tail against me. I leaned against a low wall, holding onto his soggy lead, waiting while Sam fumbled for his mobile. It stopped ringing. He swore and retrieved it from where it had been buried in the pocket of his Barbour. It rang again. 'Yes?'

Max's tail thudded against me again. 'Wait, Max.' I bent down and ruffled the fur around his collar. 'Wait a minute.'

Sam held the phone tightly against his ear. Who could it be this time? Work? He stood listening, not resuming the ramble. Zach? There had been no warning bells, no real danger signals. If there had been, they had been obscured by Sam's return from a trip to visit him in South America. Now what could have happened?

I picked up the lead. Max nuzzled me and we walked on. Sam continued the conversation, a gentle droning of words. Whatever it was, he could deal with it. I looked around me. It was still warm, muggy, a touch of rain in the air. Plenty of people were about, walking dogs, strolling, jogging. Tourists, their heads buried in street guides, evaluated the distance between bench and coffee shop, figuring out their way around the Heath, tracing the route to Parliament Hill, planning to check out the view. Others were being route-marched around the area, in raincoats, under a swarm of umbrellas, to be lectured on the finer points of local history. It was that time of year again – time shifts and altered daylight.

I heard Sam calling me. I pulled at Max's lead and twisted towards him. A regretful smile played across his face. He put the phone back into his pocket.

'That was a guy called Scott,' he said, 'an Aussie.'

I watched while he pulled at his zip. 'Well?' I asked.

Sam laughed quietly. 'His girlfriend sent him an email this morning. She has a friend in Ecuador, a guy called Shane, who's been in touch with her. He asked her to find me. She found my phone number on the firm's website. She knew where I worked.' I knew what was coming, although to someone other than me it would have seemed unimaginable. Sam had only left our son a few days ago. 'It's Zach,' he told me. 'Again. He's gone nuts. He's in hospital in Ecuador.'

I had forewarned myself but I admit that even I was taken aback. So soon? I stared at Sam, unable to say anything. He lifted his hand as if to wave at me, then lowered it and shrugged his shoulders. 'Who'd have thought?' he mumbled. We walked home, forgoing any thoughts of stopping off for something to eat or drink. My eyes hardly lifted towards the heavens. I saw the sky but it made no impression upon me. My heart was sinking like a stone. A hospital in Ecuador. Further away than Greece. What was I to do? We said little to one another. Sam knew only what Scott had told him. He had the email address of the girlfriend, a phone number.

We faced another chapter in this endless saga of madness and mind-altering substances. But why now and what could have happened so quickly? When we had heard from Zach, his emails had been bright and cheery. This was someone enjoying his life.

From: Zach
To: Mum
Date: 14 July 2001

Subject: Hello

I'm just writing to say Hi and to let you know that I am alive and well (apart from the fact that I still haven't quite got to grips with the local food!). San Pedro [Guatemala] was amazing and I can't wait to go back there . . . that is probably where I'll do my Spanish lessons . . .

Zach had decided that while he was in Latin America it would make sense to go to school, learn Spanish. He wanted to have something to do on his return. Language skills would help him to get a qualification to teach English as a foreign language; it would make the trip worthwhile.

From: Zach
To: Mum
Date: 26 July 2001

Subject: Manic Days

We've had five manic days of travelling. First we went to Semuk Champey, an isolated natural collection of pools and waterfalls in the middle of the Guatemalan rain forest. Yep, I spent a night sleeping rough in the jungle! (If that's not trying to confront one's fears, then I don't know what is!) The insects were quite scary (and I never knew that ants could cause so much pain). Then it was what ended up being a two-day trip up to Tikal via a two-horse town called Las Casas (imagine Gallup, New Mexico, with lots of aggressive wild dogs). We stayed in an isolated – very isolated – bungalow, three miles from the nearest 'town', with no electricity, in the jungle – real jungle, very loud insects, mostly nice! Apart from the swarm of bees that decided to make a new home out of my hammock and mosquito net . . . Rickey and Leo[17] got stung and I didn't (that was probably because I was cowering in a corner, scared shitless!).

> We then had a nine-hour journey all the way down to Guatemala City in time for the next day's journey to San Salvador. Overnight in a real shit-hole, then a fourteen-hour coach ride over two new international borders to Managua, Nicaragua, which is where we will be spending at least four or five days. I've got a flight on the 3rd August from San Jose, Costa Rica, to Panama City and then (are you ready for the good news) a flight on the 6th to Quito [Ecuador]. (Yep, I'm NOT GOING TO COLOMBIA!!) Rickey and Leo plan on spending a few weeks there so I will do a Spanish school in Quito. It looks like I will have at least three weeks on my own in Ecuador before going to meet the nutters in Peru. Leo flies back on the 7th.

Life continued in London. The emails went back and forth. It was great to hear from Zach so frequently. Over the breakfast table, first thing in the morning, I would ask Sam and Beth, 'Heard from Zach?' Generally, one or other of them would nod, Beth's bright, shiny blue eyes excited at the thought that Zach was away and happy. She would toss her hair back, laughing at the concept that Zach had to deal with ants, flies, bees and mosquitoes. He used to bat away flies, avoid wasps and generally try to ignore anything with more than four feet. There was very little at this stage to indicate whether his moods would change.

> From: Zach
> To: Mum
> Date: 4 August 2001
>
> Subject: I'm very lazy . . .
>
> San Jose was horrible, sleazy, absurdly expensive, over-policed, nasty. Panama City, on the other hand, is great. We have just arrived (after a lovely flight). Forty-five minutes compared to fifteen hours overland . . . IT'S NICE.

I am really enjoying being abroad. For example, our hotel here costs $11 each, with air-con, cable, a swimming pool on the roof and with great views of the city.

Obviously, I miss the family but otherwise nothing else really. Anyway, hunger calls. Speak to you soon.

He sounded so good, so full of life and the possibilities offered by travel. The emails followed quickly on one another. Things seemed to be on the up and up.

From: Zach
To: Beth
Date: 6 August 2001

Subject: Wassup lil B . . .

Well, here I am in Panama City, possibly my favourite city. The guys have just left on their way to Colombia, so here is where the journey really starts for me. Fortunately my Spanish is improving and I fly to Ecuador in about seven hours.

Last night Rickey and I won over $400 in the casino, on roulette!!! That's good news, seeing as we were conned out of a lot of cash in a strip club on Friday night! The show was rather tame, compared to some of the things I've seen but, hey, we're on holiday and it was our last weekend together for quite a while.

Yesterday we went to a ridiculously beautiful national park. Saw monkeys, vultures, a tarantula eating a cicada and the park also had the best view of Panama City (which is kinda like Tel Aviv but with lots of casinos and Latinos). Very modern. Wicked skyscrapers, Pacific coast, Panama Canal. It's hard to believe that there was a totalitarian regime here only a few years ago. In fact everywhere I've been was in a state of turmoil during our lifetime. The civil war in Guatemala only ended six years ago. Nicaragua was also in quite a bit of a state. It's totally different now.

The view from the hill in the park was equivalent to Parliament Hill, only instead of a couple of trees and a few squirrels, it's dense rain forest. (I'm even getting used to the insects!)

Last night when we were walking along the street we were approached by a couple of local cops. They asked us for proof of ID and then tried to be intimidating. Basically wanting to mug us. They asked if we had any money and then asked us to hand it over. However, when we asked them why they wanted the money, they seemed totally stumped. Couldn't come up with any explanation, looking kinda embarrassed, and sent us on our way. (Obviously they thought we were Americans who, at least the ones I've met out here, are totally paranoid about the 'horror' stories of corrupt cops.) The whole situation was like a scene from a funny movie . . . cops trying to mug tourists and basically making arses out of themselves . . .

Anyway, I'm rambling. Give everyone lots of hugs and kisses from me and do please write soon . . . as I'm now all alone . . . soon to be in the southern hemisphere.

Beth heard from Zach again a couple of days later. She brought me a copy of his email. 'Typical,' she said, pulling a face. 'Typical lazy Zach. Don't suppose he bothered with checking out the bloke selling the stuff or whether it actually looked appetising!' Being Zach, he suffered numerous bouts of food poisoning. His impatience was such that he would rather not waste time taking even the most basic precautions regarding the cleanliness of food or water. I'm only surprised that to date he's not developed amoebic dysentery.

From: Zach
To: Beth
Date: 8 August 2001

Subject: Don't feel crap . . .

. . . Feel kind of shitty right now here in Quito. I got severely ill last night (must have been the dodgy meal in Panama City airport). Puked up four times in the night and spent the whole day in bed. Struggled to even get out. I'm slightly better now.

It could also have something to do with the altitude (after all, since leaving Guatemala, I've basically been at sea level the whole time and now, all of a sudden, at 9,000 feet). I've been feeling dizzy and can't even really eat. Oh, well, I must stop moaning. I've found a really nice place to stay and hopefully will wake up tomorrow, feel fine . . . start sorting shit out . . . Send my love to the family and let them know that I am alive and (erm) well?

Obviously, travel will always have its highs and lows. Another email from Zach explained that he no longer wanted to stay in the big city and that he was lonely, especially as he knew no one and his language skills were still at a relatively basic level. However, he bought a new guitar and headed towards the mountains. Presumably, the guitar was to alleviate the loneliness.

From: Zach
To: Mum
Date: 10 August 2001

Subject: Result!

I'm now in Banos and it has turned out to be just what I needed – a small town in the middle of the mountains. My hotel includes en-suite bathroom and balcony overlooking mountains, church, waterfall, etc . . . for the princely sum of $3 per night. Loads of good food and horse riding, rafting, mountain biking – seems good to me. And the hotel is next door to the Spanish school. I start manana.

However, and there is always a however, things changed over seconds and minutes, and twenty-four hours later the following arrived:

From: Zach
To: Mum
Date: 11 August 2001

Subject: Altitude . . .

Well, I was going to stay here for Spanish school but have run out of cash . . . anyway I'm sick of the cold, rainy, Londonesque climate, even if it is ridiculously beautiful, so tomorrow it's back to the jungle. Weird, I'm actually looking forward to the Amazon jungle . . . fate, eh? Very strange.

So it'll be back to worrying about ants, bees, mosquitoes, etc. but at least it'll be hot. Have made friends with a geeza from Tottenham who now lives in Quito. Got pissed last night and went white-water rafting today. No rest for the wicked! I did actually have one Spanish lesson . . . still can't speak it . . . bit of a waste of $20 . . .

He moved around with various fellow travellers – more trekking and a World Cup qualifier football match between Ecuador and Argentina:

From: Zach
To: Mum
Date: 16 August 2001

Subject: 2–0 Argentina

Went to the game and stood behind the goal with the 'yellow army', who did actually seem to shut up once Veron scored – apart from when cursing the ref, the opposition or indeed their own players for showing the finishing prowess of, say, Yeovil, on a bad day . . .

Beth heard from him again. She came into the garden where I had joined Max in a game of pull the garden hose from the oh-so-jolly dog's manic grip.

'He's got ants,' she told me.

'What? What do you mean, ants?' I quizzed her.

'Off on another nuts expedition.'

From: Zach
To: Beth
Date: 19 August 2001

Subject: Hey, hey lil B. How's tings . . .

I've just set off on a crazy journey. Aim to be in La Paz, Bolivia, in four or five days. Just about to hop on a Peru-bound coach. Two or three days in Peru, including a desert paradise, lagoon and sand dunes that you can board down. I had never heard of sand boarding but it sounds fucking cool . . . I'll have to buy a camera now and show you the pics. Have to find out what sand board music is. Hopefully not the same shit they play on the radio here . . . well . . . Backstreet Boys came on just as I wrote that.

Got news from Leo and Rickey – they've found themselves a couple of Aussie chics and still seem to be livin la vida loca . . .

I tried to have a chat with this sweet Ecuadorian guy who told me he was a communist. Cool as fuck . . . Everytings gonna be all right.

Lots of love,

Give el dogo a big kiss from me and say high to Charlie [an old boyfriend of Beth's] . . . if he's still about?

'High' sounded about right. 'He can't spell,' I mused. 'All that money at public school and he can't spell.' We laughed. I wondered whether *he* was being ironic! Then came the 'madass' journey to Peru and all that ensued:

From: Zach
To: Mum
Date: 19 August 2001

Subject: Muppet boy forgets to get his passport stamped!!

Hey there, I've been travelling pretty solidly for the last three days (on my own) and am now in an Israeli hostel in Lima . . . all the signs are in Hebrew!

Left Quito with the intention of getting to Bolivia before meeting with the guys in Lima on the 4th. Alas the Gods conspired and I have come to the conclusion that it is just a tad unrealistic to get to Bolivia and then all the way back . . .

We crossed the border at night. I was half asleep and didn't get my passport stamped on the Peruvian side. Apparently you are meant to walk across a bridge after getting the Ecuador exit stamp. No one told me, so here I am, in Peru, with no entry stamp. Wot a muppet . . . I've got the number for the British Embassy and will call them tomorrow – shouldn't be too much trouble (I hope!).

I should've just gone to the beach instead of chasing the wild dream of my ideal city in the mountains – oh, well, you live and you learn, eh?

So this is my new plan (yep, another one!): get my passport sorted tomorrow and head for the desert – Ica, Nascar, etc. – and then meet up with Rickey and Leo (in about two weeks).

Just started writing again – probably a way of dealing with being on my own (which has certainly been an experience). Did you know that I actually spent two whole days without seeing another Gringo . . . and everyone I meet (locals) seems to think that I'm from Argentina!!! Until I start speaking, that is . . .

Anyhow, I'm fit and well and still haven't shown any signs of going high . . .

Of course, receiving this email, I wondered whether his fragile psyche could maintain its equilibrium in the face of adversity. Travelling like the plague. Spending the night on buses, probably not sleeping for more than a few hours. Being stopped in the middle of the night for security searches. Diminished food supplies. It would be physically demanding and mentally enervating for the healthiest of explorers, which Zach was not. More was to come. I became concerned for him.

From: Zach
To: Mum
Date: 20 August 2001

Subject: Possibly the most stressful day ever . . . but . . . SUCCESS

What a day . . . Woke up at 8 a.m. facing the daunting prospect of a trip to the embassy, then immigration. Phoned the embassy, who initially suggested that I return to the northern border with Ecuador (17 fucking hours away) and explain, with my piss-poor Spanish, why I didn't get a stamp! I almost cried . . . anyway . . . a trip to the embassy (where I got to read some old Daily Telegraphs, including the one about Genoa . . . even the Torygraph was on the side of the protesters, the Italian fascist police must have been REALLY bad). Anyway, nice lady in the consulate gave me details of immigration and nothing could have prepared me for what lay ahead . . .

An absolute mad house, which made a psychiatric ward seem like sobriety. Hundreds of non-English-speaking refugees (and that includes the people that work there!) being herded from one queue to another . . . and all with the distinct advantage over my humble self: they could all understand the answers to questions they asked and the literate ones, of whom there were a few, could even read and understand the blasted signposts. So for me it was over three hours of hell (and it would have been substantially longer were it not for the ever-so-friendly English-speaking clerk who could probably see that I was on the verge of a breakdown to rival all known breakdowns in the history of humanity). I was so frustrated that I almost punched the O-so-rude policeman who persistently ignored my terribly polite, if grammatically incorrect inquisition. So basically, everything is now fine. I've got the stamp, I'm legal, I've got my ticket for Ica, Business Class (!) which leaves in about three hours . . . AND as Tony Blair once said, 'Things can only get better'!!!

And don't complain that I don't write enough in my emails . . . ALL RIGHT.

I tried to ignore my misgivings. It sounded awful. I doubted whether I would be able to cope with the tensions involved with visas and embassies and power-hungry policemen and the strangeness of being in an environment where I was the only one who spoke English. Maybe that didn't reflect well on me but at least I owned up to it. I reminded myself that Zach had taken himself away and that it was an integral aspect of travelling alone that one has to take responsibility for oneself in every way. Beth received another email from him very shortly afterwards. She was happy to hear from him so often but was becoming anxious herself. 'Where does he get the energy from?' she asked rhetorically.

> From: Zach
> To: Beth
> Date: 25 August 2001
>
> Subject: Back in the mountains
>
> Life is good at the moment. Currently in Arequipa in the mountains and tomorrow I am going to Colca Canyon, the deepest one in the world! Have met some good people and have been trying to enjoy myself. Even got me a bird . . . Went sand boarding a few days ago, which was wikid apart from the fact that you had to climb the fucking sand dune each time that you want to go down. No chairlifts! Spent a couple of nice days in the desert – Huacachina – with the sand boarding and Nascar, where I had a mad trip in a four-seater plane, over the Nascar Lines (which are huge drawings in the sand, thousands of years old). Not as impressive as I had hoped but still . . . The flight was fun. The pilot (a crazy Peruvian) kept flipping the plane through 180 degrees. I'm just pleased that I didn't eat breakfast . . .

Trains, buses, planes. There was no end to it. He moved on continually, never seeming able to spend more than a few days in one place. It was hardly surprising that money was beginning to get tight but it didn't stop the continual trawl over miles of scrub, desert, mountains and valleys.

From: Zach
To: Mum
Date: 28 August 2001

Subject: BOLIVIAAAAA

Hello. I'm in Cobacobana with my new lady friend and her mate. It's nice . . . Am going to La Paz for a few days and will try and get a last-minute flight to Lima to meet up with the boys. Very expensive email here, so have to keep it short. Just to let you know that I'm alive and have all appropriate stamps in my passport!!!

Why did I feel so . . . insecure? I replied to his emails, trying to be subtle while attempting to reassure myself that he was fine, not losing his grip. One of my biggest worries was the rate at which he was spending money. Looking at the credit-card withdrawals, we wondered what was behind it. Of course, he could simply have been paying for food and travel but he tended to squander money when his mood was high and there was always the possibility that the cash was going on drugs. My impression was that he was aware that he was spending large amounts; but, as usual, he had excuses.

From: Zach
To: Mum
Date: 31 August 2001

Subject: Money

Hello, I'm in La Paz with my new lady friends. Bolivia is an amazing country. Spent two days in Lake Titicaca on the Bolivian Isla del Sol, which was one of the most beautiful places I've ever seen. On day two we took a wrong turning while trying to find a beach and ended up hiking down a rock face, with all our bags, guitar, etc . . . We must have looked a funny sight to all the peasant farmers . . .

La Paz is a fantastic and very cheap city with a really good, very spiritual feel about it.

Re your queries: I am totally stable and my overspending has been due to various tourist costs. Lots of travelling, plus a few guided tours and even a couple more Spanish lessons. I will endeavour to spend less. Due to money limitations I will not fly to Lima but do ANOTHER 20-hour-plus overland journey . . .

Lots of love, your mentally stable and happy son.

Was he? I wondered. Zach was spending what money he had at a tremendous rate and ATMs worked infrequently; I was anxious that he would end up stranded without any cash. He was also travelling for hours, almost days, at a time.

From: Zach
To: Mum
Date: 1 September 2001

Subject: Still here

I don't know where you got the idea that my new lady was from Brazil (she's actually from exotic Leicester!), although I did get a kiss from a beautiful Peruvian lady . . . Anyway . . . Becky and Sara have gone back to meet up with their friends in Cusco [Peru] and I have planned to see them again in Ecuador.

I am going to Peru via Chile (it's quicker to go via Arica than Cobacobana) and will arrive in Lima on the 5th. My plans after Ecuador (seeing I've pretty much 'done' Peru) will probably be spending six or seven weeks exploring Bolivia . . . which could be the best country I've seen so far . . .

Last night we ended up in a bar for rich Bolivians (it was funny trying to guess which were politicos and which had coke money, though I guess this applies to all politicos anyway . . .). The guy that owned the bar now lives in London and was keen to give us free drinks. I'm going over to his house today (where I will probably be spoiled rotten) to watch the match that is being shown on ESPN. I'm looking forward to seeing the posh area of La Paz.

Anyway, gotta go . . .

Looked as though he was having fun with his 'rich Bolivian' friends. And he sounded well, too. Was he putting me in my place?

From: Zach
To: Dad
Date: 2 September 2001

Subject: Germany 1 England 5 (special bulletin) I know, I saw it

I was fortunate to catch the game at the rich Bolivian's luxury flat on ESPN Latin America. Juan, who now lives in London, seemed to get almost as excited as the commentator (oooowennn gooooooooooooooolllll iiiiiinglaaaaaateraaaaaaa) for real.

I am heading back to Peru (via Arica, Chile) on the 4th. Just got word from Rickey that he is already in Lima.

Anyway, I just wrote to say high.

The money problems continued to be a source of anxiety for him. We had injected some cash into his account but it took time to arrive. It was a wire transaction but he was unable to make use of the funds until the account reflected the new sum. Because of this, I now worried whether he was actually eating and sleeping, and I pictured him standing alone, his backpack and guitar at his feet, somewhere along a cracked road, hand out, waiting for a kind soul to take him somewhere for free.

From: Zach
To: Mum
Date: 3 September 2001

Subject: ATMs . . . S.O.S.

I'm currently in Tacna . . . [in the] south of Peru and am down to my last 20 sols . . . fortunately I have procured a ticket to Lima, where I know the whereabouts of Rickey. I have enough for a cab to his hotel and maybe even some breakfast but then I will have to rely on his good nature. I just went to the bank, where I was informed that (just as the ATMs have been saying) my bank would not allow me any money (though I was able to pay my hotel bill this morning with it).

I have been travelling all day (and now have a Chile stamp in my passport). Only another 20 or so hours to go . . .

I have been far more economical with my (or distinct lack of) money . . .

How did he do it? Traversing the continent by bus. Madness. Where did he find the motivation, the energy? Obviously, the difference in sunlight, space and oxygen was a great stimulant – too stimulating, I was beginning to think.

From: Zach
To: Mum
Date: 5 September 2001

Subject: Yeah, right . . . I really took FORTY FUCKING HOURS ON A PLANE

Hey, I'm in Lima, with my pals. Had 40 HOURS SOLID ON BUSES. I didn't get the plane because it would have been too expensive. Why does Lima always have to involve PAIN? I was literally down to my last 4 sols (80p) that meant that I didn't eat, apart from popcorn, for over 24 hours . . . couldn't afford to get to an Internet (the roadside service stations in the middle of nowhere had no Internet and DON'T TAKE VISA). However, am now at a nice hotel in a miserable, cold, GREY city and yet again can't wait to leave. LIMA IS ALWAYS GREY.

I didn't call either of you yesterday because I was travelling peasant class. The bus was stopped and searched by the police TWICE and must have been the slowest vehicle on the road. It really is soul destroying when, after non-stop travel for 30 hours plus, other buses on their way to Lima seem to wiz past, especially when one is hungry, cold, unsure if one can even afford the taxi to the hotel . . .

17

A Tilting of the Axis

Within three days of arriving in Lima, Zach was back in the rainforest along with the ants and bees and beetles. He had met up with Rickey. By this time, the gremlins were working away in my stomach. I pretended to myself that everything was fine and dandy.

From: Zach
To: Mum
Date: 9 September 2001

Subject: Hi There

I might come home a few weeks early. Have seen enough beauty for a good while and considering that I will be spending about six months in Asia next year, it would be nice to spend a bit of time in London with friends, family, etc. I DO NOT look like Che Guevara, though he seems as popular as ever down here. I actually think I look quite sexy (and this has been backed up by at least a couple of chicas!).

Given that Rickey's leaving on the 30th October, I might come back then . . . I KNOW that there is no room for me in my parental home . . . so a possibility could involve [finding] a nice/shitty one-bed flat for me and Rickey before we return. Remember, we will be making LOADS of money in Japon and will be able to reimburse you . . . HONEST . . . NO . . . REALLY . . . REALLY . . .

Anyway, something to think about.

I was bothered. I felt that something was in the air. On 11 September, the World Trade Center was violently and sadistically pulverised. I emailed Zach. I had no idea whether he would have heard the news. His reply was bizarre in the extreme. I got the impression that he was unable to comprehend the enormity of the disaster. I told him of the numbers dead. I recounted what had happened: how aircraft, flown by calculating fundamentalists, had been rammed into the twin towers; how human beings, in their desperation, had thrown themselves from parapets and windowsills hundreds of feet above the ground, terrorised; how thousands had died and many thousands more had been targets. I told him how the horror had affected me, how it had affected my sister in New York. It did not make its way into his consciousness. I received a reply from him that I no longer have. It was a 'plot', he said. It was a concerted effort by the Republicans to start a war. It had nothing to do with fundamentalism. I was not to believe what I saw, what I heard, what I read. The email was so sickening in its denial of the truth and so full of invective against everyone and anyone, and especially America in general, that I deleted it. It was obscene. How could someone I had helped create display such callousness?

As a family, we had always engaged in discourse and debate. In the past, many nights had been spent arguing over our beliefs. One of us would generally play devil's advocate. It was a ploy, a game we indulged in. We didn't always agree about politics but none of us would have reacted to world events with a tirade of abuse. That he should have responded in such a completely unreasonable and hysterical manner was an indication to me that indeed he was not thinking rationally. It was completely at odds with how he would normally have reacted. What was he thinking? In my fury, I wrote that I hardly knew him. He had changed so much. He must be unwell, unhinged. Obviously, being so far away had had a negative impact on him. I sent my reply – I was angry – yet something unseen rebuked me, reminding me that he could be seriously losing it again. I knew he was beginning to unravel. I didn't know how much. Maybe he could control it. Maybe he would realise what was happening. His subsequent email did put my mind at rest – to some extent.

> From: Zach
> To: Mum
> Date: 13 September 2001
>
> Subject: Sorry
>
> I AM NOT UNWELL
>
> I did not realise the extent of the tragedy when I wrote the email.
>
> It's not so easy to get accurate news out here.
>
> I have friends who are currently in New York. One of them is currently 'missing' . . . I AM NOT A HEARTLESS BASTARD.
>
> The real tragedy is that America will retaliate and cause at least twice as many more innocent civilian casualties in Afghanistan or wherever.
>
> I did eventually get to see the news footage . . . OK.
>
> How you can judge the state of my mental health based on the tone of my emails is beyond me . . . but Mummy knows best . . . I will call you so we can talk.
>
> We both have very different political beliefs (what with me being an anti-capitalist revolutionary, or whatever) but I still love you . . .
>
> Sorry if I sounded MANIC but you really upset me suggesting that I had no compassion for human life . . .
>
> All I know is that a great tragedy has happened . . . my friend Jane was in New York . . . literally running for her life as the building collapsed. Obviously I feel bad about what has happened and I know that you never did appreciate my black humour . . .

A few days later another, more poignant email expressed remorse because the attacks had affected someone close to him. Now he could empathise, to some extent. But his views have changed little since that date, especially as there has since been a concerted effort to rewrite history.[18]

From: Zach
To: Mum
Date: 16 September 2001

Subject: Just another view

Hello there . . . Just got wind of some tragic news . . . Rickey's god-brother was in the Trade Center and is now dead. I've never seen Rickey cry before and it has certainly brought the tragic events there much closer to home. I'm really sorry about my initially heartless response to the bombing. I know that we have good friends and family in New York. I really feel like such an asshole for the blatant vitriol I expressed and am really sorry that I did not have the foresight to realise how this would affect you . . .

During the early part of September, before the world tilted on its axis, Zach had suggested that Sam join up with him and that they travel around together for a few weeks, taking in the Andes and Ecuador. He wanted to see the Galapagos and there was no way that he could afford it himself. 'Hey, Dad,' he asked, speaking from a payphone opposite a lake. 'How about it? Why don't you come out and we can see the boobie birds and the lizards and the giant tortoises?'

I was still worried about Zach's health but I tried not to think about it. 'Why not go?' I said to Sam. 'He probably wants to see you, especially if it's you who pays!' Sam investigated the options. He could spare the time but was in no mood to squander more money. Air miles were called in and the chance of a free round-trip emerged. Another bonding session over horizons new – Zach was delighted. He suggested that Rickey join them and they travel together to the Galapagos. Zach organised the boat trip. It gave him something to do.

Sam boarded a plane to Madrid in late September. During the two hours he had to wait at the airport before his flight to Ecuador he called me and told me he wondered whether he was doing the right thing. When I next heard from him, he was positive, said that they were having a great time. It was now October, three weeks since 9/11 and the craziest of emails. I was still unsure of the situation. In spite of Sam's apparent dismissal of my fears and his very encouraging feedback, I knew in my core that there was something tipping the balance.

From: Zach
To: Beth
Date: 2 October 2001

Subject: Jungle is massive

I have met a very special girl out here and hope that something proper comes from it (only problem is that she's got a boyfriend at home). Am meeting up with her when Dad leaves . . .

Just got back from the Amazon rain forest. Fucking amazing (and not really any mosquitoes). Saw monkeys, climbed vines, walked through swamps. Don't think Mum would have enjoyed the basic accommodation so much but you would have . . .

I got a wikid cheapo Canon camera in Quito for ten quid, with film, and have already had one film developed. There are even a couple of photos that you'd be proud of. Can't wait to show them to you.

It looks like I'll probably be staying here until the New Year. You should come and visit at Christmas. I've already been invited to Christmas dinner in Lago Agrio (I could take you to the jungle . . . or the mountains. Whatever . . .). My Spanish is coming along pretty well as well.

Anyhow, get back to me soon.

Sam's last email related where they had been, what they had done. The trip to the Galapagos was 'truly awesome'. Zach and Rickey enjoyed it immensely. They returned to Quito. Rickey departed, having given Sam chapter and verse on the new (older) woman in Zach's life, who, Rickey believed, was having a negative impact upon it. He believed that she was 'bad news'. Sam's email was indicative to me that something was brewing, although, as so many times previously, I denied it, pretending that all was fine and dandy. Was I reading too much between the lines, being neurotic? But the fluctuating plans indicated that Zach's mood was changing subtly.

From: Sam
To: Ros
Date: 2 October 2001

Subject: Hi there

This has been an enormously beneficial trip in many ways. Zach is now acting like an eighteen year old [he was twenty-two], though can, on occasions, reach the giddy heights of twenty . . .

I managed to get Rickey on his own yesterday, which was very insightful.

I still don't think that Zach has finally and unconditionally rejected the drug culture that has so fucked him up.

I don't think that Zach has used much more than the odd bit of marijuana since he has been out here.

Rickey thinks that Sophie (the older woman) is bad news. I think that Zach is generally in control but is not out of the woods yet.

He has not yet formulated any plan. There are lots of different ones. Now that we are alone for five days, I can try and get him to focus.

Generally we had a good time. The Galapagos trip was extraordinary. The boat and people were fine, although Zach and Rickey managed very easily to piss off the 'authoritarian' figures, as well as some of the other passengers!

Zach had told Beth he would be in South America until the New Year but then told Sam he was fairly certain that he wanted to return to London at the end of November. He suddenly felt homesick and by the time November came around he would be ready to return. His plan was to focus on his music. He no longer wanted us to help him financially. He would find somewhere else to live. Although I did have qualms regarding his sanity, maybe I was exaggerating these uncertainties. Maybe he *was* all right. Sam arrived home. Another Sunday, another trek around the Heath on a warm autumn morning, dog in tow, in anticipation of a lethargic afternoon spent doing little. Another phone call from another stranger. Groundhog Day.

* * *

I could hear Max barking downstairs. Something in my subconscious troubled me, although something else had woken me up. Not unusual, really. What was it? The fact that once more Zach was in prison somewhere, or even – who knows? – another psychiatric ward? Or could it have been the row that Sam and I had had before going to bed? Zach's tentacles reaching out to us, manipulating us once more so that whatever accord there had been between us recently was now discord.

Then the phone rang. It was 2.00 a.m. Selfishly, I wanted to let it ring. I had no desire to find out what was happening. Sam turned over, moaning in his sleep. I pulled at the covers. The clock face shone out, its luminescent dial proclaiming the hour. The ringing stopped. Then it began again. This time, I answered it, reaching over for my tumbler of water and spilling drops as I cradled the handset.

'Hello,' I said quietly, not wanting Sam to awaken.

'Hello!' shouted a strong male voice. I could hear that the caller was speaking from some distance.

I moved around to face the wall. 'Sorry I didn't answer straight away,' I responded. 'It's the middle of the night here.'

I could hear muted laughter. 'Yeah, I know. I didn't know when else to call. I'm leaving tomorrow. It's Shane here. Shane Jones. I met Sophie when she was trying to get help for Zach.'

Sam stirred. 'Who is it?' he mumbled. 'Is it Zach?'

I turned around to him, covering the mouthpiece. 'It's someone called Shane. I think he's calling from Ecuador.'

Sam sat up, pulling the sheets to his chin. 'What's he say?' he asked.

I moved my hand off the mouthpiece. He was still there. 'Do you know what's happened, Shane? Is Zach all right?'

Sam moved closer to me so that he could hear. I held the phone between us. The line crackled. 'It's like this . . . Zach was arrested by the police the day before I arrived in Vilcabamba. I met up with Sophie and we got talking and she asked me to go with her to the police station to sort things out . . .' Shane's voice faded then reappeared. 'From my first impression,' he continued, 'I thought the whole thing was about the local cactus juice. That stuff's lethal. But Sophie told me it wasn't. We only managed to spend a short time together but I think I built up a very honest relationship with her. I really don't doubt her for a minute.' I looked towards Sam. He raised his eyebrows. 'Anyway, the cacti are pretty rare now.'

I moved myself further up the bed so that I could rest against the headboard. Shane continued speaking. 'I just thought that I'd let you know that Zach's in good hands. The second hospital appears to be pretty professional. I've worked in homeless shelters in London and you know how many people on the street suffer all sorts of mental problems.' I knew only too well. It wasn't too difficult to ignore the shuffling mental refugees throughout the city. Shane's voice broke into my thoughts. 'Zach was pretty delusional the entire time that I spent with him after we got him out of jail and then the other hospital. He was manic. He needed to be sedated because otherwise there was a danger that he could do something pretty awful – to himself, though not to other people, especially.' I recognised that aspect. Sam nodded his head in agreement. 'He was generally out of control,' Shane added. 'But anyhow, Sophie's with him now and they don't need me, so I'm going on.'

One thing intrigued me. 'When you say "second hospital", Shane,'

I asked, 'what happened in the first hospital? Were you there then?'

Shane's voice came back to me over the airwaves. 'Yeah, the first hospital . . . you really don't want to know about it!' He laughed sardonically. 'You wouldn't wish it on your worst enemy – a great big bloody fortress of an asylum full to the bloody rafters with the residue of society. It was like Bedlam without the psychiatric ward, just a load of buildings for every sort of disease. They didn't know what to do with Zach. They dosed him up with Largactil and that meant that he could hardly stand or do anything. He was just dribbling and drooling. It was disgusting.' My eyes pricked. I felt a hammering in my chest. 'They weren't exactly empathetic, you might say,' Shane added. 'We couldn't let him stay there. He was pretty badly bruised and cut – they'd beaten him around a bit when they arrested him. The place he's in now is private, so it's better – for here.'

My head felt constricted, the tightness pressing against my temples, a headache beginning. 'It's really good of you to call us, Shane,' I said to him. 'We really appreciate it.'

'That's OK,' he murmured. 'Anyway, I'm off. Just wanted to be in touch.'

We had a harrowing time until we heard from Sophie. When the phone rang, the stabbing ringtone heralding another bad-news day, I jumped for it. Sam and I tried self-deception, believing, hoping, that Zach's decline was in fact purely a result of the local cactus juice, laced as it is with all kinds of hallucinogenic goodies. He had in all probability made prodigious use of sellers of his new favourite tipple. However, we realised gradually that it was more likely that the relapse was a consequence of travel, stress and homesickness, Sam's return to London and time. That time of year again. October.

Zach draws strangers to him. His good-looking charm had obviously resurfaced somewhere in South America, along with his humour and bonhomie, and as a result Sophie forfeited the next four weeks to be there, around Zach's lunacy, while we toiled in what sometimes seemed a futile attempt to bring him back home again.

Repatriation. We had been there before. Not so long ago. Would it be any different this time? 'They don't know what to do with people who suffer from mental illness here,' Sophie told me during our first conversation, over the blips and farts of overseas communications. 'The police were brutal when they arrested him. They didn't have a clue what was wrong but they beat him up anyway. He was all bruised and cut and bloodied when I first got there.' I felt sick hearing about it again. She continued, her small, distant voice wavering. 'Because of his weird behaviour, they took him to prison. Bloody idiots. Then obviously someone with a bit more intelligence pointed out that he was sick in the head, so they took him to the hospital. It was an absolutely vile place. I don't know how anybody could get better there.' We could only speak for a limited time. Her voice faded in and out. The connection was fragile.

Sophie was at her wits' end. She'd managed to get various telephone numbers from Zach's travel documents – those he hadn't discarded. Delving among what was left of his belongings, she found a few notes and some change among the cartons of cigarettes and packets of medication. She called the insurance company, whose number appeared on the back of his membership card, attempting to explain the situation in Ecuador to a woman in a call centre in Newcastle. How Zach needed to be repatriated. Utterly depressing. The woman was unhelpful and the money was being devoured by the moment. 'I'll call you back tomorrow,' Sophie groaned. 'There's no point in this conversation. Let me know if you have any good news then.'

Another call, to the British consulate, where a man with a strong tenor voice took all the details and told her to wait by the phone. 'Let me just get this clear,' he said, before disappearing into the ether. 'This young man is in a private clinic and needs to be repatriated?'

'Yes, he needs to get back to London. He's very sick. Can you speak with his family?'

The official ended the conversation. 'Let's get back in touch tomorrow. You can let me know how he is then.'

The funds that Sophie had found among Zach's things had gone, on phone calls to us, the consulate and the insurance company, who, Sophie hopefully anticipated, would be prepared to send him back home. She was at the end of her travels and had spent over and above her resources. Now she was coming up against obstacles everywhere she turned. The clinic in which Zach was languishing demanded that she guarantee their remuneration of $100 each day. 'I've made arrangements to stay near the hospital so that I can visit Zach,' she told me, 'but I leave so late from there that I can't get a bus. I have to take taxis and they cost a fortune.'

In addition to her financial problems, Sophie was also troubled by the indiscriminate distribution of mind-numbing medication. The drugs prescribed were nauseating in the extreme. 'I've tried to get them changed,' Sophie explained. 'I keep speaking with the psychiatrist. Zach's totally tranquillised but the doctor told me that the only way we can get him back home will be either like that or in a straitjacket!' My blood ran cold. I saw visions of horrific Hollywood movies and padded cells. 'They were so scared of Zach in the other place that they locked us up together. They wanted someone to be with him the entire time. When they prescribed him Largactil, it broke my heart and I spent the whole night crying.'

Sophie spent her time running between villages, talking to the police and lawyers. 'The local governor has his passport,' she told me. 'They want to deport him to Peru. So I've got to deal with that too. It's so hard having to make decisions about someone's life without their consent. But I promised Zach that I'd wait and go home with him.' A month earlier, she had been travelling around South America without a care in the world. What was there in her stars that had led her to this place, stuck in hospital with a guy whom she had only recently met? She had become caught up in a production playing out on the boards of a theatre far removed from our orbit. I somehow managed to get through to her every day, settling myself down with a coffee and paper and pen, so that I could make notes of our conversations. Max would sit at my feet and I'd bend down and stroke his silky ears as I strained to hear her voice. One of the first things I really wanted to know was what exactly had happened to bring him to this latest arrest and captivity.

'It was really cruel,' she began. 'We'd been travelling around together. Then I went off on my own for a bit. We'd made arrangements to meet up again in Vilcabamba. I'd been there before. I'd stayed in this rank hostel where the scuzzy owner tried to break into my room during the night. I think he wanted to rape me. When I found out what he was trying to do and told him to fuck off, he wasn't too happy . . . I think I must have told Zach about this, because when he arrived in the village, he checked into the same hostel!' Idiot, I thought. Why did he have to go and search for trouble? 'Anyway,' Sophie continued, 'Zach was pretty delusional, even at this stage. He thought that the owner would have it in for him because he was my friend. But the most bizarre thing is, the day Zach arrived there, the revolting man had a terrible accident that left him in a coma. So it followed in Zach's head that this was because of him!'

Sophie explained the events in sequence – well, as much as she could remember. Zach checked into the hostel and then checked out, meeting up with her at another hostel. For some unknown reason, a light glimmered in his brain and he actually remembered where she said she was heading. When they met in the narrow bedroom overlooking a mountain pass, she took one look at him and realised that he was not the bloke with whom she had been travelling. 'I gave him Valium and hoped that a good sleep would calm him down. We went to bed but when I woke up in the middle of the night, he was gone.'

Zach managed to find his way to the local hospital. Unbelievably. He knew that he was unravelling and, deep down, recognised that he needed more than a sleeping pill. He found his way to A&E but was unable to make himself understood to the staff there. His fractured countenance frightened them. All he wanted was medication but they were obdurate. Instead of simply humouring him, they argued and shouted, and consequently he disintegrated further. The police were called and they arrived with all guns blazing. A nun attempted to pacify Zach but it was too late. He became violent and hit out, thumping a large cop when he attempted to arrest him. Shouts, screams and fisticuffs. A broken window and an extremely agitated young man. He legged it back to the hostel, where, followed by the police, he was arrested in the midst of a violent altercation. Almost naked, scratched and bleeding, Zach was thrown into the back of a police van.

For two days, he was held in a jail cell, raving and crying for help. The police were uninterested in his plight. They had his passport and were threatening to deport him – in the state that he was in – over the border to Peru. It was only because of pressure exerted by Shane and Sophie that he was finally released to the local hospital. His mental state was now even more fragile than before and physically he was a mess. The authorities had neither fed him nor dressed the wounds that he had suffered during the fight.

I listened to Sophie's story with my eyes shut, in despair. Max was now resting his head in my lap. I recognised the pattern of events and could see in my mind's eye what Zach must look like. What he must have looked like to them. It was all so horrible.

'No one seems to know what I'm going through here,' Sophie said sorrowfully to me. 'People are amazingly intolerant of mental illness. The villagers in Vilcabamba think Zach is doing this deliberately but I know he's ill. He's been completely knocked out by the drugs but he knows I'm here. I usually just lie next to him and cuddle him while he slips in and out of consciousness. He can't even go to the toilet by himself. Even so, he keeps on trying to attack the nursing staff. One doctor has a big scratch on his arm and I've a few bruises of my own!'

Clearly, Zach had realised that he needed medication. But he had waited far too long and had lost any opportunity of getting hold of it at a stage when it could realistically help him. He relied on Valium to get to sleep. He carried lithium with him but it is unlikely that he took it when he should have done. Once a breakdown is in full flight, he generally refuses all antipsychotics. This aspect of the illness does not change. His clash with the authorities and his outbursts of violence were consequences of his mania. Obviously, as had been the case in Greece, no one was prepared to help him. No one wanted to have personal dealings with a madman. Had he been suffering an obvious physical ailment, the appropriate aid and advice would almost certainly have been forthcoming. Instead, because of his mental state, he was treated like a criminal and then abandoned.

18

Emails and Money

In London, the phone calls began again. To the consular official in Quito, the Foreign Office in London, the hospital in Vilcabamba and Zach's South American psychiatrist, who, to our dismay, did not speak any English. All conversations involved translation – challenging work. However, the doctor came highly recommended and Sophie made the point to me that without the input of Dr Jueves things could have been even worse. The time difference contributed to the daily grind of it all. Some days were better than others. It was always a question of one step forward and two steps back.

'I've managed to get Zach's drugs changed,' Sophie told me one afternoon, while a huge thunderstorm unleashed its fury around me.

In his panic, Max took himself off and hid in the bathroom, pulling the bath mat over his head and spilling an open shampoo bottle onto the tiles. 'Oh, God,' I groaned at him, 'I'll deal with you later.'

Sophie could hear the thunder clapping above me. 'I can hear that! Anyway, Zach was getting better, I thought. Then today he attacked two of the medics. He wanted to escape. He ran up to a window on the fourth floor and tried to climb out but the nurses pulled him back in.' I could hear a sort of sob in her voice. 'Now he's back in his room but they've dosed him up with haloperidol again. And they tied him to his bed. It's like fucking *One Flew Over the Cuckoo's Nest*!'

I asked myself whether there was anything else Sam and I could do, apart from speak with Sophie on the phone each day. I knew that it was no use either of us travelling to South America. It would have been a pointless exercise.

'What else?' I asked Sophie. 'What else happened?'

She took a deep breath. I could hear it catch in her throat. 'Oh,' she said sadly, 'there's so much stuff but I just can't tell you all of it . . . the treatment of the mentally sick is inhumane.'

'That doesn't appear to differ throughout the world,' I agreed. 'Nothing seems to change, wherever you are.'

'Before I got his drugs changed, I had to take him to the toilet and hold him so that he didn't piss all over himself,' Sophie continued. 'He's so frustrated by this. He just wants to be a human being.' She paused. 'At least you'll find this funny,' she said bitterly. 'I spend most of my time here lying next to Zach and singing to him – although I'm absolutely certain that my singing voice would drive the sanest person nuts!'

It was financially crippling. We had to wire funds through the embassy to pay for the hospital bills, doctor's bills, nursing bills and extra cash for Sophie. Zach had reverted to type. He wanted cigarettes and cola and pizza and chocolate. Local cigarettes were cheap but junk food was not and, in his heightened state, only American cigarettes would do. 'He's not a cheap person to look after,' Sophie complained to me, 'what with his passion for all things imported.' Then a further, not unexpected bombshell: the insurance company informed us that they were not prepared to repatriate him again, effectively closing the door. We were left to foot the entire bill.

Surprisingly quickly, we were notified that Zach would be able to fly back sooner rather than later, although he would have to be accompanied. Sophie would return with him and the embassy stipulated that his psychiatrist was to come too, which meant that we had to pay for the eminent psychiatrist's flights, as well as a short stay in London. What choice did we have? Leave Zach there and continue to pay up for God knows how long? I spoke to Sophie, who maintained that he had to leave and come back to London. She took it upon herself to make the travel arrangements – only for them to be abandoned. As a result of 9/11, security was so tight it seemed likely that, given the state he was in, Zach would have been hustled away from the other passengers to a safe area.

During the course of one of our excruciating conversations, she informed me that, as well as being fully sedated, he would probably be flown home cuffed.

'Cuffed?' I exclaimed. 'What, in *handcuffs*?'

I think at this point she was frustrated with me too. 'We've *got* to get away from here!' she cried. 'But I don't know when it can happen. He thinks he can leave at any time but they've got three people watching him and they've still got his passport.'

Emails, phone calls, money. But we really had no idea what was going on. Our only link was Sophie. We had to trust her implicitly. What else could we do? She experienced the same highs and lows as we did during Zach's manic phases and was also manipulated and deluded by his fluctuating moods. 'You know,' she told me, 'I almost thought he was back down to earth. You know – an amazingly fast recovery. So I told him that if he agreed to stay in hospital for another week and not try and escape, then the doctors would hold back on the really revolting medication. But then yesterday he got out of his room, into a lift. He was practically away when one of the orderlies noticed.'

I listened to her with bated breath. 'What happened then?' I asked, my heart palpitating.

'This orderly rugby-tackled him to the ground. Both of them caught between the doors. There were plants all over the place and soil and magazines. He's got a bloody great gash in his leg now.'

I no longer wanted to imagine just what was happening there. How could it be happening to a son of mine? 'Jesus,' I whispered.

'Anyhow,' she went on, against the buzzing line, 'I'd taken him in his guitar and today he gave the staff an impromptu concert. I think they liked that! I think they're quite surprised to see that there's a human underneath. You know, I don't *think* that he's much of a risk any more but I'll keep an eye on him. He told me that this episode took him far higher than previous ones.' So he admits to those, I told myself. 'He also said that he felt high when he was with Sam.' And Sam noticed nothing? How could he not? 'You're lucky that he's still alive,' she said, 'because if they'd deported him to Peru with no clothes, no money and no ID, then God knows where he could've ended up!' I shuddered at the thought. It hurt me to think about it. 'I've asked him not to travel alone again and I've also said that he's probably allergic to puff and is better off avoiding all drugs in the future.'

Sophie's observations regarding Zach, marijuana and his use of narcotics made good sense.[19] It was neither the first nor the last time that such advice would be proffered. But her recommendation that he terminate his love affair with drugs did not penetrate the foggy haze of Zach's brain. Exasperating and frustrating as this is, it is not unusual among bipolar disorder sufferers. 'The substance-abuse problem takes on a life of its own,' writes Francis Mark Mondimore of Johns Hopkins University. 'The mood disorder and the substance-abuse disorder start feeding on each other, and a vicious cycle of mood symptoms, increased substance abuse, and even more severe mood fluctuations takes over until it's impossible to separate one problem from the other.'[20]

Zach rarely, if ever, takes advice. Rickey told me later that he thought Zach was hypomanic the entire time they were travelling together in Central and South America, and especially when they were with Sam.[21] In her innocence, Sophie believed that he had made 'an amazingly fast recovery'. He was to prove her wrong.

'As for miraculous recoveries,' Sophie grumbled the following day, 'I may have spoken too soon, because Zach's turned into a manipulative bastard who keeps insisting he'll be allowed out of hospital before he flies home. It's hard to know what to believe with Zach,' she continued, in the same angry tone of voice. 'He seems to think that I'm off having fun the whole time I'm not with him. So, right now, I could strangle him for not realising how fortunate he is!'

Someone else would have given up. Given in. Gone home and left him to get on with it. What motivated Sophie to stay in Ecuador with a guy who was now in total meltdown? It occurred to me that one would have to be seriously masochistic – either that or unbelievably altruistic – to stay there and suffer with him for any reason other than family ties. Why was she doing it?

Two days later, she called sounding elated, her voice sparkling with relief. 'You won't believe this but I've just met this guy in the clinic who's an American psychiatrist. He's here for a few weeks and he's going to see Zach and do something about his meds!' I wondered why Dr Jueves had been unable to be proactive here and why Zach was reliant on a complete stranger to take control of the most basic medical problem. However, Sophie gave me the American's number at the hospital and I managed to speak to him, although, as was the case with all the phone calls, we were mostly drowned out by the cacophonous noises accompanying us.

'I was very surprised to find Zach here,' he told me, after I had given him a potted version of the past few years. 'We've managed to converse reasonably lucidly.' I could imagine the tone of *that* discussion. 'Primarily, I don't think that lithium is the right medication for him,' he continued. 'He doesn't like it or want to take it and, quite honestly, I don't think it works.' I was gratified to hear that someone was finally taking a different view of the pharmacological treatment. I *knew* that lithium didn't work. I hated it as much as Zach did.

I could just about hear the doctor shouting at me in the distance and banging the receiver against something. His voice faded and then burbled up into my ear. 'Can you still hear me?'

The hisses and clunks resounded. 'I can hear you!' I yelled back at him, irritated at the continual technological gremlins. 'It sounds as though you're in another solar system!'

'I know. Communications here are pretty unreliable. In any event, I'm going to start Zach on a relatively new medication. It's used a lot in the States and has few, if any, really nasty side effects. It's Depakote, or semisodium valproate. I think that Zach will benefit from it.'

I was grateful for his input and relieved that the ghastly lithium was banished. For the millions who respond positively to lithium, it is a wonderful drug. But Zach was patently among those who do not react well to it. Evidently, there is the argument that it had to be tried on Zach. When he began the course, no one could know what the outcome would be. But it turned out to be a complete waste of time. The months of enforced medication compliance and the myriad blood tests on his liver and kidney functions were for nothing. Zach was happy to comply with the change. Anything rather than having to be subjected to lithium's sinister torments. It was now a question of waiting to see whether or not the Depakote would work. At this juncture, time was not on our side. In Zach's ongoing delusional state, he believed that any day now he could leave the hospital behind him and set off on his travels. Sophie's and the various medical professionals' assertions that he was too unwell to continue his Latin American journey and that he needed to be escorted back to London fell on deaf ears.

'Zach's only admitted to me once or twice that he thought I was doing the right thing,' Sophie told me. 'The rest of the time he's had a go at me for interfering in his life. He reckons he'd be free and happy right now if it wasn't for me but I don't think the police would have let him go so easily if I hadn't been there. You don't hit a cop in any country and get off lightly. I'm worried that if he's discharged from hospital into my custody, I'll end up losing him, because I can't force someone to stay by my side at all times.' I empathised with her. My experience with Zach in Athens and over the past four years had taught me that he should not be discharged until he was on the way to recovery. Sophie's energy and motivation diminished the longer she was stuck in Ecuador. I know how debilitating and exhausting it is to contain Zach when he is psychotic. He might not agree with this criticism but to those of us who have, unfortunately, been witnesses to his overexcited and hyperactive moods, his behaviour resembles that of a wilfully perverse, intractable adolescent.

It was now up to the embassy and the hospital to decide when they thought Zach was sufficiently 'down' to travel but a date had to be agreed upon, a day in the not too distant future when, realistically, Zach might be able to board a plane, accompanied, not so ill that he might get into an altercation, resulting in more grief and despair. It would, in some ways, have made far more sense for Zach to remain safe and cared for in the clinic until he came down to a maintainable level but we were under the impression that the Ecuadorian powers that be were pressurising the hospital to get shot of him in any way possible, even if this entailed his having to travel back to London in leg irons.

One possible route home was via Newark, New Jersey. Not an appealing thought. Sam's disquiet forced him to write to Sophie: 'I certainly don't fancy the thought of him ending up in an American jail if he plays up on the plane.' I knew that, in the light of the worldwide situation vis-à-vis air travel, that was exactly what would happen if he did: a trip to Newark's on-site lock-up. Sophie's response said it all: 'I think I've dealt with enough police and authorities recently to last me a lifetime.'

The consulate insisted that things were moving on apace but, in spite of their assurances, obstacles were constantly appearing in the way of progress. Sophie boiled over with irritation and disappointment. The embassy refused direct contact with her, preferring email or elongated and expensive phone calls to either Sam or me. This was idiotic. Sophie was there. She could drop everything and be at the embassy within hours. 'They're driving me nuts,' she exclaimed to me. 'They won't speak to me and the guy I'm dealing with is a complete idiot!' A date was decided upon but on the day prior to departure the embassy came up with another caveat: Sophie would simply not do; she was not family. Out of the blue, and without first having consulted us, they informed her that Beth would have to fly to Ecuador and that she accompany Zach in Sophie's place. What insulting nonsense. Poor Sophie!

This was a whole new strand to the drama and no one was benefiting from it. And who was making up the rules on the hoof? Why make Zach stay longer if they had decided that he was well enough to travel? Why bother changing all the air tickets? My mind went back to Athens, when I'd believed that relief was on its way, only to find that greater forces had stymied it. I called the embassy and spoke to the vice consul. He made soothing noises. I spoke to Sophie. She was irate. I managed to speak to Zach. He wanted to continue his travels, didn't understand what all the fuss was about. The American psychiatrist had gone to visit other patients further along the coast. There was no one else to whom I could speak.

More days passed in this fog of uncertainty and, of course, the fallout meant that Zach's apparent restoration to better health deteriorated. Sophie's exasperation and helplessness combined with Zach's truculent ill humour resulted in an explosive mix of passions. Sophie stridently gave me chapter and verse on the problems, forcefully letting me know that her patience was dwindling. 'I know this isn't a particularly nice thing to say,' she almost shouted at me, 'but did you ever give Zach a seriously good hiding as a kid? Because I would really like to do so now!'

'What now?' I asked. 'Has the adolescent resurfaced?'

Scorn entered her voice. 'I realised when I took this on board that it might drag on and on,' she told me, 'but I'm finding it really difficult to relate to the sort of spoiled-brat behaviour that Zach displays on a daily basis. We fell out yesterday. Zach's frustrated – understandably. He believes that he shouldn't be in hospital and I almost agree.' Oh, yes? I wondered. 'He thinks he's in a fit state to travel by himself and I don't agree with that. Anyway, he ended up screaming at me. So I gave him the silent treatment. He's got no concept of money and he hassles everyone if he doesn't get what he wants from me. He almost begs other patients for money! And then he spends it as fast as he can when he has it! He seems to think that the whole world revolves around him and it's embarrassing and disgusting. Everything I've done has been totally by myself, on my own, and when the shit hits the fan, I don't have the luxury of ringing home for help!'

I knew why she was feeling like that. This revolting persona, this demon, now resided within Zach. In order for it to abandon his fragile psyche, he had to get better. It would take time but eventually he would return to himself. The Jekyll-and-Hyde being would be replaced once more by the person we almost knew. But what an intriguing illness this is! Is there one simple, concise reason that explains why someone who suffers from bipolar disorder displays such a total transformation of character and personality? How is it possible that a previously rational human being's nature and disposition can revolutionise themselves so dramatically as a consequence of a chemical imbalance in the brain? And why is it that often only the worst aspects of the sufferer are revealed? Again, what comes first? Is the response an exaggeration of the underlying personality or something new introduced as a result of the mania?

Zach is not unique. He shares his personality traits with some illustrious predecessors. A quote from one of Lord Byron's physicians explains in more detail the fluctuation of moods and the distended personality:

Those only, who lived for some time with him, could believe that a man's temper, Proteus like, was capable of assuming so many shapes. It may literally be said, that at different hours of the day he metamorphosed himself into four or more individuals, each possessed of the most opposite qualities; for, in every change, his natural impetuosity made him fly into the furthermost extremes. In the course of the day he might become the most morose, and the most gay; the most melancholy, and the most frolicsome . . . the most gentle being in existence, and the most irascible.[22]

I would like to think that the more revolting character traits that manifest themselves in Zach when he is psychotic are not really a reflection of his underlying disposition. However, I must admit that it's possible they are a part of his true self. Maybe we should all suffer from some form of psychosis that would fully mirror the inner soul. Who knows what would show up?

Just as we were feeling so despondent and low, suddenly they were on their way. The embassy sent us the last of the invoices for Zach's expenses (Sam and I had come to refer to these as 'ransom notes'), and Zach, Sophie and Dr Jueves – whose presence had been insisted upon by the embassy – were put on a plane back to a dismal, icy England. There was, indeed, a brief touchdown in Newark, where a severely frazzled Zach tried to have a smoke. 'They grabbed him by the arms,' Sophie related to me later. 'Two burly policemen with all the silverware and handcuffs and truncheons on their belts homed in on him as if he was some kind of serial offender and then they led him to a separate area of the airport.' In order to avoid any further altercations, they made sure that he smoked his roll-up away from the scrum and accompanied him onto another aircraft, which sped above the world, where he slept for seven hours, under the spell of the psychiatrist's alchemy.

At 5 a.m., Sam and I drove across London towards Gatwick. The sky was black, scattered with the remnants of night stars. A chill wind blew brittle leaves and straggly fragments of paper and discarded cartons around the pavements. A Saturday in November. The morning frost had laced itself over the leafless trees and hedges, and delivery vans made their way down the motorway, passing lay-bys filled with articulated lorries and their somnolent drivers. Few cars were about at this time and the thunder of the early-morning planes had yet to fill the sky. We watched out for the signs to the airport, then made a left turn onto the slip road. Sam parked at the terminal and we trudged through the shadowy car park into the gloomy depot.

Other greeters were there. A few rumpled strangers gathered around the exiting travellers, cups of cooling tea or coffee secured in their hands, their coats and scarves in stark contrast to those arriving from sunnier climes, whose tans, shorts and T-shirts created an impression of a divide between haves and have-nots. I walked over and stood at the barrier, watching the holidaymakers, wondering whether Zach would have changed much. I was apprehensive, relieved and sad. Apprehensive about which mood I was about to witness, relieved that he was back at all and sad that yet another journey had been a disaster.

Within moments, I glimpsed his form over at the exit doors and watched while he stopped and hesitated and looked around for someone he recognised. Then he saw us. Grinning, he came over, taking long steps, his back stooped as though he were in some pain, his arms outstretched for a hug. He was still Zach, albeit more tanned and with more hair than when he had left. His only luggage was a plastic bag that contained cartons of duty-free cigarettes and his wash bag. He was thin and fragile. His cheekbones jutted out once again but his eyes shone brilliantly, although they were heavy-lidded and ringed with dark shadows. He wore a threadbare sweater that I did not recognise over a thin, mangled T-shirt and dirty, fraying jeans. The anorak that we had bought together before the trip reflected his battered soul: the pockets were torn away from the body, the hood at a less than jaunty angle, ripped and hanging loose. I hugged him to me, feeling his slender bones beneath my hands. I looked over his shoulder and saw a young, blonde woman in boots and an alpaca jacket. She guided the celebrated Dr Jueves towards us.

19

Back

Zach slumped in the front seat. His conversation was stilted, disjointed. I sat in the back with Sophie and the doctor. Worn out, they slept for most of the journey. The doctor spoke little. Sophie translated as best she could. After an hour or so, we turned the car into a narrow, winding avenue. The hotel sat back off the road, opposite a curious block of flats, the epitome of Victorian Gothic, faux minarets flanked by flamboyantly carved gargoyles, flying buttresses and pointed columns. I gasped at its audacity – a pure romantic folly. The hotel was a poor Regency imitation, replete with box hedges and hanging baskets. Sam pulled up and we sat still, gathering ourselves together.

After some moments, I guided the doctor into the hotel. He carried a small bag and an umbrella. All smiles at the comparative elegance of the mock-Regency mansion, he removed his hat and handed me a file. I opened it and saw that it contained a wad of papers written in Spanish, with graphs and statistics and medical terminology. Of what use was it to us?

I smiled at him bemusedly, while Zach hovered close by, his fingers rolling one of his ubiquitous cigarettes.

'Where's his room?' he asked me, gesturing towards the doctor.

The receptionist gave me the key. 'It's on the third floor,' she told us.

We took the lift up to show the doctor his room. It was a gracious pink-and-white medley of florals and leaves; a blast of enveloping warmth hit us as we opened the door. The doctor mewed with pleasure at the sight of the en suite bathroom, the velvety nap of the fitted carpet and the canopy above the bed. A small table housed a tray with cups and saucers, teabags, biscuits and milk. He went over to it, lifting the china cups and examining the choices. Beaming, he indicated how grateful he was. But Zach wanted more. He wanted to spend time with Dr Jueves and to show him the parts of London that were important to him. That would give the doctor an insight into the person he had been treating these last weeks. However, to his disappointment and ours, the psychiatrist refused any further discourse and our invitation to a meal. He had done all he was willing to do, so he bade goodbye to Zach and Sophie and that was the last we saw of him.

There was no other choice. Zach came back to our flat. I had assembled a camp bed in the corner of the sitting room. Clean towels lay on top of the pillow and the new T-shirts I had had the foresight to buy alongside. The fridge was full of the foods that I knew Zach would eat. I had already put in a call to the crisis team and they were due later, during the afternoon. Eschewing my advice that he shower and change, he draped himself over the bed, pushing the clothing and his bag to one side.

'I need to sleep,' he told us.

I looked over towards Sophie. 'Don't worry,' she said, grinning at Zach. 'I'm staying with friends and I'm really tired and dirty.' She went over to him and he put his arms around her, giving her a deep hug. He then lay down again, closing his eyes. I saw her to the door. 'See you later, Zach,' she called over to him. He was already asleep.

Despite the intensity of the conversations that we had had and the emotional journey that she had taken with Zach, Sophie seemed hesitant to fully engage with us or explain why she had put her life on hold to stay with him. She was a conundrum. I wasn't suspicious of her, just curious. It wasn't as if she had known Zach all her life or even as if they had expressed undying love for each other! We saw her once or twice while she was in London. She turned up at the flat, seeming carefree, her short blonde hair shining, a slight, petite girl with a permanent smile and lively eyes. But she appeared unwilling to divulge her true feelings and open up to us. While Zach remained relatively calm, we took them out for a meal but I could not sense any romantic feelings between them. They laughed when they spoke about the weeks in the hospital in Ecuador and the journey that had led them to it. Sophie was happy that they had both made it out of the Andes and that they were safely in London. I think maybe Zach would have wanted to pursue the relationship but she was not interested. After a few days, she left.

Zach was back in one piece. That was indisputable. But, to our chagrin, he was not on the way to recovery. However much we tried to put a spin on it, the fact was that he remained elated and bloody-minded. He refused to admit himself to hospital, maintaining that the facts were skewed and that it was not his fault that he had been hospitalised in South America. Nothing new there, then. He was ill but adamant that he did not need to be cared for on a psychiatric ward. We had been in touch with the local authority, and three social workers had arrived at our home the first afternoon and attempted, unsuccessfully, to explain to Zach that he really needed to be in an environment where he was safe. 'No way!' he barked at me, as if, again, it was as a result of my intervention, my contribution to his life, that he was ill.

One of the team asked him, 'If we came in every day to give you your medication, would that be a way around it?'

He pondered for some moments and agreed. 'If you find me here,' he added.

His previous flat he had vacated so that he could travel. Now he was homeless again. We were under pressure to make sure that he had a roof over his head but I hated the camp bed and resented being on the front line in the re-emerging battlefield. None of it was encouraging, especially as we had already made the point that we were not a happy family when living in close proximity to one another. Admittedly, this was a very selfish and single-minded response to his illness. Beth tried to avoid him as much as possible. She was so obviously vulnerable to his moods. She loved and hated him in equal measure and took what she perceived to be his lack of respect for her incredibly badly. He saw her as easy prey and made her life miserable. We were all miserable. Sam, as so often in the past, stayed later and later in the office, using every excuse to avoid the war of attrition that was wearing down our souls. But I had to be around. Whatever else I wanted to do, I felt that I owed it to Zach to ensure that he ate and washed. I particularly wanted him to sleep, at least for a few hours of the day or night. Although he took medication, he did not improve. Indeed, his mood swings escalated and we knew from experience that they could only point in one direction: drugs.

He had no income and no savings but it was obvious that Zach was finding the drugs somewhere, along some dark, dingy passage. Who in their right mind would finance him? Give him the stuff? It was impossible to keep him in if he wanted out. Each day he would leave, rushing into the pouring rain, wearing a thin vest and fleecy top, his bag hurled across his back, oblivious to my entreaties that he stay in, be safe, get well. 'I have to go out!' he'd yell at me. 'You can't keep me in!'

But, of course, the outcome was that he got into fights. The first night, he came back with his clothes in disarray. 'Someone thumped me,' was the explanation. The second night, a phone call alarmed us and a taxi arrived outside the block with a bloodied Zach inside, aided by a young man, who, recognising that he was ill, insisted on accompanying him to safety. Another Samaritan.

A shivering, sodden Zach stooped into the flat followed by a deeply tanned, dark-haired man in a long suede coat. I was utterly shocked to see the gash above Zach's right eye and the rivulets of blood that dripped down to his chin and onto his vest. His face was bruised and turning yellow and purple. 'I'm Denny,' the young man said, coming towards me, his hand outstretched. 'I'm really sorry to bring Zach back like this but I thought that he needed to be home. Be somewhere secure. He got into a fight.' I could see the kind-hearted compassion in his eyes. Maybe he had a relative like Zach or he himself suffered the pangs of desperate moods. 'I think he was thrown out of the club,' he continued, sounding somewhat embarrassed for Zach. 'He got into a fight with one of the bouncers.'

A hollow, sad laugh from Sam. 'I wonder who won,' he remarked ironically, looking at the blood now staining the white fabric of the armchair across which Zach lay, propping himself up on the armrest. Sam was past caring what others felt. He could only live in the present. Resent the past. Be cynical about the future. I could see the ire in his face. 'Zach,' he hissed, 'get up! Look what you're doing!' Zach removed himself dazedly, languidly, totally unaware of his surroundings and of the bit-part players on his stage, including the stranger who'd helped him. I stared around at the mess of humanity. Should I reprimand Sam for his anger or Zach for his mind? I was stunned and felt almost as if I were in some kind of parallel universe where such events were ordinary and those day-to-day realities experienced by my friends were no longer the norm.

I struggled to resist the temptation to deny the reality surrounding me by quietly removing myself from the proceedings. Pinching myself in an attempt to return to the now, I went into the kitchen, where I found a damp cloth that I could use to try to remove the blood from the chair and, maybe, my feelings of total inadequacy and guilt. There was an air of all-pervasive acrimony in the room. I sensed that Denny wanted to go, to escape the enveloping currents of hostility. Who could blame him? I guided him to the front door. 'I don't know what to say,' I said. 'This keeps happening. It's so repetitive, so boring.' He straightened his wavy black hair, pushing his fringe away from tired black eyes. I thought maybe he was Italian, Greek. 'Let me pay for the taxi,' I offered.

He wanted nothing. 'No, it's fine,' he told me. 'I don't know him. I just wanted to make sure he was all right.' He took my hand in his again. 'I think he needs to go into hospital, or somewhere.'

I nodded my head. 'Absolutely,' I responded. 'He needs to go into hospital. But how? That's the bigger question.'

I made sure that he got into the taxi and closed the front door behind him. I returned to Zach. The cut continued to ooze blood, his clammy vest now stained with crimson Rorschach patterns, an illustration of our disconnection, our unreliability as parents. How sad. 'You need to get this fixed, Zach,' I said to him, trying to clean his forehead with cotton wool. 'I can't do this. You have to go to hospital to have it fixed.'

He pressed at the cotton wool in an attempt to staunch the flow. Pointless. 'I know what you want to do,' he said, contemplating my position. 'You want me to go to hospital and then you'll get me sectioned.'

It had occurred to me. Awful mother. Betrayer of sons. 'You've got to get it stitched,' I reiterated. 'I'll take you,' I added.

Of course, he was right. This was the only way – so long as they would take him. He gave in. I think deep down, fundamentally, he knew that the game was up. There was no point in continuing further here. He knew that eventually he would end up in hospital. Maybe he recognised that it would, in some way, be safer to be watched continually by strangers than to be the constant object of our unhappiness and disappointment. He picked up his things, all the while holding the bloody rag to his head. Once more, I took the reins while Sam and Beth looked after the dog, the flat, themselves. We drove to the hospital in silence. I felt desperate.

Here we were again. The black night, the rain teeming down, made me feel ragged, empty. There was no one around. It was late. I drove into the hospital car park and stopped the car. Zach got out and I came around to the other side of the car to help him. He rebuffed me and strode off to the emergency department. He was given stitches to stem the blood and, with his notes to hand and his mental health assessed, he was assisted upstairs to the first floor. Another two months.

* * *

'The Priest' was a recommendation. 'You'll love him,' we were advised. 'He's helped them all.' He was a big bearded bear of a man whose past endeavours included treating those disorganised, dispirited souls tired of life careering along the glittering, gruelling channels of drug addiction and mental instability. He had succeeded with so many, seen so many, and he recognised the symptoms, the results and effects of pharmaceuticals and narcotics. His attempts to get through to Zach were manifold. He had written a seminal work; his knowledge was immense. So, Wednesdays, I would get Zach up and force him out of his new studio into the lifeless, grim mornings, watching while he lethargically donned his jacket and hat and scarf, coercing him into my car, this unwilling participant in my pursuit of a cure. In spite of his protestations, I would wait for him while he spent a fruitless hour in the tiny cottage overlooking the exhilarating panorama from the top of verdant Highgate over towards Alexandra Palace and beyond. A pungent aroma of washing detergent and pipe fumes would spill forth from the doorstep of a home more reminiscent of *Pride and Prejudice* than *The Three Faces of Eve*. I would peer at Zach while he sadly shuffled in, head down, hands in his pockets or cradling a cigarette. The grotesque melancholy had hit him again.

What could we do to help? I asked the guru. What more was there available for us, for him? 'He has to fall,' was his expert advice, stroking his asphalt beard, his eyes looking towards the ceiling, the fireplace, outside. 'He has to fall as far down as he can go and only then will he pull himself up. Only then will he think of doing something with his life.'

'How much further can a person descend?' I interjected, reflecting that he had already fallen pretty far: homeless on the streets of London, seedy squats in Tower Hamlets, jail cells and psychiatric wards. How much further do you have to plummet?

He had no answers. He had no new advice. 'Let him fall.' This was not news to us. This we had already done, to the detriment of our feelings of responsibility as parents, out of love and out of self-protection. We believed it had worked. It did, for a time.

You hear of other families finding 'the one', the indispensable human being who has all the answers, and then – boom! – everything falls into place and hey presto, everything works out. You tend to find this in the American memoir. 'Oh, I found the *most wonderful* doctor who put me on this or that medication and I finally turned the corner!' All those books where lithium is the wonder drug. If only.

I recalled a time, not very long before, when I was walking on the Heath with Max. In the distance, dragging himself slowly along a path towards the summit of Parliament Hill, I spied a young man. I think that he was young. It was difficult to tell from a distance. The bent figure shambled slowly along, a thick, heavy coat strewn across his shoulders. His trousers were tattered, the soles of his trainers flapped as he walked. He had a huge, dark thatch of curly, filthy hair, falling from forehead to chest, completely obscuring his entire face. It was as if he wanted to draw a veil across his humanity. What was he doing here, wandering around on his own in this distressed state? Why was he not with his family at home, in a hospital ward or at least being cared for in a hostel? I was shocked and saddened. I wanted to go over to him, to help him somehow, in the knowledge that this youth – for he couldn't have been any older than twenty-five – needed urgent intervention. But I held back. Who knew whether my intrusion into his existence would be welcomed or repulsed? So I left him, that sad, disheartening son of a mother who had given him up. Was this what I, too, was supposed to do? Leave Zach to 'care in the community'?

So we said adieu to the Priest and organised things as best we could. Someone, finally, was designated to deal with his benefits; a social worker was allotted, who would make appointments to see him, appointments that he seldom kept. He was supposed to have meetings with the ward psychiatrist, which would have been an added benefit, but they were rare and were invariably postponed for weeks at the last moment.

In spite of being overwhelmingly in denial about his illness at that stage, Zach continued to take the Depakote. At least, when I made an appointment with the GP for him and ensured that he had a prescription, he took it. I was always surprised by this. Why would he bother to take medication that he insisted had no beneficial result? He said that he experienced no side effects from the drug and therefore there was no reason not to take it. He rarely, if ever, had blood tests, liver or kidney screenings, or sufficient medical intervention to ascertain that he took the correct dosage. The only time this was sure to be checked was when he was in hospital during those generally three months of the year when he would be incarcerated on some ward or other.

Then summer arrived, a damp spring heralding the spectacular efflorescence of warmth and sunlight, and Zach's happiness returned. He started going out with a friend, Sylvie. He had met her a couple of years earlier but at that time did not want a full-time relationship. She was very young and he wanted to wait a while. They shared confidences but their times together were fraught. He ventured out with friends. Music appeared to be played, written and performed again and that ambition resurfaced. He met up with the old school crowd, and Dominic and Jack were once more on the scene. I spent a lot of time on the phone to Maggie, Dominic's mother; we would discuss her hopes for Dominic's future and my aspirations, not yet crushed, for Zach. Dominic still lived at home, having finished university, and he was at a crossroads, unable to decide upon a particular profession. But he assiduously found himself work. I wished that Zach could apply himself to some kind of career, anything that would give him some long-term security. Maggie advised me not to give up hope. I tried not to. And then Zach did indeed find himself a job that he didn't disdain and stayed employed until September. Rickey was in Thailand with his girlfriend, Anna. Of course, Zach had to join them, rekindle the spirit of adventure. He saved and scrimped and borrowed some more, and another journey loomed in the distance.

* * *

Sam, Zach and I sat in the car. The rush-hour traffic steamed ahead then halted. I opened the window. It was a still, sultry Monday night in late September. I had asked myself countless times whether it made sense for him to travel now, especially at this time of year, but each time I had brought up this point I had been gently put in my place.

'Why can't you trust me?' he asked plaintively. 'Why d'you think only *bad* things happen when I travel?'

Should I be surprised at this reaction? 'It's not a question of trust,' I responded. 'It's this time of year. You know what happens.'

He looked around at me. 'What?' he interjected. 'What d'you think's gonna happen?'

I stared at him. Would he never get it? Why was there always this absurd refutation of the obvious? I looked out of the window, reluctant to be drawn into further argument or anger.

An hour or so later, we accompanied him into the terminal and waited in line while he checked his baggage. Other travellers smiled when they heard us remind him to protect his travel documents, buy health insurance and look after his money. 'Bloody kids, eh?' grinned an elderly Aussie in front of us. 'First time?'

I looked over to where he stood, noting the lively green eyes peering out of his bronzed and leathery face. I made a wry face and laughed with him. 'I wish.'

So we said our goodbyes and good lucks. This time Zach was heading in the other direction. To Rickey, Thailand, Laos and the rest of South East Asia.

20

Apocalypse Now

From: Zach
To: Mum
Date: 2 October 2002

Subject: Football

I've just organised my visa for Laos which is where I'm heading in a couple of days (despite the flooding, hurricane etc.). It should be an adventure . . .

I've managed to spend a small fortune these last two days but hopefully that should stop when I leave. The food here is amazing but too many tourists mean that I don't talk to anyone. Oh, well. Is nice . . .

Love Zachareeeeeeeeeee

Uh-oh! Now, why did I infer that something was wrong already? He had only been gone for a matter of days. Could it have been the way he'd signed his name, that little play on words? Was it just a little insignificant fooling around with the keyboard? An in-joke perhaps? Sam had already received a spate of emails with reference to the Premier Division. Who had scored the most goals? Who was now at the top? Who had been injured? What was happening in whatever European football league? They didn't, on the surface of it, suggest that there was anything to worry about. But the focus on one particular subject was somehow disconcerting. And here was another anxiety-inducing, worrying email. What on earth was happening?

From: Zach
To: Mum
Date: 3 October 2002

Subject: Plan of Action

To be perfectly honest it has taken me a few days to get used to how things work over here, overcome jet lag, but I'm going to visit my friend Ella on the tropical paradise island of Ko Phi Phi (which has a reputation for being touristy) but it's NOT peak tourist season and I met someone who has just got back from there (sexy broker lady from London) who bought me a drink yesterday and I figure if there are people like her there, it must be worth it!!!

I guess it's a week beach holiday followed by a flooded rain forest adventure. I'll be going down the Mekong on a slow boat and probably stopping at a couple of places in Northern Thailand en route to Laos and then back to Bangkok (which is as filthy as you'd imagine). I've eaten 'street food' and even had ice a few times and not even close to getting the 'runs' (by this stage in Guatemala I was writhing around in agony!).

I now own a very professional portable stereo system (long playing/recording) mini-disc player, SONY, Made in Malaysia, bought from authentic exclusive Sony dealer. Under warranty and I even get cash back at the airport (tax back).

Anyhow. I hope that this email has been more substantial and informative than the previous correspondence.

Hope to hear from you soon.

Love, ZachO.

(ps A Thai tarot reader told me that my father was a very good man and had always been very good to me . . .)

There is a negative side to immediate communication. Sometimes the message received is not what you really want to hear. In previous decades, when the world was in many ways a far less stressful place, your offspring could go away and then, unless something really dramatic happened, you'd be none the wiser as to what they were up to. It was so much easier then. We could all be so much more selfish. So many evenings, you could wonder, 'Where is he? What's happening? Is he all right?' And then you could settle down with a cup of tea and a biscuit in the hope that the fact that you hadn't heard anything meant that all was right with the world. Not any more. The impact of the instantaneous email means that we are glued to our computers, laptops and terminals with a zeal greater than that of the average Grand Inquisitor. But emails from Zach were a double-edged sword: I was happy to know that he was actually alive and able to find an Internet café but dubious about whether what I would find when I read the text would make sense and reflect the sane embodiment of my reliably unreliable, delightful son.

From: Zach
To: Beth
Date: 8 October 2002

Subject: Greetings from the beach

Wassup Lil B.
I am currently on Ko Phi Phi which (along with a little island nearby where I spent two days previously) is where 'The Beach' was filmed. Very beautiful tropical island. Very tanned, wikid food (I ate fresh barracuda the other day). But there are too many tourists.

Tomorrow I go to Ko Lanta (which is meant to be much more quiet). I've been with a good little group of people (from England, Ireland and Norway).

After a week or so on the beach I'm heading up to Laos (I've got a sixty-day visa so that means that I can go at any time).

You must come and visit sometime . . . You'd love it here!

Give my love to everyone and let the crew know that I'm alive and well and no food poisoning yet!

We didn't hear anything more for a few days. Seems that he was on yet another island, soaking up the sun and meeting up with whoever was travelling that particular stretch. So many were, a constant stream of young people always on the move, in flux, travelling from island to island, coast to coast, in the search for the perfect beach, the greatest crowd, nirvana. It was as if there was no reason on earth to return to their homes and find any kind of employment that would keep their interest for any length of time.

From: Zach
To: Beth
Date: 11 October 2002

Subject: Heading to Laos . . . the weed here isn't actually that strong

Have just been to Ko Lanta for three days. Very chilled . . . Just got to Trang (to start a two-day train journey) but the trains are all booked for the next two days. Not that nice here SO I bought a flight to Bangkok, then to Chiang Mai tomorrow. Cost about 70 quid . . .

Weather generally very hot, sticky, etc. Very tanned . . .
Some hardcore monsoon-style rains . . . is nice . . .
Don't have much time . . . gotta find Trang airport.
Speak to ya soon. Email b4 Laos.
Love and stuff.

Beth called me to her room to show me the email on her computer screen. 'What do you think?' she asked me, her penetrating eyes wide with anxiety, once more having to absorb worries created by the sprite thousands of miles away. 'Do you think he sounds all right?'

I looked out of her bedroom window, into the street below. The truth was I wanted only the most positive news. 'I don't know,' I said, looking back at her. 'I think he's all right but, you know, he's playing with words again . . .' My antennae were twitching, sensing trouble. We were asking ourselves the right questions. It was only a matter of time, we opined. Only time.

From: Zach
To: Mum
Date: 17 October 2002

Subject: Nothing special

Can't be too long but just to let you know I got to Laos safely. Didn't go to Luang Prabang and am now in Luang Namtha. Last night was spent on the banks of the Namtha river, staying with a very hospitable local family who cooked for us (me, a geeza from Bournemouth, an Aussie and a Dutch girl) and put us up for the night. The food here is excellent and is outrageously cheap. Am heading up to some annual Buddhist full-moon celebration.

Will send email when next I find a computer.

Rickey and Zach had arranged to meet up somewhere in Laos or Thailand or Burma. Unfortunately, they kept missing each other. Rickey and his girlfriend, Anna, were in one place, Zach in another, and usually at opposite ends of the country. Rickey and Anna had parted ways, deciding that they would travel around separately and meet up again later along the line. Coincidentally, before he left for Laos, Zach stumbled upon Anna in a bar on a beach in Thailand. They would therefore travel those now well-worn roads together. Rickey continued in another direction. Then Zach made some strange telephone calls, asking us to let Rickey know that 'things were fine'. What did that mean? I asked Zach when he called me late one night. 'I don't have much time,' he said. 'I'm calling from a restaurant and they're watching me.'

I asked him whether he was all right. He sounded far too zany for my liking. Hypomanic. Smashed. He laughed me off. 'How's your sanity?' I asked him. He replaced the receiver.

Then came another phone call from Zach, from another café. This time I could hear the sound of loud laughter in the background and the boom of a television spewing forth in a language unknown. Anna had left Rickey, he told me, gone off with another someone whom she had met in a bar in Luang this or Prang that. Zach was with her when she did the dirty deed. He told me that he felt terribly bad for Rickey. They were good friends and had been for years. They'd done stuff together that I didn't really want to know about: shared nasty, dirty squats in London, done the music festivals, got drunk and extremely high together, too. They'd maintained a good relationship throughout their travels together. Now Zach was travelling around with Anna and she had betrayed Rickey. Two weeks later, I heard from him again. Now I knew that in some way the earth had tilted once again.

> From: Zach
> To: Mum
> Date: 29 October 2002
>
> Subject: Finally in a City
>
> I've met some amazing people. Loads of northern Laos. I stayed two miles from China . . . Great times . . . there's bad news for Rickey . . . all plans chaos . . . have been writing loads . . . found a cheap studio in Thailand . . . already played one gig. I think that this travelling experience has been fantastic so far . . . real life experience.

'All plans chaos'. Was that more a chaotic mind? What did he mean about a 'cheap studio in Thailand'? I thought he was in Laos. Did he intend moving there? Now what? I received another email on the same day, just one hour later. From it, I could detect that he was not dealing rationally with the emotional fallout from Rickey and Anna's love life. That their emotions should impact badly on him was not surprising but it made me even more anxious for him.

From: Zach
To: Mum
Date: 29 October 2002

Subject: Dark times

Great news in dark times. I'm now in Laos with Anna and Vikram (HER NEW BOYFRIEND . . . TRUST YOU NOT TO MENTION ANY OF THIS TO RICKEY). Vikram is as cool a guy as . . . You'd really like him. So would Rickey BUT . . .

I've written some great tunes/songs and am going to go to Pai (Northern Thailand) to record in proper studio there. Vikram lived there a while and could maybe sort me a few gigs. The HUGE dilemma is the Rickey situation. Rickey loves Anna . . . Anna loves Vikram . . . I love all of them . . .

Please don't tell Rickey. Let Anna break the news to him . . . PLEASE . . . Heartbreak on the horizon. I'll check mail later probably, 'cos there's loads of Internet cafes in LUANG PRABANG.

Later that same day, a bizarre email, written by both Zach and Anna, protested Zach's sanity. In the face of all the current emotional turmoil, it did not render a reliable analysis of the situation and did nothing to dissuade me from hurriedly phoning Sam and expressing my doubts. 'I dunno, Sam,' I said to him, hearing his intake of breath, his irritation at the other end. 'If it were anyone else, then I'd ignore all the phone calls and the weird emails. But he just doesn't seem right.' My suspicions, I felt, were about to be proven. But how?

From: Zach
To: Mum
Date: 29 October 2002

Subject: Sanity? What sanity?

We've sent Rickey mail now . . . and have put him totally in the picture. He knows all the options about who/when/where to meet/fly to, etc.

ANNA WANTS TO TALK NOW . . . (Doesn't this remind you of something . . . Ecuador, etc.!!!)

Hey: We've never met but I know you know the score with what's been going on . . . I've told Rickey now (via email, which sadly is the only way because I felt it was a matter of urgency). Anyway. I just want you to know that your son Zach has been the strongest, most grounding soul I could ever have near me right now. He has done nothing but fill me with clarity, reassurance and positivity. Kept me feeling strong within myself. Every single person he meets learns straight away what an absolutely amazing person he is. Just in case you were anxious or curious about his own state of mind right now: I'm telling you he is well beyond 'stable' (he wanted me to use that word).

Anna.

So there you go, Ma . . .

Could I believe this? None of it rang true apart from the fact that Zach *can* be 'an absolutely amazing person'. When he wants to be. He can charm the pants off everyone. When he is well. He did not sound well. What did she mean that he was 'beyond "stable"'? Did she not protest too much? Then, the next day, another email came reprising the sentiments of the first. There was no real surprise for either Beth or me, nothing in it that made us raise our eyebrows. It all went hand in hand. His emotions were running haywire. It was not a case of reading between the lines. Not now.

From: Zach
To: Mum
Date: 30 October 2002

Subject: Words of wisdom

While I'm upset for Rickey, I am so happy for Anna (she's my best friend too) so this puts me in a big dilemma. PLEASE don't worry about it affecting my mental health . . . it's really just provided me with artistic inspiration. Vikram is a lovely bloke.

Oh, and more bad news . . . one of Anna's friends died yesterday. But then again Vikram's friend is about to have a kid. I guess that's how this whole life death rebirth thing keeps rolling on . . .

The dude abides . . .

Later that day, masochistically, I checked again and saw that yet another email had navigated cyberspace.

From: Zach
To: Mum
Date: 30 October 2002

Subject: Finally in which city?

I'm in Luang Prabang right now. Good Internet access.

Rickey's gonna be in Bangkok in a week but I wanna be in Pai (with Vikram . . . my other new best friend and Anna's new love) . . . how complicating. We think that Anna should go and see him in Bangkok but maybe I should. We don't know if she's gonna call him or what. It's all so tragic but beautiful at the same time. (They're already talking about getting a dog together . . . bless.) At least I've written a beautiful song.

Don't know where any of us are going or with whom. We are not going to 'Nam now anyway. We don't know anything but that Rickey's got heartbreak and I'll have to be there for him AGAIN . . .

BUT I'm having an amazing time. The last few days have played havoc with my bipolar inclinations but I'm as strong as an ox and I know when to take my lithium . . . don't worry about me.

Lithium? Zach had stopped taking it in Ecuador. Was he trying to placate me? I was worried and said so in a follow-up email. I had no idea whether he would actually read it. I had no doubt that his 'bipolar inclinations' were by now severely screwed and would soon be causing all sorts of highly stressful problems. His reply arrived on the same day. This was so unusual. In the past we had generally been lucky to get mail every few days. To get six in two days . . . The email indicated that grandiosity was creeping in, adding to the overall picture of the symptoms of mania emerging.

> From: Zach
> To: Mum
> Date: 30 October 2002
>
> Subject: <*no subject*>
>
> Please Mum, don't worry about my sanity. I'm a big boy now. I've been a pillar of support to Anna and Vikram. I've got olanzapine [antipsychotic] anyway . . . You know I love you and I won't be getting any of those electric shocks (I can even barely communicate in Laos and Thai now).

I had the telephone number of Rickey's hotel in Bangkok and got through to him. I guess I was interfering – something I had vowed not to do. Rickey had heard from Anna about the Vikram affair but was not too concerned. He didn't think his relationship with Anna had been anything deep or intense, although in his present mood Zach seemed to consider it akin to something out of *Dr Zhivago*. 'It was just one of those relationships that you strike up when travelling,' Rickey told me. 'She wasn't the love of my life.' He added that he thought that Zach was pretty disturbed by now. The worrying tales of Zach's behaviour related by Anna made him particularly troubled. 'We've emailed each other, although he hasn't responded to my latest. I told him not to worry about Anna but I've not heard back from him.' I asked him how concerned he was. 'I'm more worried now because I think he's going to fly to Hanoi. You know he's meant to be meeting up with Harry? They organised it months ago. I was supposed to go, too.'

I'd completely forgotten about it. 'Rickey,' I said to him, 'he hasn't stopped travelling for the last four weeks. I think he's getting worse.' He agreed with me. 'Let me know if you hear anything.' He said he would.

21

Sanity?

Nothing. Then a peculiar email arrived in response to my appeal that Zach make for Bangkok and join up with Rickey rather than venturing further east to Vietnam. I knew that should he attempt to fly to Hanoi and be picked up by the authorities because of his odd behaviour or strange appearance, nothing we could do from London would be of any help to him in the short term. Each time I allowed myself to imagine what might pass for a psychiatric ward in a hospital in that former Communist enclave of South East Asia, I became sweatily clammy. The notion was not at all attractive.

From: Zach
To: Mum
Date: 3 November 2002

Subject: Sanity

LOOK . . . First. I'm fine and balanced (my friend Jenny can explain) . . . she's lovely . . . she's been ill too . . . she will write to you tomorrow . . .

Second. Rickey is a big boy. He can fly to Hanoi. No problems. Bangkok is too, too far and Harry is in Hanoi on the 11th. Have told Rickey I'll be in Hanoi by the 8th. I've already dragged myself on a 40-hour journey from La Paz (one of my favourite places) to

Lima (one of my least favourite places . . .). Fucked if I'm doing that from Laos to Bangkok. No one met *me* off the plane. He's been there many times. I've got a year (mas or menos) with the pendeco [idiot]. I've told him this in an email he hasn't responded to. Let him know about Hanoi on the 8th please . . .

Love ya loads . . .

November. Although he was in another hemisphere, on another timescale, the compass points made no difference to the overall nature of the illness. Why should I think they would? It was the natural wishful thinking that clouded my mind whenever I tried to envision a future for Zach. Why couldn't he be like everyone else? I was terribly, remorsefully upset for him and utterly depressed to think that he was losing it so far away and at such a pace. I sat at home on the settee, crying into packets of Kleenex, nearly distraught at the thought of what might be happening to him. I had no idea just how delusional he was becoming. I knew that the trajectory of the disease meant that drugs would be involved and that that could mean the police and the authorities. I wondered how long it would be before things took a real turn for the worse.

In the hope of determining the extent of his illness, Sam emailed Zach to ask why he had changed his mind and decided not to meet up with Rickey as planned. The reply he received did not bode well.

From: Zach
To: Dad
Date: 4 November 2002

Subject: <*no subject*>

Explanation . . . I am fucking miles away from where Rickey lands. I am in a state of total natural balance . . . in a country where my heart feels settled.

Rickey is an experienced traveller and the ORIGINAL plan was

> that he and Anna would meet and I travel on MY OWN at least till Christmas. What has happened between Rickey and Anna is nothing to do with me. I've sent him mail saying that I WILL meet him in South East Asia THIS month but have already arranged LOCAL rendezvous (look at a map if you want to understand why I don't wanna be in Bangkok on the 6th . . .) with Harry (you know, MY OLDEST FRIEND IN THE WORLD).
>
> The nature of Rickey's previous email to me suggested that he wanted to fuck straight off to Burma India Nepal (with or without me). Now he's saying that you think I'm being a cunt and should come home. If only you knew what opportunities there are here . . .

I dreaded to switch on the computer, fearful that there would be nothing from Zach or another, even more irascible screed. Regrettably, a further email advised me that he had bought his flight from Vientiane, the capital of Laos, to Hanoi and that he was 'NOT OVERLY ELATED . . . JUST HAPPY'. Oh, really? He wrote that he was going to make his way south slowly and take a plane to Hanoi on 8 November. My mind buzzed. Where was he now? What was he doing? Why did he need to go further? Why not stay in one place, see a doctor maybe?

I called Rickey again. He was sitting in his hotel room in Bangkok, waiting to hear from Zach, out of his mind with worry. 'He hasn't rung or emailed me. Nothing,' he told me plaintively. 'So I'm gonna go to Burma. It's doing my head in here. Have you let Harry know what's happening about Vietnam?' I affirmed that I had, the fear gnawing at my belly that Zach would try to board a plane while totally manic. 'It's unrealistic to go to Laos without knowing where the hell he is,' Rickey continued. 'It might be worth contacting the Oz Embassy in Laos, though. If I hear where he is today or tomorrow, I'll try to go to him.'

Rickey rang later that day to see if we had heard anything at all. Over an appalling line, where fizzes and crackles brought back memories of previous difficulties with long-distance communication,

I managed to make myself heard. 'No, nothing!' I shouted down the line. There was a muffled expletive, then a void as if I were speaking into a crater. 'I'll call you back tomorrow, then . . .' I murmured disconsolately.

Rickey felt trapped in his room, unable to leave it or go anywhere until he had some information. I was grateful that he was there, looking out for Zach – at least he knew the lie of the land. The following evening, while I was preparing dinner, I received another phone call from Rickey, made from a payphone in the corridor of his hotel. This one bestowed on me all the details of the story. Once again, Zach had relapsed: the wear and tear of neurotransmitter, the adrenalin rush of serotonin and freefall. The jigsaw puzzle was almost complete.

'I'm with Anna now,' he told me, while I stopped peeling and turned down flames under pans. Max lay in my way, at my feet, hoping for falling produce. I sat down again, pouring myself some of the Sauvignon that I had put on ice. The glass clinked on the granite surround. 'I think I've got most of the story,' Rickey explained further. 'Zach was well high before all the shenanigans with Anna and the other bloke. Anna's been going through hell with him. There's a whole disjointed story about a party in Zach's room and noise and music and drugs.' Surprise, surprise. 'Apparently the police were called and found stuff in the room. Anna put up £100 to stop them from taking him away and did everything she could to try to convince him to come to meet up with me in Bangkok but he wouldn't leave with her. The one time she confronted him about his mental state, he got very aggressive and threatening and scary.'

Ugh. Yes, I knew about that very well. 'You know what he's like then. He just won't listen.' Total obliviousness to everyone else is what was usually the case. Whether it was conscious or not, I never really knew. I usually gave him the benefit of the doubt.

'It turns out it was more of a case of her trying to follow him than them travelling together.' I finished the first glass of wine, then poured myself another. Who needed sobriety? 'We're doing our best here to try and email people in Laos who Anna and Zach met along the way,' Rickey continued, 'see if there's any news of him. I can't go anywhere until I know he's OK. I'll do whatever I can. You can rely on me. I've got my own life but it has to be on hold right now and when this is all over and everything is OK, I'm gonna give him such a piece of my mind!' He wasn't the only one. There was a queue of us waiting to do the same thing.

But why had Anna bothered to write that everything was fine? That Zach was 'strong' and 'grounding'? It made no sense. Was she frightened of him? She had made the decision to leave him even though she knew he was ill. Then she had made her way to Bangkok to confront Rickey with her news. The implication was that Zach was at the stage where it was almost impossible to spend any length of time with him. Now she was in Bangkok – with Rickey. There was, clearly, no serious breakdown in their relationship. Friends, it would appear, they remained. Zach's irrational fears regarding their situation had been yet another delusional manifestation of his incipient insanity.

When I next heard from Rickey, I understood that he too was, not surprisingly, experiencing the effects of the emotional roller coaster. 'I never went to Burma,' he told me, his voice breaking up. 'I've been in Bangkok the whole time, having a nervous breakdown. I'm still at the same hotel, in the same room. I don't really know why Anna's still here but thank God she is.' I just could not understand these kids. So many God-awful things happened to them and they somehow dealt with them. 'Anna said that if she had sent that email to you twenty-four hours later, then it would've been a different story altogether. I honestly believe there was nothing more she could have done.' Well, that was the answer to my question!

The lines of communication between Zach and us died. We heard nothing more. Then a completely off-kilter transmission arrived. I had no idea where Zach was now, apart from being somewhere in Laos, making his way 'south' for his flight to Hanoi. If there had been any doubt that his mind was unbalanced, this email indicated that all our fears were grounded. He sounded completely manic. An absolutely dreadful, sickening feeling descended to my innards.

From: Zach
To: Mum
Date: 11 November 2002

Subject: <*no subject*>

Eh! . . . the same day Anna told Rickey . . . I had three motorbike crashes . . . AND TO BE PERFECTLY HONEST I AM FUCKING SICK OF YOUR SELFISH WORRYING ABOUT ME . . . I am more concerned for Rickey . . . I AM NOT sick . . . I HAVE ALL THE FUCKIN meds I need . . . SO PLEASE . . . FOR THE LOVE OF GOD STOP FUCKING WORRYING . . . THAT'S THE KIND OF SHIT THAT MAKES ME SICK . . .

I've even had a nice meeting with a professional CPN [community psychiatric nurse] from London.

I am coming to London for Christmas/New Year . . . b4 continuing my journey and would like to see the gang . . . I would also definitely like to go to Israel . . . have been studying the Martin Gilbert book intensely and feel I might be able to give MOSSAD a bit of a hand and kill Arafat myself (I SHIT YOU NOT) . . . doesn't it sound like I'm HIGH . . .

ps thanks for sending me Rickey's plans LAZY BASTARD DIDN'T TELL ME . . .

I'm in LP [Luang Prabang] still . . . recovering my wounds (third time I have had the stigmata!?!) . . .

took LITHIUM olanzapine and natural herbal shit and valium and beer and weed and slept like a baby for 15 hours . . . just woke up . . . very calm

quit worrying . . . I explain more in letter . . . got good business out here . . . am coming back to London to pick up some cd's, books

> etc. for my FIRST new house (YEP . . . I am now OFFICIALLY a PROFESSIONAL tourist guide) and have a house in LP . . . gonna see Harry in a few days . . . is nice . . .
>
> ps found good gemstones and gold and silver (typical businessman) . . . maybe Uncle Dod might want to do some business in Laos. I'd like you to come and see my house. I have done a lot of work (labouring) . . . and I saw Grandpa last night [My father died when Zach was six.] . . . he told me to tell you he is content and is sorry for the pain he has caused you . . .

My mind's eye shifted onto grotesque visions of Zach distractedly careering from one Internet café to the next, his belt adorned with the customary paraphernalia – the knives and keys and sunglasses and whatever else he viewed as necessities – his mood changing, becoming more labile the less he ate and slept, the more he ran, his thoughts colliding, in the crush of travellers, hawkers and police. I knew that by now he would be unable to determine whether what he did made sense and that he would be following his own peculiar focus. Renting bikes and smashing them following dramatic skids tens of metres along bamboo-strewn roads was also typical behaviour. This was now the third continent on which he had suffered accidents of this kind. Would he survive the bikes, the mania, the drugs and, perhaps, the intervention of the police?

In his hotel room, pacing, enervated, watching interminable repeats of *Friends*, Rickey had made contact with the Australian Embassy in Laos. In a drained, hoarse voice, he expressed his relief that something was happening, positively, somewhere. 'They're gonna keep an eye out at the airport in Vientiane,' he told me. 'There's a guy there who's actually gonna go and make sure he doesn't get on the plane.'

I was duly impressed but doubted anyone could find Zach in the scrum at the airport. 'Sam's spoken to the British Embassy in Thailand,' I told him, 'to the vice consul in Bangkok. He said she was very understanding. He's told her the story. The usual, you know, that

Zach intends travelling further, to Vietnam. That he has his ticket. How concerned we are about his state of mind.'

I wondered how understanding she could be. What was her experience in matters of this kind? 'I told her,' Sam informed me later, over dinner, with much wine to dull our anxieties, 'that we both shuddered at the thought of him being hustled off a flight by either Laotian or Vietnamese police. What kind of an ordeal might that lead to? It could make the Greek hospital look like a holiday camp. She said she would contact the Australian Embassy to see what they're going to do and then be in touch with us.'

There was relief in the knowledge that we were not alone in our pursuit of Zach, that there were people trying to locate him who would attempt to help him, make sure that he would no longer be in danger. But I continually worried that he would do something so dramatic that he would be killed. I wrote to him again. Maybe he *was* still accessing emails. Maybe he *would* gain some kind of insight into our worries, our concerns. Maybe he *would* let us know where he was and what he was doing – anything to relieve my doubts and uncertainties.

From: Ros
To: Zach
Date: 11 November 2002

Subject: Please get help

Zach, it's so hard not to worry when I get an email from you and you are obviously completely manic.

Please get help, otherwise you'll be picked up by the police – as is the usual course of events. Anna is with Rickey in Bangkok. Rickey wants to help you. Please contact him and arrange to meet up. He has more meds with him.

You won't be allowed on a plane while you are manic.

I presume that you are still in Luang Prabang??? Please try to take care of yourself.

His response to me implied that he had read the email and ignored it. Then, having made arrangements with a visa-wallah that involved a $20 fee and the handing over of his passport for a stamp, he found that it had been impounded.

> From: Zach
> To: Mum
> Date: 11 November 2002
>
> Subject: Thanks to you and Anna and Rickey conspiring . . .
> I now have found out that my passport is in the Australian Embassy
>
> Give it up already . . . if you are that concerned, come out and see how calm and UN MANIC I am. I know how to look after myself. You STILL don't understand me. One day you will. You don't seem to realise that I know how to medicate myself and now, thanks to the three of you conspiring, I will have to endure unnecessary hassle . . . THANKS a lot. Didn't you once promise that you would not get involved . . . ?
>
> Please stop meddling in my life . . . Rickey and Anna can do as they please . . . I am getting on that plane to Hanoi . . . except now . . . thanks to you I'll need to see another fucking shrink . . . thanks a lot, mum.
>
> I still love you . . . I am not 'high'. I'm just very spiritual . . .

It was all quite absurd. It had a Keystone Cops element to it. Zach was in Laos, we believed, having a major psychotic episode. Rickey was in a hotel room in Thailand, restlessly and fearfully waiting to hear from the Australian Embassy whether they had found a grandiosely manic young man in Vientiane attempting to board a plane for Vietnam. We were in London waiting to hear from them all. We had emailed Harry to let him know the situation. He was waiting in Hanoi, just in case Zach made it across the border. All so utterly crazy but so expected. When Beth and I spoke about it, we almost collapsed in hysterical laughter. It was ghastly. Awful. We were fed up with it. We wanted it all to end positively but there appeared to be an almost nihilistic quality to the events happening so far away and out of our control. Out of Zach's control, for certain.

22

Crocodile Dundee

'I'm rushing but I managed to get a flight to northern Thailand!' Rickey shouted down the phone at me while he shoved his belongings into his backpack. 'Then I can get a cab to Laos. It's about an hour away. I know what flight Zach plans to get on. I'll see how he is. The Australian Embassy bloke's told the police where he's off to, so if he gets into trouble, unless it is a drugs thing, he'll be treated with understanding.'

I wondered how the police would treat Zach even if drugs were not involved. However, the idea that they were onto it, converging on him from right and left, towards Wattay International Airport in Laos, made me feel less disturbed. I told Rickey what Zach had written, how he sounded, about the bike crashes. 'I'm on my way now,' he said. 'I'm just so pleased to be able to do something. Whatever it is. Whatever it takes.' Beth asked rhetorically what I myself queried a hundred times a day. 'Why does he bother?'

When Rickey arrived in Laos, he met up with the Australian consular official. 'The main guy, Ed, is very nice,' Rickey informed Sam. 'He's going to give me all the help I need and soon enough, when Zach gets better, he'll realise that we've only done what we have out of love.' Rickey had to be one hell of a good friend to go so far out of his way and endure these hardships for love! But he also knew what the fallout might be. 'I'm sure I'm the bad one at the moment and I'm very nervous. But I'm confident it'll all be OK.'

Later that day, in Vientiane, the charming French-influenced capital of Laos, out of a clapped-out, fume-belching taxi climbed Zach, accompanied by two young French travellers. Rickey and the Australian consul, Ed, had been waiting at the airport for some considerable time, having anticipated that Zach was planning to take an earlier plane. There with them, in the embassy car, was Suk, the driver. I imagine that this was a first for him, the first time that he would be confronted with Western insanity. The sun was baking hot and the forecourt was crowded with the flotsam and jetsam of international backpackers, diving in and out of taxis and buses and leaving mopeds and pushbikes secured to railings for the wild dogs to use as latrines. The three musketeers, tired and thirsty, wanted to go somewhere for a cold beer. 'We were about to go,' Rickey explained to me later, after it was all over, 'then I heard the unmistakable squawk of an excited Zach!' Rickey turned to see Zach running towards him from the ancient taxi, the two French guys at the rear.

He was a bizarre apparition that would not have been out of place in a comedy horror film. In one hand, Zach carried two half-drunk cans of Red Bull, in the other, a can of Coke. Under his arm, he cradled a large plastic water bottle. A broken cigarette dangled dangerously from his lip. The ghoul was foaming at the mouth, having ingested a large tube of green toothpaste. His hair, in a parody of fashion, was shaved in patches that resembled a draughts board and there were bloody grazes and scratches and weals on his arms and legs, a consequence of the latest tangles he had got into with motorbikes. He had rubbed toothpaste into the wounds and these oozed green slime. At his waist was tied a large, black shirt, Ninja style, the pockets torn away, hanging from threads of cotton. In one of the pockets, a torch slouched precariously; attached to his backpack a football hung in netting and a small guitar was thrown over his shoulder. The ever-present sunglasses adorned his forehead, and sweat and grease crept down his cheeks.

'You fucking star!' he shouted, running towards Rickey. 'You fucking star!' he repeated, a huge grin on his face, clasping Rickey in a crushing embrace. 'We're gonna be millionaires!' he continued yelling. 'I've got a guesthouse in Luang Prabang!' Amazed, Rickey pulled back to stare at him. Ed and Suk snorted in disbelief. The two French guys, while amused by Zach's antics, also seemed concerned for him – touchingly so, given that they had probably never come across this type of eccentric behaviour before. They had been sharing his space for some time now; what might have been happening in the taxi to the airport?

Gulping down air and pulling himself up to his full height, Rickey extricated himself from Zach's suffocating clutches and attempted to take him to one side. He was at a loss as to how to begin. 'Zach,' he started, 'you shouldn't be going to Vietnam. It's dangerous there for you.'

Surprisingly, Zach was quick to agree to this advice. 'Cool,' he responded. 'I know this great five-star hotel nearby that has everything inside: pool, pool tables, you know, everything. Let's go.'

Rickey pulled him back before he rushed frenetically off. Ahead of the meeting, he had hoped that maybe his fears had been exaggerated, that they could continue travelling together once Zach had been put on the right medication and had a good long sleep. After only a matter of minutes, however, he realised that his fears were in fact spot-on. Zach was completely loopy. He had to go to hospital. 'You gotta listen to me, Zach,' he appealed. But Zach was past discrimination, past the moment when he could have stopped and paid heed to advice. He grabbed at Rickey, partly in affection but also brutally, as if he wanted to hurt him. 'I could feel him willing himself desperately to get control over himself,' Rickey related to me, appalled that Zach could demonstrate a hitherto unknown capacity for cruelty. Zach held on to Rickey, yelling at him, 'Only if you listen to me, you gotta listen to me!'

Standing together outside the taxi, and having paid the bemused driver, Zach's travelling companions, Yves and Jean-Paul, remembered that they had a plane to catch. They noted that help had arrived and that others were involved who would ensure that Zach was taken care of. Hoisting their bags over their shoulders, they began walking over towards the terminal. 'Zach,' called Yves, 'we have to go!' He stopped. 'Bye, Zach!' he shouted again. 'Look after yourself.' Jean-Paul saw Rickey tug at Zach so that he would see that they were leaving. He walked quickly over to Rickey, his face showing a marked concern. 'Take care of this guy, Rickey!' he implored. 'He needs help.'

Rickey's eyes filled with tears at the friendship these two had shown Zach. Although he was frantically manic and unwell by any standard, he had been able to show his innate personality through the illness. 'Don't worry, mate,' Rickey called back, his voice breaking. 'I'm gonna do everything I can!'

On the concourse, watching as Yves and Jean-Paul made their way over to the busy terminal, Zach jumped up and down frenziedly. He yelled over to them in broken French, making everyone around giggle. He then bent over his backpack and pulled the football from its net. Placing it on the tarmac, he aimed a low cross that miraculously took flight, avoiding the teeming humanity and parked cars. The boys laughed aloud at these antics and, scuttling to meet the ball, Jean-Paul returned the shot so that it landed at Zach's feet. The consul and the driver continued waiting, leaning against the embassy car. Rickey could see the fear etched on Suk's face. Ed appeared unfazed, hiding behind his aviator sunglasses.

Rickey had to make a rapid decision. How best to handle the situation? Humour and subterfuge were the obvious answers. 'OK, Zach,' he replied to the hotel suggestion. Anything that proscribed further air travel. 'Yeah, let's go to this hotel of yours. I've got a lift with these blokes.'

Zach stopped jumping and babbling. He stared at Ed and Suk.

There was some glimmer of intelligence. 'What's an Aussie doing here?' he asked Rickey, after being told Ed was from the Australian Embassy. 'Where are the Brits?'

Ignoring further disjointed discourse, Rickey propelled him towards the embassy car. 'Don't worry,' he said. 'Let's go now.'

Still hostile but less frenzied, Zach gathered up his belongings and climbed in. He shoved the backpack onto the floor, juggled with the various cans and stuffed the football onto the seat next to him. Once in place, he commenced a long, rambling, monotonous monologue that incorporated his admiration for all things Australian, humorously having a dig about the Ashes – or was it a rugby victory for England? When Rickey tried to interject that maybe at this juncture Zach should consider the idea of hospitalisation, it brought forward a belligerent retaliation from Zach: 'Mum had to bring in Rickey to hijack me, didn't she!'

The car, haphazardly directed by Zach through the Vientiane streets, arrived at the 'five-star' hotel.

'Is this the place?' asked Ed on arrival.

Rickey was surprised. Was he going to abandon them now, after all this? He lifted his eyebrows in a gesture of interrogation, his eyes widened in fear. 'Yeah, but . . .'

Ed turned to him. 'I know,' he said quietly, looking directly at him. 'It's all right.' He shifted around and took Zach gently by the shoulder, confronting him while at the same time trying to keep him calm and not antagonise him. 'Let's go and get you checked out. You ain't right, mate.'

Zach responded angrily. 'What d'you mean "checked out"?' he shouted, his face contorted, trying to escape from the car. 'I'm not going anywhere to be checked out!' The consul understood the situation. He realised that he had to do more than make a mere suggestion. Pondering, he made a more conciliatory request. 'At least,' he said in a measured tone, 'let's go to the Australian Embassy clinic and get your wounds cleaned up.'

Zach sat down again and stared at Ed, thankfully not taking advantage of the opportunity to take a swing at Rickey. He gazed around him, at Ed and Suk, and considered this advice, looking down at his legs and scratching at the oozing grazes. 'All right,' he said after a minute, 'but that's all. I just need some plasters.'

Ed nodded his head towards Suk and they made their way towards the clinic.

There was no let up in the teeming life on the Vientiane streets during the journey. In comparison to other South East Asian countries, Laos is less crowded and frantic but dodging the rickshaws, bicycles and pedestrians en route enervated the entire company. Then having to coerce the reluctant Zach from the inside of the vehicle took much guile and energy. He had changed his mind again. He wanted to continue his travelling. What was the point of all this? he asked more than once, angry and threatening.

Ben, the embassy doctor, waited on the steps, shielded by the fronds of a banana tree, traces of perspiration appearing on his brow. Having stepped out of the fiercely air-conditioned rooms of the modern building into the sweaty tropical temperatures, he adjusted his shirt, pulling at the wet collar. He watched while Suk drove into a space and stopped the engine. The driver opened the car door and stepped around to where Ed was gesturing at him to stand. Ben watched curiously while they leaned over to admonish and cajole a young man from the back seat, where, it was apparent, he was determined to remain. Finally, Zach was removed from the car. His possessions came after him in dribs and drabs, followed by a red-eyed, tousle-haired young man who was yelling and swearing at Zach to 'Listen!'

After one look at Zach, Ben would have known that they had a problem on their hands. He would have understood the nature of the emergency and he was at the ready with medication. He must have appreciated that he would have to be extremely diplomatic here in order to avoid doing or saying anything that would create meltdown. He approached Zach and held out his hand. 'Hello, mate,' he said to him convivially, 'let's go inside in the cool. It's bloody hot here, isn't it?'

He opened the door and Zach stepped into the clinic, placing some of his belongings on the marble floor. He smiled at Ben, stepped back and lifted his T-shirt to reveal a tattoo. An Egyptian eye, beautifully coloured and designed, graced his upper chest. 'You the doc?' he asked Ben. 'If you're gonna give me liquid Valium, then could you shoot me up in here?' he said, pointing to the tattooed eyeball.

The doctor stopped suddenly, shocked at Zach's bizarre request. Other members of staff and patients who were shuffling around the reception area stared at Zach. There were one or two giggles of shock, disgust. Ben reached up to his clammy salt-and-pepper hair and ran his fingers through it, combing it back off his face. He took a deep breath. 'Come on, mate,' he said to Zach, steadying him with a tanned, gnarled hand. Rickey had made his way in and was now waiting and watching. Ben turned Zach around and led him over to a small room off the main waiting area. 'I'm going to give you something to calm you down, mate,' he said, sitting him down in a squat metal chair. He went over to a small refrigerator and opened the door. Drawing out a glass phial that contained clear liquid, he walked back towards Zach, who stared at him, his T-shirt still rumpled above his chest. Ben withdrew a syringe from a closed sterilised packet and filled it with the liquid. Zach grinned and held out his arm. The doctor administered the shot in silence.

A deliberately numbing dose of Valium, together with the olanzapine that Zach swallowed down with huge gulps of water, should have taken the edge off his mania. Eventually, it did, but it took its time. Until then, hyper-animated and irrepressible, Zach was unable to suppress his wild movements. He rhymed and punned and constantly changed his babbling from one topic to another so that it was impossible to follow his train of thought or make sense of his increasingly random associations. He strode relentlessly and hastily in and out of the reception area, where his bags and bottles and cans and belongings lay strewn about the terrazzo.

At one point, he dropped down to the floor, pulling his backpack towards him. Rooting through it, disembowelling its innards, he reached in and abruptly pulled out a knife. Screams and gasps of fear came from the direction of the receptionists. 'Put it away, Zach!' Rickey shouted, running over and holding onto him. 'Put it away, they don't know you!'

Hearing the commotion, Ed hurried purposefully towards them. He stood in front of Zach, preventing him from lifting his arms. 'Put it away, mate,' he said to him forcefully, all conviviality now vanished.

Zach looked up at him, grinning wildly. He pushed him away and, in a strong, guttural Australian accent, he laughed, 'Call that a knife? THAT'S A KNIFE!!!'

Ed stepped back cautiously and watched while Zach slipped the knife back into the bag. Then, recognising the allusion, he began to guffaw. Ed, Rickey and Ben, all having watched *Crocodile Dundee* umpteen times, laughed until tears ran down their faces: at the joke, at Zach and at the surreal circumstance in which they found themselves. The receptionists and Suk looked on forlornly, confused. They obviously did not understand, in the midst of all this fear, this insanity, what all these strange people were now laughing at.

Zach's emotional state changed at ferocious speed from phenomenal euphoria to profound depression. He laughed and cried and could not calm down. He knew what was ultimately going to have to happen but he hated the thought of another hospital stay. 'You know how long it took me to get over it the last time,' he sobbed bitterly to Rickey during one break in the mania. 'But I'm not sad,' he added, disconcertingly refilling his mouth with toothpaste and foaming again, his cigarette cast aside for this peculiar purpose, 'I'm just emotional.' The medical staff and the receptionists, unused to this kind of highly eccentric behaviour, were fascinated and appalled by the continuing instalments.

Ben watched Zach carefully. Although he had been dosed up with enough medication to relax a rhino, there was nothing yet to indicate that Zach would be coming down from his high any time soon. Rickey was as unnerved as anyone else. After some sixty minutes of entertainment, Ben drew Rickey away from Zach. 'Rickey,' he said, 'can you come into my office, please?'

Ben sat down, drumming his fingers on the desktop, causing his milky tea to spill over into the chipped saucer. 'I'm afraid for Zach, Rickey,' he explained. 'He's obviously seriously ill. I think that he's a danger to himself and, by extension, will be a danger to other people.'

Rickey flopped down in a chair, picking at the hairs on his chin. The day was becoming longer and more confusing. What now, what did this mean? 'I know what you're saying,' Rickey answered. 'God knows I've seen him like this enough times before.'

Ben pushed the cup and saucer out of the way of a notepad. Strange sounds wafted into the surgery, sounds of someone banging a metal implement onto a stone floor, the echo reverberating around the building. 'I've given Zach a huge sedative injection,' continued Ben, ignoring the rhythmic clanging. 'It'll calm him down pro tem but he has to go to hospital. I don't know for how long but he needs to go as soon as possible. He can't stay here. The nearest decent hospital is over the border in Thailand, miles away.'

Established to cater for Australian Embassy staff and Australian citizens in Laos, the Vientiane clinic was the only medical facility in the area that provided a Western standard of care. There was an informal agreement to assist British citizens in an emergency. The local hospitals are not used by travellers unless it's absolutely necessary. It did not take too much imagination to see what they might be like. Naturally, the clinic in Vientiane was ill equipped to care for Zach, even for a short period. There was no mental-health provision and the medical care, wonderful as it was for the average traveller, was not specialised enough to deal with his specific problems. 'I've called around and there's a hospital in Bangkok that's agreed to have him,' Ben told Rickey, consulting the writing on the tea-stained notebook. 'There's no way that Zach can stay here, we simply don't have the facilities for him. We'd better let him know.'

The two of them walked out of the office to where Zach sat sprawled on a deep, well-worn brown-leather settee, his personal belongings around him, intermittently strumming at his guitar. Three half-finished glasses of water were discarded on a scratched, stained teak bench, juxtaposed with an unfinished bar of Cadbury's best. He looked up at them. They confronted him with the news. He would have to travel to a hospital in Thailand and check himself in. Rickey was afraid that Zach would simply get up, gather his possessions and leave, refusing to take this advice. However, slightly calmer now, he agreed to go. 'All right,' he responded, to Rickey's wide-eyed astonishment. 'I'll go. So long as I can have a private room, and a bottle of wine and a pizza for the journey.'

Ben was equally astounded, patting Zach on the back to show his pleasure and giving a silent high-five to Ed. 'You go and organise the stuff,' he said to Rickey, striking while the iron was hot. 'Take Suk and we'll see you here later.'

Ed ambled over to them, reached into his pocket and brought out a bundle of damp, crumpled notes. He handed them to Rickey. 'Whatever it takes, mate,' he said.

'Meanwhile,' said Ben, walking back to his office, 'I'll confirm the arrangements with the hospital. By the way,' he added, 'you're going to have to go overland.'

The situation, by now, was volatile. Although Zach was calmer than he had been some hours previously, he was still combustible, raging against the 'injustice' of it all. Given his state, neither Ed nor Ben was prepared to put him on a plane. In any event, it was doubtful that any airline, after one brief look at Zach, would have been prepared to endanger the lives of their other passengers by allowing him a seat. Irrespective of who was accompanying him, he was far too dangerous a proposition. The only option, then, was to transfer him by ambulance.

When Rickey returned to the clinic armed with piping-hot pizza and bottles of good Bordeaux, Ben manoeuvred him away from Zach. 'I've spoken to the hospital,' he told him, relaxed now that he knew there was an answer to his concerns. 'It's all confirmed. It's an excellent place, with good facilities and a renowned psychiatrist. They'll take Zach but they insist that a psychiatric nurse accompany you. They'd also prefer him to be heavily sedated during the journey.' Rickey grimaced. Ben continued, ignoring Rickey's expression, 'I've managed to get someone.' He stopped, smiling to himself and then at Rickey. 'It was a bloody hell of a job to find someone who was willing.' He took a deep breath. 'As you can guess.' Rickey could. Who'd want to be stuck with a nutter for hours at a time? It would have to be a very well-paid journey.

Oblivious to the time and effort expended on his behalf, Zach now objected to these conditions. Having initially agreed to go to Thailand, he now baulked at the idea of his trip to Hanoi being curtailed and blamed Rickey and the Australians for their involvement. He had no appreciation of how his latest performance had impacted on those around him and no perception of how his mood swings regulated his entire existence. 'Lao society does not have a very good understanding of mental illness,' the Australian consul wrote to me later, 'and he could quite easily have been locked up for a significant period before the embassy was informed.'

Rickey gazed up from where he had been speaking with Ben. Lights were playing across the walls of the clinic. Rickey slowly walked towards the source of the flickering lights: Zach. Rickey let out an involuntary chortle. Zach had created a light sabre. His little *Star Wars* episode. He'd somehow managed to collect enough sticky-back plastic to tape his two torches together in a gummy embrace. He ducked and wove and wended his way around the chairs, tables and plants, adding the required 'whoosh' sound effects as he went.

Suddenly, he stopped, sensing Rickey watching him. He rushed over to him, light dancing from his hands. Zach's face was thrown into stark relief by the beam from his makeshift toy. 'Look what we've got for the journey, pendeco!' he cooed, delving into his pocket and bringing out a little box. He opened it with jittery fingers. 'Lookie here . . .' It was stuffed with weed and opium.

Grinning, he crammed the weed back into the box and closed it tight, shoving it once again down into his raggedy trouser pocket. Rickey was aghast at this idiocy and snapped at him, 'You can't take that over the border!'

But Zach huffed and sulked and glowered at Rickey, getting pissed off with this perceived failure of friendship. He wanted Rickey to 'go loco' with him as they had done so many times before. 'Yeah, well,' he said to Rickey with a smirk, 'we'll see.'

23

Definitely Drug-Fuelled

Inside the converted minibus, Zach, Rickey, the driver and the psychiatric nurse hastily employed at an exorbitant fee made their way towards the Thai–Laos border. In the knowledge that the wine, pizza and his opium-laced weed were at hand, Zach was tranquil, for the moment. Dusk. The night was drawing in around them and the road that headed towards the Friendship Bridge was dusty. All along the verges, people were cooking their evening meals and the air was clotted with the embers and smoke and smells from individual fires that burned bright in the fading light.

The nurse, sitting in the front of the van, presented a friendly persona, especially to Zach, ingratiating himself so there would be no discussion when he offered his medical wares once the journey had begun. 'I was panicky that there would be the usual grief,' said Rickey later, 'but Zach took whatever the guy offered him, basically because he didn't know what it was.'

Once the ambulance crossed the border, there having been no problems with guards or police, they cracked open the wine. The pizza had been demolished by this time and a heady garlic and tomato aroma still filled the van. When the joints were lit, the smell changed once more. 'We asked the nurse to join us,' Rickey told me, 'and he accepted straight away. Somewhat surprisingly.'

The first town that they approached was Nong Kai, where they found a 7-Eleven. Rickey asked the driver to stop and they pulled up. He dived out while the others waited and watched. Zach slumped back in the seat, a large opium-packed fag cupped in his hand, sated. Rickey returned with plastic bags hanging from his arms, filled with munchies and Cokes. Up until this point, the journey had appeared to be going along swimmingly. The sultry night air wafted warm, pungent breezes into the van. The three passengers passed small talk between them. Zach remained in his dreamy state. Then, suddenly, he sat up straight in his seat.

'What was that fucking hideous shit you gave me?' he demanded, staring at the nurse. 'Aagh, it's fucking horrible!' He pointed towards himself, gesturing wildly at his stomach, his chest and his head in an attempt to describe the appalling reactions he was experiencing. The nurse, startled by this, tried to explain what type of medication he had administered. Now extremely animated, Zach shouted at him. 'Disgusting!' he spat. 'Don't ever give this to anyone! Ever again!'

The fury in Zach's eyes terrified Rickey. He held on to him, trying to pacify him and stop him from hitting out at the nurse or the driver. All they needed now was to crash. 'Zach, he didn't know!' he shouted at him. 'He was just trying to help you! He's just fucking stupid!' He glared over at the nurse, whose wide eyes displayed a mute horror as he nodded fiercely in agreement. Zach sat back again and tried to relax but every few moments he would sit up ramrod straight in his seat, stare angrily at the nurse and yell epithets. Then he fell asleep.

The journey continued. Rickey smoked joints, becoming sleepier as the time passed. In the front, the nurse's head wobbled up and down, every so often emitting loud snores. The debris and bumps that littered the road threw the passengers around until they resembled a carton of raggedy dolls, their movements heightened by the glare of oncoming trucks, bikes and buses. Once more, Zach awoke but this time he started to cough, heaving and convulsing on the seat. Unable to stop or to catch his breath, he grabbed at his throat, tearing at his flesh. Virtually unconscious, the nurse sat there, nonplussed, unable to do anything. Now fully awake and terrified that Zach was going to choke to death, Rickey yelled at him to help them. 'Aren't you going to do anything?' He sat still. 'NURSE!' cried Rickey once more. Thoroughly frustrated and disgusted at the man's total inadequacy, Rickey shouted at the driver to stop the car and pull over.

Still coughing and heaving and panting for breath, Zach fell onto the floor of the van. Rickey leaned over him and grasped the handle, sliding open the wide metal door. Bending down, he put his arms around Zach's waist and dragged him outside, both of them falling onto the ground in a heap of sweaty, smelly arms and legs. Extricating his arms from Zach's embrace, Rickey heaved himself up to standing. Zach's coughing gradually began to subside once the clear night air coursed into his lungs and they were away from the weed and opium fumes of the 'ambulance'. In an effort to straighten himself, Zach grabbed onto Rickey with one hand. Standing, he then lit into Rickey, slugging him around the face and chest. In his delusional state, everyone was the aggressor and even though Rickey was his saviour and best friend, nothing would stop him from thumping him over and over again until, destroyed with the physical exertion, he crumbled to the ground. Rickey's head reeled from the not-so-weak punches, the wine, the weed and the draining experience.

It was two in the morning, in the middle of nowhere, Thailand. The brilliant night sky surrounded them, but an eerie quiet filled the void. They were stuck on the bank of the road and only the sounds of monkeys and insects and unknown animals broke the silence. They were alone. No one else was around, apart from the occasional car or lorry hurrying past. The driver and the nurse sat in the ambulance listening to the tinny, whiny radio. After some moments, during which he regained some semblance of strength, Rickey bent down and yanked Zach into a standing position. He pushed and shoved at him and propelled him back to the van. Turning him so that he was pinned against the metal, Rickey reopened the door, engineering it so that Zach fell indecorously onto the floor. He collapsed and fell into a deep stupor.

The wine was finished. The not insignificant amount of weed and opium that was left was used up by Rickey and by the time the ambulance arrived in Bangkok it was daybreak and he had not slept a wink. The streets were crammed with cars and bikes and commuters and hawkers swarming from all directions. The noise was deafening. The last part of the journey had been spent in relative quiet while Zach passed in and out of consciousness and Rickey related his life experiences to the thoroughly worn-out and bewildered nurse. He eventually closed his eyes, desperately trying to ignore Rickey's hoarse tones. The driver negotiated the streets and after a short while the hospital loomed up before them. The van stopped outside.

'I so desperately wanted the nurse to take charge and help us and make arrangements,' Rickey remembered, 'but the dumb idiot woke up stoned and confused and totally fucking useless.' In his wired, dazed state Rickey had to compose himself. He somehow had to get Zach into the hospital. Half leading Zach and half propping himself up against him, he navigated the wide, white steps, flanked by huge overbearing palms, heading towards the reception area. The opaque glass doors swung open as they approached and they just about tumbled into the foyer.

An old nurse with a mean face greeted them, looking incredulous at the state of them. 'This is Zach,' croaked Rickey. 'He has bipolar. Did you get the message from the Australian Embassy?' Before she had a chance to answer him, Zach broke away from Rickey. 'No, no,' he protested, 'that's not right. I'm not bipolar. This is Rickey. He's bipolar. I may be schizophrenic but I've been wrongly diagnosed!'

The mean-faced nurse continued to stare at Rickey, ignoring the tirade. 'No, no message here,' she said to him in broken English. 'Wait, I go get doctor.' Something had sunk in. Zach's distinct lack of composure and unconventional appearance had struck a chord. Zach continued to remonstrate with Rickey while she was away. He waved his arms around, shouting that there was nothing wrong with him, there was no need for him to stay there. Rickey looked around, despairing of getting help from anyone. Then two burly male nurses trundled up the corridor towards them. They approached Zach and linked their arms into his. Both smiling like cats, they forced him towards the doors of a spacious stainless-steel lift. One of them nodded at Rickey: 'Do you want to bring his stuff upstairs?' He coerced him gently into the arriving elevator. 'Come on, Zach.'

A bright room overlooked a courtyard with coloured pots and bushes and exotic trees. A pond with tropical fish enhanced the back lawn. A motorway could be heard, the early-morning Bangkok traffic hooting and screeching its way to work. Rickey looked out and saw an area that had been made into a small football pitch. Perfect. Over the next four weeks, many games of football would be played with the other hospital casualties and a steady stream of visitors, adding to the inventory of Zach's holiday experiences.

* * *

There was no health insurance to cover his insanity. A chronic casualty who will almost certainly require emergency aid is refused. Of course, one could argue that his breakdown was self-induced. We were charged by the Aussies for tracing Zach to the airport, by the clinic in Vientiane for the doctor, the nursing staff, medication, phone calls and the transfer to the border (the ambulance was a private-hire car). The so-called psychiatric nurse cost hundreds of dollars. Rickey's hotel room in Bangkok, his flight to Laos and all his other expenses vis-à-vis Zach we were obliged to cover. There was no problem there. He did a remarkable job. Then further invoices covered the hospital in Bangkok and the psychiatrist, plus all the medication and the two flights back to London, one for Zach and one for an accompanying nurse. This 'travelling experience' cost us thousands of pounds. It made us sick to our stomachs.

During the last conversation I had with Rickey while he was back in Thailand, he gave me chapter and verse regarding the reasons for Zach's catastrophic breakdown. It was no surprise that he had fallen apart so badly: he had completely discarded the bipolar standard plan of action for travelling alone. Why were warnings ignored, recommendations disregarded? 'Anna reckoned he was pretty weird, overexcited and hyper when she first met him,' Rickey told me from his hotel room, once Zach was in the hospital and Rickey hooked up to Sky TV. 'But after they went to Laos he started taking yaba [an amphetamine popular in Thailand] and there was also ganja and opium and a litre of rice wine a day. It's locally made and God knows what's really in it.' Unbelievable, I thought. When will he ever learn?

'He also told me that he took some other hallucinogenic shit,' Rickey further informed me. Was I disappointed? I wasn't surprised. 'I feel like a bit of a telltale tit. But fuck it! I'm sure that Anna's exploits had some impact on him too. He tried telling me that he worried himself sick about me but he never phoned me. I do love him loads, obviously, but he needs to realise that he's not special and his actions have consequences. Everyone's really angry with him for leaving England so healthy and then acting recklessly like that. I told him this: if he takes hard drugs and ends up in hospital again as a result, no one's gonna have any time for him. Everyone else has grown up. It's like being with an angst-ridden sixteen year old sometimes with Zach – so frustrating. He'll surely be back in hospital again soon, because he won't fucking learn! Maybe next time he'll have to be kept in for longer, to the point where he realises he can't play ridiculous games with his own head any more.'

Zach spent four ugly weeks in Bangkok. During that time, he never really regained his mind. He intermittently believed that he 'had a gift from God' and could 'commune with the dead'. He vehemently denied suffering from manic depression, requesting funds so that he could continue his travels 'but as a businessman

NOT as a backpacker'. The expense, the sleepless nights and the sobs of anger and despair would not be forgotten. It was, we determined, the last time. From now on, if he wanted to travel, he was on his own.

On a bitterly cold December morning, accompanied by a tiny, unsmiling Thai psychiatric nurse, Zach flew back to London. This time, I went alone to the airport. I knew from the emails and phone calls that he was far from well. Having spoken to Rickey, who was now back in Burma teaching English, and to other friends who had taken time to visit him, I knew that his volatile moods showed no sign of stabilising. Sam emailed him to say that he would have to go back to the NHS psychiatric ward and stay there until he calmed down and became rational. 'No way,' Zach replied:

> *I'll continue my travels, but have to establish a base in London first . . . 500 quid please . . . I would prefer to go straight to Laos but am cooperating with the doctor and doing everything by the book. It's my aim to have bases in Laos and Australasia. I agree to pay my own repatriation costs but NO FUCKING way am I going to have that MUPPET doctor. I'm quite happy to take the Sodium Valproate, as unlike Lithium it does not seem to have the same EVIL side effects and will carry on. If YOU are willing to pay for me to stay in the Griffin with Doctor Goode as my shrink, then fair enuff . . .*

No, we were not.

It was the busiest time of the day. From all points east and west, planes had arrived and were decanting their passengers. Thousands of travellers milled about, their baggage on wheels and trolleys and generally in the way, so that to make a space in this chaotic, claustrophobic melee meant having to use elbows and heels. I was depressed already and dreading my meeting with Zach. Why couldn't we have the oh-so-typical delight, hugs and kisses that I saw happening between other parents and offspring? Why did our meetings, now so predictable as to be almost routine, have to be so dispiriting?

I saw them coming through and waved at Zach. I pointed to an area at the back of the concourse, next to the shops. He tore across to me, shadowed by the accompanying nurse. 'I need a cigarette,' he demanded without a word or gesture of greeting. 'I don't have any and I need one desperately. I've been travelling for hours.'

I looked at the nurse. She said nothing. He continued to demand cigarettes. I could feel my disappointment and anger boiling up. I tried to direct him away from the crowds. 'Can't you lower your voice?' I asked him quietly.

No, he was not going to succumb to my control and began an outpouring of venom, of outrage. 'Why do I have to ask your *fucking* permission?' The crowds around us parted, spectators of a full-blown manic rant. They watched us while he shouted at me, his emotions out of control, his actions becoming wilder. They watched him shove me away from him.

The nurse remonstrated with him. 'Please behave, Zach,' she said to him in a small voice, grasping hold of his arm. I tried to make myself oblivious to the stares, to pretend that this, actually, was not happening. Zach pulled away from the nurse. Hurriedly, she jammed a pack of medication into my hands, looking around her so that she could make a quick getaway. 'Zach,' she repeated, 'stop it! Behave yourself!' He was having none of it and, without thanking her or attempting to apologise to me, he stormed out of the terminal towards the car.

Three days later, after another series of encounters with unhelpful barmen, unfriendly publicans, overly helpful dealers and the police, Zach ended up in the local hospital once more. Grandiosely manic, he fiercely resented any interference by the authorities in his existence. He positively hated Sam and me and despised our having been involved in his repatriation. He loathed having to face up to the fact that when he fell apart, there were always others who would end up becoming involved in the chaos that ensued. Weeks of fractious, debilitating mania led, of course, to the horrendous depression and his hospital chart repeated itself: he was out again.

24

Tosh

JANUARY 2003

The front door slammed shut. I glanced out of the steamy kitchen. Zach stepped into the hall. Throwing his keys on the dining room table, he removed his bag, his glossy wet anorak and his woolly hat. Max padded over to him and Zach kissed him on either side of his furry snout and rubbed his tummy. Max made noises of contentment, then sauntered back over to his bed, flopping down with a grunt. It was an exceptionally cold evening. Outside, the murky night sky covered a frigid, glistening city. In the distance, I could hear car horns playing their nightly concert, an accompaniment to the commuters wending their way back home. The heating system continued with its winter melody. It was a comforting sound, reminding me how glad I was to be inside in the warmth. The windows were clammy with condensation and tiny puddles gathered together in the joins between glass and wood. It was good to be inside, cosy. Zach came into the kitchen, blowing on his hands, and took a glass out of the cabinet. He went over to the water cooler and poured himself a large tumbler. I was in the midst of preparing dinner but I wiped my hands and sat down.

'I saw Tosh last night,' he said. I examined him apprehensively. Zach was recently out of hospital, not yet back down on terra firma, and appeared anxious and troubled. Once more, we were revisited by the past. Tosh had been absent from our lives for some considerable time. We rarely spoke about him but if we did it generally elicited a negative remark from me, although not necessarily from Zach.

'Where?' I asked him. 'Where did you see him?'

Zach's hands shook as he drank the water. 'I was in Dalston on my way to the pub and I saw him in the street. He was acting really weird.' No surprise there.

Zach went over to the bread bin and took out a loaf. He cut several slices, giving torn corners away to Max, who had joined us when he heard the crackle of bread wrapper. Zach went back over to the fridge for cheese, tomatoes and salad cream, then drew the chair out from under the bench and settled himself down.

'When was the last time you saw him?' I asked.

'He's been living on the coast, in a bedsit,' he explained. 'Don't you remember? I visited him once, after a football match.'

I did recall Zach describing the room occupied by Tosh: a tiny cubicle in a run-down council block, just big enough for him, his books and his television. Nothing else. I had the impression that he was on benefits and that his rent was paid for by the local authority, while all the time he continued along his destructive path. He drank to oblivion, used drugs unremittingly and remained completely nihilistic. I read between the lines that in addition he had developed psychiatric problems. Zach didn't discuss these to any extent, possibly because he simply didn't understand what they were, other than he 'wasn't right'. I thought it amusing that Zach was positing the view that Tosh 'wasn't right in the head'. This was hardly news to *me*.

Although Tosh had come up to London on various occasions over the past couple of years, Zach had made a point of not seeing him. In the past, Tosh had re-entered his life and malevolently created discord so that the relationships Zach had rekindled with old friends were once again ruptured. Tosh's malice and envy coalesced in his viewing all Zach's friends as easy prey.

Before we had made it clear to Zach that he could no longer live with us, and during times when family life became burdened with rancour and acrimony, he had sporadically settled in with friends in squats in Hackney or Seven Sisters. Being aware of Zach's whereabouts, Tosh would turn up and insist on crashing there, too. However, he was quite unlike other members of this particular fraternity, who, though amoral in their attitudes to drugs or paying a lawful rent, were generally a pretty laid-back and benevolent bunch. There was a lot of dope around and much (probably specious) intellectual debate among the squatters, most of whom were university students. In this milieu, Zach was at home but Tosh was considerably out of his depth. He no doubt suffered a massive inferiority complex, so the resentment about his own background surfaced in spiteful jealousy. He seemed to have made it his objective to transform the hazy ambience into an atmosphere charged with brooding menace.

Zach was severely conflicted. He felt he was being disloyal to Tosh but he also realised that there was something profoundly 'wrong' with this guy and that he no longer wished to share his breathing space. Months later, after we had finally given Zach the push, he told me he'd met Tosh coincidentally in the street in Hackney. Tosh had 'found Jesus' and was on an evangelical kick. Would Zach join him now that he was 'at one with the Lord'? Zach made a dash for comparative normality. The complexities of their relationship and its breakdown created an overriding belief in Zach that he had betrayed his friend, in spite of Tosh's obnoxious behaviour towards him.

'So you saw him last night?' I repeated, waiting to hear the explanation. 'I know he's weird. You know he's weird. What was so different?'

He got up and walked slowly into the dining room. I followed.

'He was on the other side of the road,' he responded. 'When he saw it was me, he crossed over and started talking.' Zach pulled out a dining chair and sat down. He started to bite into the sandwich, salad cream and tomato oozing from its creases. 'There was something really odd about him. He wasn't behaving normally. I really didn't know what to say to him, so I asked him how he was and he asked me to go back to where he was staying. I felt sort of sorry for him, so I went along.' Zach paused. He replaced the sandwich on the plate and took a gulp of water, wiping his hands on a piece of kitchen roll. Then he reached over to his bag, opened it and withdrew a long, heavy-looking object wrapped in paper. 'Look,' he said, placing the package on the table. I watched while he removed the wrappings. From inside, he took out something metallic and shiny. In fact, there were two objects: two gleaming, burnished knives with ornately carved wooden handles.

'Where did you get these?' I asked him, startled. 'They're not yours, are they?' I knew he had a propensity for knives when high; could they belong to him?

'They're Tosh's,' he replied. 'I took them off him.'

I didn't know whether to believe what he was telling me. For years, he had bought numerous penknives and had somehow managed to bring back a sheath knife from South America. But this? I was out of my depth.

'I'm telling you the truth!' Zach snapped. 'He was completely nuts. Manic. Dangerous. You think *I'm* mad! He was raving. I don't know what he needed them for but I persuaded him to give them to me. I told him they were lethal and I would look after them for him.' I got up from my chair and walked over to the table. 'I don't know why,' Zach continued, 'but he believed me.'

Zach's hands trembled. He got up and came over to me, taking me by the shoulder. 'He told me he had a list.'

I turned the knives over in the newspaper, trying not to touch them. 'What d'you mean, a list?'

Zach was agitated. He took a roll-up from a wrinkled tobacco packet in his back pocket and walked towards the balcony doors. I wanted him to finish telling me what had happened that night but I didn't want to appear too uneasy. Outside, he lit up. I waited until he had finished smoking. He came back inside. 'He said,' Zach told me, gesturing towards the knives, 'that he had a list of people he was going to murder. He had decided to become a serial killer.'

I got up from my chair and walked towards him, holding onto the table. 'A what?' I asked sharply. What on earth was all this about? I knew that Zach was telling the truth. It was too wacky for him to have made it up.

He didn't answer me directly, dancing around on one foot and fumbling in his pockets. 'The strangest thing was,' he explained, withdrawing a cigarette paper and some tobacco, 'the *weirdest* thing was, he told me not to worry. I wasn't on the list.'

I stared at the knives. What do you do with knives taken off an aspiring 'career serial killer'? I had to think hard but really I had no clue. Call in the police? But this was a crazy story. Would they believe Zach, believe me? I wanted the knives away from us and away from Zach in particular. He was still suffering the downside to the mania, still sick, hypomanic. Who knew what this could do to him.

'Are you worried?' I asked him.

'I didn't believe him,' he responded. 'I think my life's in danger.'

I tried to think. I had to get rid of the knives. Get Zach out of here. Get him away from this seedy mess. I went back into the kitchen, delved in the recycling box and brought out all the old newspapers I had. I laid them out on the dining room table and, donning rubber gloves, placed the knives on the paper, wrapping them so that, to the naked eye, they could have been anything. 'Wait here,' I told Zach, while I shoved the packages into one, two, three plastic shopping bags and then a black bin-liner. He stared at me as if I too had lost the plot. 'I'm going to throw them away,' I explained to him. He made no attempt to stop me. Gathering them up, I shoved the rest of the garbage in with them, tying the bag at the top. Who could guess? I took them down to the bins, undid one of the other rubbish bags and, speedily and shakily, dumped the whole lot inside. This was like a '50s B-picture. I couldn't believe I was doing this.

I went back upstairs. Zach was outside smoking again. I went over to the balcony. 'They've gone. Does he know where you live?'

Zach shook his head. 'No,' he answered emphatically, 'and I never want to see him again.'

* * *

Weeks later, the winter days left us once more. Sam and I took advantage of a glittering Sunday and led Max on a long walk over the Heath, now overflowing with spring flowers. He loped alongside us and when we finally reached Hampstead High Street and stopped at one of the pavement cafés, he sat down impatiently, waiting for passers-by to pat his head with the usual 'What a beautiful dog!' He was used to those words and, wagging tail at the ready, often generated snacks from waiters and generous praise from indulgent children. Today was no different, and by the time we left the café it was going on towards noon. We arrived home, retrieved the Sunday papers, discarded muddy boots and jeans, and headed for the settee and comfy chairs.

The phone rang. Sam answered it. 'Hi, Simon,' he said. It was Dominic's father. I continued reading, reaching out for the supplement and folding my legs beneath me. The sun shone directly onto me through the west-facing windows and it was difficult to see the words. I shielded my eyes from the glare. Sam had been about to sit down. He stopped, continuing to stand, and within moments he let out an anguished moan. Somehow he just folded, collapsing onto the armchair. Cradling his head in his hands, he rubbed furiously at his eyes.

'What?' He moaned again. 'What did you say happened? Oh my God, Simon. I can't believe it.' He turned his anguished face towards me and I desperately tried to think what could possibly have happened. 'Oh, Simon,' he continued, 'I'm so, so sorry.' I stared at him aghast, mouthing, 'What's happened? Has something happened to Zach?'

In his distress, Sam was unable to continue the conversation, so I gently retrieved the phone from him. 'Simon?' I asked. 'Simon, what's the matter? What happened?'

Initially, there was no response. I heard him take a shuddering mouthful of air. 'Ros,' he responded calmly, so calmly, 'I'm so sorry to have to tell you this. I don't know how to say it. How to explain . . . Dominic has been murdered. Tosh came around to our house last night . . .' Simon stopped. He paused as if he were straining for oxygen. 'Tosh,' he continued wearily, almost vacantly, 'he came round to our house and killed my son.'

It was only much later, when we saw Dominic lying on that cold bier in the funeral home, his face displaying a yellowing tinge, drained of blood, that it all hit home. His body had lain for days in a freezing cabinet, as if he were an end cut of meat. A shiny blue curtain shrouded the body. It was lifted by an attendant and the mourners shuffled past. I remember looking at him, mesmerised. It was only his face that we could see. Silent now, unsmiling. No beatific grin to his friends, no more words on his lips. The body was a cruel cipher for a much-loved friend. Almost unrecognisable. How could it have happened? What set in motion the series of events the consequence of which was the truly untimely demise of a genuinely decent and loyal friend?

It was a Saturday evening. Dominic and his family were waiting for a pizza delivery. They were sitting around the front room, chatting about nothing much: a day out, the football scores, summer holidays, the weather, wedding plans. The doorbell rang. Dominic went to answer it in the expectation of the pizza delivery-man. Opaque glass set in a Victorian surround disguised the identity of the caller. After a moment, Dominic opened the door. A surprise but not a stranger: Tosh stood on the stone steps. A baffled Dominic stood staring at him, waiting for the usual reluctant greeting. His family waited for their pizza, continuing their conversation, oblivious to the fact that their lives were about to be irrevocably transformed.

Do I need to describe it in all its horror? I don't think so. Tosh turned up in the doorway of Dominic's house and, armed with a knife and a hammer, ended Dominic's life. There were terrible noises, shouts of anger and fear. Hearing the scream from their son and then the crash of bodies, Dominic's parents rushed into the hallway, only to see the carnage on the floor tiles. Simon struggled to prise Tosh's body from the leaden Dominic, who was bleeding heavily. Although noticeably small and skinny, Tosh was wiry and he held onto Dominic in a psychotic embrace. It took all of Simon's strength to haul him away from his now stricken son and pin him down on the floor, pressing him beneath his body until the police and ambulance arrived. There was nothing he could do to help Dominic. In shock, he demanded of this callous individual why he had chosen *their* home. Why Dominic? Over and over, he posed his question. All that Tosh would say was 'Because I could.'

That first phone conversation did not last long. Between pauses for air, Simon told me what had happened on Saturday night. I was loath to interject. What was there to say? What could anyone say? Was there anything I could do? He replied that all was taken care of. There was nothing that anyone could do. His son was dead. He had been killed in the most heinous and cold-blooded manner by a ghoul dressed in leather, who had created in his mind a list of those whose lives he envied obsessively. I listened to Simon. I felt empty. Dulled. Circumstances dictated an inquest. A funeral is the healthy response to death but no funeral could take place. When it did happen, it would be private, Simon informed me. Only close family. I understood. Should he call Zach? Simon requested. 'No,' I answered him. 'We'll do it. We'll let him know. He's not well. I don't know how he'll take it.'

I replaced the receiver. Sam and I looked at each other, wordless.

'Who's going to break it to Zach?' I asked.

'I will,' he responded, more calmly now, the initial shock to his emotions having been controlled. 'I'll go over to the flat and I'll bring him back here. We can hardly call him on the phone.'

Within ten minutes, Zach was with us and we explained as gently as we could what had happened. He expressed very little reaction to the news. I could tell that he was profoundly upset but he was unable to show any kind of emotion. There were no tears, no recriminations or anger. Although Dominic was one of Zach's oldest and closest friends, he had not been a member of the band and had not lived in the squats. He was a peripheral acquaintance of Tosh, mostly because of his closeness to Zach. He had a good job, a fiancée and a caring and supportive family. There was absolutely no coherent reason whatsoever for him to have been nominated as a target. Yet, conversely, it is evident that this is the reason why he was picked.

Of course, Tosh has never given a clear explanation as to why he chose Dominic. 'Because I could' is no answer. He did not attack any of the other members of the band, although Tommy, who had also seen him within the previous few months, remembered the 'list'. But who would have thought that he could have meant what he said? He had a list. So what? Yet Zach believed him and avoided him. Tommy met him but didn't believe him.

So now he is detained at Her Majesty's pleasure. His overwhelming sense of inadequacy manifested itself in a desire to eradicate anything or anyone who was good and who represented success and happiness, neither of which he would ever attain. It was for this reason that he destroyed Zach and the band, and it was for the same reason that he murdered Dominic. He desired the obliteration of anyone who represented the antithesis of his own vile, warped persona.

Epilogue

In the spring and summer of 2003, Zach moved into a new flat with Sylvie. He seemed to be doing well and all appeared to be going smoothly. However, by the end of October, our heightened senses and canny antennae were beginning to pick up warning signals. Two or three small words here and there. The odd sentence thrown in among those that continued to be lucid. Beth and I only had to look at each other to know that we weren't imagining it and to see that we were thinking the same thing. Her anxious eyes betrayed her inner fears. The mannerisms, the bizarre ideas and the strange ways he related his thoughts to one another. The spending, the sweaty face, the filthy clothes. *Here we go again.* Maybe this time it would be different. Maybe this time he might manage himself so that none of us would have to endure another spell of enforced captivity.

By the second week of November, when the nights had drawn in so that by late afternoon an eerie black mantle smothered the daylight, Zach began to unravel, to disintegrate, to climb the crazy stairs. We could all see it, apart from Sylvie, who persisted in her own better judgement that he was not mentally ill, that all he had was a 'drug problem'. We were fighting a losing battle on two fronts. All we could do was repeat ourselves ad nauseam: '*Take* the fucking olanzapine. Do us all a favour, five milligrams at night so that you don't go through the usual crap and don't screw up everyone else's winter. It's only for a few weeks. Surely that would be better than spending Christmas in hospital.' No, he wasn't interested. There was no way he was going to take the antipsychotic. Valium, lovely. Sleeping pills of any variety, even better. Then we found out that he'd decided, well, hell, why not succumb to the pleasures of ketamine? Why not indeed? It only took one hit, one small baggie, one toke, and off he went again, into the wild blue yonder.

His flat was in a squalid mess. Zach was not in the least bit house-proud. The bathroom was never cleaned and dirt accumulated around the shower, the sink, the toilet – ingrained dirt that would have to be systematically scoured off. Dirt and dog hair and matches and ash were ground into the carpet; crockery piled up in the kitchen sink, unwashed; putrid food caked on festering plates. Dirty clothes lay in piles; unwashed bed linen, bathroom towels, kitchen cloths festooned the floors. Zach had kicked in three doors. Great wide holes had been smashed through into the rooms beyond. Unable to control himself, he would kick out at anything in his way. Other furniture, too, bore the brunt of his anger and frustration: the bedroom chest of drawers was now front-less, the kitchen cabinets door-less. Lamps and ornaments and even guitars lay in broken heaps. It was depressing to see it. To him, it was 'art'; to us, it was pure destruction.

There was no more that anyone could do. Zach's repetitive illness was there for the duration. The lucky ones may have one quick, small episode. There are those who may have two or three during their lifetime and although their lives are dealt a heavy blow, they survive and maintain a pretty decent lifestyle. Then there are other sufferers who go from mania to depression within months or days, or even hours, their lives a profound burden to themselves and those around them. However, all the above may well take their medication and at least try to gain control of the disease rather than allowing the disease to control them. Zach's particular brand of bipolar disorder, the dual diagnosis whereby he was also addicted to cannabis and other street drugs, meant that his life was a balancing act. We could only hope that age and maturity might one day bring to bear a recognition that there is more to life than searching out the next hit. Maybe the right medication, combined with a disavowal of drugs, could lead to an understanding that a home and a family are more important. But I didn't know if the portents were there.

Then, surprisingly, there was a hiatus: eighteen months with no nuthouses, loony bins, asylums, no drugs, no alcohol. Just sobriety. An occasional problem with gambling but that didn't lead to a section. It was more than we could have wished for. We hoped it was wisdom come with age. It wasn't down to any lotions, potions or pills – although he did agree to take the Depakote, on an ad hoc basis. We had no idea how long it would last but it was wonderful not to have to mentally preview every conversation to ensure that it would not end in acrimony and conflict.

Zach travelled again – India, Asia and the Middle East – and he came back in the same frame of mind that he had set off in. No ambulance to meet him at the airport, no middle-of-the-night phone call from a stranger in an embassy telling us that our wayward son needed succour. There was a rekindling of affection between Zach and Beth, and of the long journeys that father and son used to take together to watch whatever sport took their fancy.

Sylvie remained on the scene then, a potent presence, someone who loved Zach unconditionally. We were appreciative of her and of her patience and tolerance. They had their moments but on the whole appeared to be happy together. We thought that there was a happy ending on its way but soon enough we were disabused of this notion: the summer of 2007 was the worst yet.

Another journey to the Far East. We thought that, having managed his travels so well for nearly two years, Zach would be able to cope with this trip without any serious problems. I really didn't expect the email from the Foreign Office to say that he had been held once more on the Thai–Laos border – this time having had his passport impounded by the authorities. Nor did I anticipate that he would be beaten up in jail yet again. Only after I'd informed the authorities that Zach was likely in trouble because of his mental-health problems was he taken to a psychiatric hospital – yet another psychiatric hospital – in Thailand. This time, both Sam and I had to travel to Chiang Mai for three days in order to arrange for his repatriation. The psychiatrist there wanted to keep him in hospital and, frankly, that is where he should have stayed. He would have ridden out the psychosis; he would have been safe and clean and fed, and he would have had no recourse to illegal drugs. What happened instead was that we brought him back to London, where he disintegrated to such an extent that he became grandiosely manic and hooked on heroin. Eventually, after he'd invited half of London's homeless and junkies into his flat, which we had bought and where they set about creating a Third World slum, we threw him out. History repeats itself.

The NHS psychiatric team couldn't help us. They refused to section him this time, as he no longer fitted their 'criteria'. Apparently, despite his addiction to drugs, he did not present a danger to himself or other people.

'Why *didn't* they section me?' he asked me plaintively later on.

'Why?' I replied. 'I've no idea. They didn't think that you were a danger to yourself . . . '

He fell further and further into the gutter. Finally, when Zach was arrested and cautioned by the police, the possibility that he might face a jail sentence shocked him for the first time into actively seeking help with his addictions.

* * *

I remember taking Max for a walk on a sparkling, frosty morning not so long ago. A brisk north wind battered the leafless trees and emergent spring flowers. I pulled my scarf tightly around my neck. Max lumbered slowly beside me, his arthritic legs holding him back from any enjoyable scampering ahead. His tail wagged rarely now, unable as he was to walk on the Heath and spend time with younger, more agile dogs. We meandered along towards the bottom of the lane. Through traffic was prohibited, although cars were parked on one side. At the end, a lone father and son were playing football. An attractive young man in his early thirties, he was explaining to the boy how to stop the ball with his toes. He gently kicked it towards the toddler, who successfully sent it back, with great skill and gusto. He was good! He knew innately where to put his foot to kick it back expertly. He was perhaps no more than three years old. He wore a pair of denim jeans, trainers and a bright woolly jumper. Although it was bitterly cold, he wore no hat or scarf or gloves. His soft cheeks were ruddy from his exertions and he giggled with anticipation each time the ball came towards him. He had talent, this boy!

A short time ago, in the midst of his winter depression, Zach came to see me. He was unable to remain alone in the flat where he now lives. 'I'm so lonely,' he explained to me. 'I'm so lonely and depressed, and I don't know what to do with the rest of my life.' He sat down on the settee and shed tears of misery and despair. I sat still and watched him. We had played out this scene for years now. There was no deviation. I repeated the hollow words I had said so many, many times before. Take the meds, have counselling, seek proper help; get a job, change your lifestyle, make new friends, be positive. Were these platitudes falling into a void? Was something within him preventing him from helping himself? Was it a fear of success or a fear of failure? I couldn't work it out. This time, as he was now finally in some kind of rehab and addressing his addictions, would there be any light, any real hope? Was I deluding myself? I just wonder at the futility of it all.

I remember when Zach was three years old, and Sam and he

would play football for hours. He wore a pair of denim jeans, trainers and a bright woolly jumper. He giggled with anticipation each time the ball came towards him. He knew innately where to put his foot to kick it back expertly. He had talent, that boy.

London, January 2008

Appendix A

Some Frequently Asked Questions

The following represents an overview from my point of view as the mother of a young man with bipolar disorder. It is, of course, advisable to consult further sources for a more involved analysis and for advice tailored to your situation.

What is bipolar affective disorder?

Bipolar affective disorder is an acute psychiatric disease characterised by severe and generally cyclical mood swings. The pendulum swings from the highest elation and euphoria (the manias) to the lowest, most debilitating lows (the depressions).

What are the symptoms?

Symptoms of mania

- Decreased need for sleep
- Reduced appetite
- Racing thoughts
- Pressured, fast speech
- Distractibility
- Loss of judgement and self-control

- Grandiose and unrealistic beliefs
- High, elevated and irritable mood

Symptoms of depression

- Weight changes related to an increase or decrease in appetite
- Sleeping too little or too much
- Loss of interest or pleasure in activities
- Inability to concentrate
- Feelings of guilt or worthlessness
- Decreased sex drive
- Suicidal thoughts or actions
- Tearfulness
- Excessively low mood or sadness

Who does it affect?

It affects men and women equally, adults and children.

At what age does it usually occur?

It typically begins in the late teens or early twenties. However, bipolar disorder has been diagnosed in children as young as three years of age and adults over the age of seventy.

Is there a genetic predisposition?

It is arguable that there is a strong genetic element to bipolar disorder. An initial evaluation of the sufferer will in many instances throw up a history of some kind of mental instability in the family.

How would I recognise it in my relative/friend?

Bipolar disorder does not suddenly appear overnight. The symptoms build over a period. It could be months, weeks or days. It is generally the case that one recognises that someone is acutely unwell only when the episode reaches its peak: that is to say, when someone is either unnaturally high in mood or almost unrecognisably low. It is not always easy to discern a shift in temperament. Some warning signs include the following:

- excessive expenditure
- inappropriately sexual, garrulous or intimidating conduct
- an excessive desire to be up all night and to sleep during the daylight hours, thus reversing the sleep cycle
- unusual and excessive use of alcohol or drugs
- being unnecessarily overactive and restless
- ideas of grandiosity whereby he/she believes that he/she knows 'the answer to everything' or that 'God speaks through' him/her
- unmanageable behaviour – so much so that it is difficult to spend time in his/her company
- being so low in mood as to be unable to get up in the morning and go to work or study
- feeling so dispirited and wretched that all he/she wants to do is to cut him/herself off from society
- an innate feeling of utter worthlessness and/or an overriding sense of inadequacy and failure
- such abysmal feelings resulting in suicidal ideation

What should I do in the first instance?

Establish whether the person recognises that he/she is unwell. Even if he does not believe that he is ill, then at least make an appointment with the GP in the hope that he will go once contact has been made with the surgery. Try to accompany him to the GP to make sure that if the GP concurs that he is suffering from a psychiatric disorder, an appointment is made for the earliest possible meeting with a psychiatrist at the local hospital. If you are covered by private health insurance, an appointment should be made with a recommended psychiatrist as soon as possible.

How far is the GP involved?

A GP can establish whether someone is suffering a psychiatric crisis. For depressive illness, a GP can prescribe antidepressants and recommend further therapies. There are far more difficulties encountered when someone is suffering from mania, especially once the mania has intensified into a full-blown psychosis. GPs are often reluctant to become involved at this juncture or to prescribe antipsychotics. If it is the case that the sufferer is deemed a danger to himself or others, then the GP will arrange for a crisis visit.

What about hospitals?

The level of care differs from hospital to hospital throughout the country. For someone suffering mania, a hospital may be the best and safest place to be. It is extremely difficult, if not practically impossible, to care for someone who is suffering extreme mania at home. Psychosis that incorporates delusions and hallucinations does not go hand in hand with bed rest. That is not to say that every patient who suffers from bipolar disorder will exhibit these symptoms.

What medication is available?

There are numerous medications available to treat the depressive and manic elements of the condition. The best advice is to ask the relevant questions of your GP/psychiatrist and fully research how the medication works and whether there are side effects that will need to be addressed.

How effective is medication?

Medication can work extremely well. It is a balancing act and an experimental game. What works for some will not necessarily work for others. Lithium is believed by some to be a 'miracle drug' but much evidence shows that there are many who do not benefit from it. Medication for psychosis is essential. Not all antidepressants work.

Mood balancers other than lithium can work well. Ultimately, it rests with the patient to work with his/her psychiatrist to obtain the best possible result.

WHAT SIDE EFFECTS ARE THERE FROM MEDICATION?

Most medications have side effects, even the simple aspirin. Individuals vary in their sensitivity to each medication prescribed.

WHAT IS BEING SECTIONED?

When a sufferer is extremely ill but will not stay in hospital voluntarily and is considered to be a danger to him/herself or others, then, on the recommendation of two doctors and a social worker, he/she can be detained under a section of the Mental Health Act. There are various sections. For a complete overview of the Act online, go to www.mhact.csip.org.uk (CSIP, the National Institute for Mental Health in England).

FOR HOW LONG DOES A SECTION LAST?

For a review of all the particular sections, see the Mental Health Act at the website address above. Two sections that are frequently used are:

- Section 2: Application for Assessment
  A patient can be admitted to a hospital and detained for a period not exceeding twenty-eight days in the interests of his/her own health and safety and the protection of other people. This section is generally applied when a sufferer is taken into hospital for the first time.
- Section 3: Application for Treatment.
  This section can last up to six months from the date of admission. During this time, the doctors can assess what is wrong and plan the appropriate treatment. The patient can be discharged before the end of the six months if the doctor agrees or the order can be cancelled if the patient agrees to stay

in hospital voluntarily. If a patient's nearest relative does not agree to the section and wants a discharge, application is made to the Mental Health Review Tribunal with the request that they reconsider the section. This request has to be filed within twenty-eight days of the advice from the doctor that he/she views the patient as a danger to him/herself or others and does not wish to discharge him/her. The patient is also at liberty to apply to the Tribunal if he/she wishes to be discharged from the section. There is usually a legal representative on the hospital ward available to help with this.

What happens if my relative/friend is violent?

Call the police. Tell them that there is an emergency. They can be invaluable. Try to cajole your relative/friend into going to the A&E department at the local hospital. Alternatively, call the local authority mental health crisis team, if they have previously been involved. Depending on how well led and managed they are, and to what hospital they are affiliated, there should be a positive outcome. However, they are often reluctant to become involved in cases they have never dealt with before and advise that the patient is instead taken to A&E.

What is self-medication?

Generally, abuse of alcohol and street drugs in order to 'control' or 'take the edge off' mania/depression. Bipolar patients are particularly at risk of self-medication when they are manic or hypomanic. It is not unusual for a severely manic patient to want to prolong and intensify the high by using drugs.

What is a dual diagnosis?

Bipolar disorder is notoriously difficult to recognise. When drugs or alcohol are involved, the problems are exacerbated. Bipolar patients should always be asked whether they indulge in either drugs or alcohol. As many psychiatrists have only a basic knowledge of the dangers associated with drug or alcohol abuse, most prefer not to get involved in this aspect of the illness and will treat the bipolar symptoms in isolation. However, to a great extent, the primary illness and the substance abuse go hand in hand. It has been estimated that 'more than 60 per cent of persons with bipolar disorder also suffer from alcoholism or drug-abuse problems'.[23]

There is yet again the oft-asked question: what came first? Does a diagnosis of bipolar disorder make an individual more likely to abuse drugs? Does an addiction predispose an individual to other forms of mental illness? Is there a genetic cause for both? There is evidence that the answer to all these questions is 'yes'. In any event, there is cause for concern. Taking street drugs and drinking large quantities of alcohol will unquestionably alter the effects of medication. A dual diagnosis will invariably lead to a need for inpatient treatment. There is also a far greater risk of suicidal tendencies. Substance abuse creates distinct problems. It takes on a life of its own and can lead to the mood disorder and the substance-abuse disorder feeding off each other. Once the illness and the substance abuse are symbiotically entwined, it is extremely difficult to separate one from the other and to distinguish whether a 'high' is due to mania or drug-induced psychosis.

How do I recognise if there is a drug/alcohol problem?

As can be seen from the above, great difficulties can be encountered in distinguishing a mood disorder from a substance-abuse problem. However, there are many warning signs that could indicate that drugs or alcohol are involved, including:

- Moody, irritable or erratic behaviour
- Excessive tiredness
- Lying or secretive behaviour

- Loss of appetite or loss of interest in day-to-day living
- Withdrawal from society
- Poor immunity to coughs, colds and a general 'malaise'
- Dilated or pinpointed pupils
- Stealing from friends or family
- Drug paraphernalia

How far should I go to help my relative/friend?

Learn all you can about the illness. Help your relative/friend to get a diagnosis and embark upon a course of treatment. Try to encourage him/her to participate in the treatment. Offer emotional support, understanding and patience as far as you can but don't continually blame yourself if you cannot. If your relative/friend is depressed, then encourage him to try to go out, if only for a short walk to buy a newspaper or get a cup of coffee, to go to the cinema or the shops. Anything so long as he is not incarcerated in his room for days on end and totally cut off from society. Create some kind of plan of action so that if your relative/friend relapses then someone can help in the first instance. Keep notes on his behaviour so that you can differentiate the 'good' moods from the 'bad'. Keep a chart of mood swings.

Help him so far as you are able but without reducing the freedom of the sufferer to take control of 'his' illness. It is sometimes advised that you should intervene only if your relative/friend is a danger to himself or others, for example if he is likely to put himself in a life-threatening situation. There has to come a time when your relative/friend realises that he is able to take control. It might take years.

What can trigger an episode?

Many life events can cause episodes, stressful situations in particular. Causes might include:

- Exams
- Leaving school
- Starting at university
- Marriage, childbirth or divorce
- Changing employment
- Death of a loved one
- Seasonal triggers

There is the additional complication of the 'kindling' effect. Once a patient with bipolar disorder has had several episodes, it can take very little for a relapse to occur. The patient becomes highly vulnerable to stress and past episodes are easily 'rekindled'.

Is there a cure?

To date, there appears to be no 'cure'. There is prevention and there is medication and therapy – all kinds of therapies. From art, dance and drama to CBT (cognitive behavioural therapy), from hypnotherapy and water therapy to nutrition and acupuncture. Treatment and management are the best 'cures'. Exercise, sleep and eating healthily help enormously. Keeping stressful triggers to a minimum can help avoid a relapse. However, it is up to the individual to create a method for dealing with his/her illness. Denying the disease will not make it disappear. Years of denial and blaming the illness on others will not eradicate it. Medication can help prevent relapses. It is inevitable that there will be setbacks but medication compliance can help to ensure that these setbacks are less severe.

Can I make him/her better?

No. You can only help as much as you physically and mentally wish to – but without enabling your relative/friend in his/her illness by taking control. There is only so much that you can achieve with help and advice. If ultimately your relative/friend does not take either, then you must realise that it is up to him to take control of his own life.

What is the usual prognosis?

There is no prognosis per se. Each individual will suffer his/her own version of the illness. Some people may have only one episode in their entire lives; others may suffer on a monthly or yearly basis. Rapid-cycling bipolar disorder sufferers may experience as many as four episodes (depression, hypomania, mania or mixed state) in one year.

What help is there for me as a carer?

There are various organisations and self-help groups available (see Appendix B). The Internet is a great resource. It is worthwhile being in touch with other carers. The carer should not feel abandoned, in a vacuum. Many people still recoil from mental illness and many are unwilling to speak about it. However, there are many organisations producing leaflets and booklets about the illness that are of much assistance. Many books are published in the USA by sufferers from bipolar disorder and by carers. There is remarkably little in Britain. Remember that as a carer you, as well as your relative, are entitled to get help from the social services.

The good news

Many bipolar disorder sufferers are fascinating people. They are often creative and artistic and wonderful company when they are well. When suffering from mania, they are rarely consciously violent. As this is generally a cyclical illness, there will be times when the sufferer is not ill. You can then spend time with them in order to create a plan to ensure that all is not lost should a relapse occur. Hopefully, more resources will be provided to research foundations so that new medications will eventually be forthcoming.

Appendix B

Some Useful Organisations

This is a small selection of what there is available. In order to get help, you have to be steadfast and determined. This is especially the case vis-à-vis the benefits system. A good social worker is essential, one who knows his/her way around the incessant form-filling.

BABCP

(British Association for Behavioural and Cognitive Psychotherapies)
Victoria Buildings
9–13 Silver Street
Bury
BL9 0EU
Tel: 0161 797 4484
Email: babcp@babcp.com
www.babcp.com

The association's website includes help in finding therapists and information on their areas of competence.

Carers UK

32–36 Loman Street
London
SE1 0EE

Tel: 020 7922 8000
Email: info@carersuk.org
www.carersuk.org

Established to improve the lives of those who provide unpaid care, looking after a partner, relative or friend.

Crossroads Association

10 Regent Place
Rugby
Warwickshire
CV21 2PN
Tel: 0845 450 0350
www.crossroads.org.uk

Established to help carers by allowing them to have a break from looking after their relatives or friends.

Depression Alliance

212 Spitfire Studios
63–71 Collier Street
London
N1 9BE
Tel: 0845 123 2320
Email: information@depressionalliance.org
www.depressionalliance.org

A self-help organisation. Provides information and support, working with healthcare professionals to seek the right help when needed.

Forresters Respite Centre

Southampton Road
Hythe
Hampshire
SO45 5GQ

Tel: 02380 843 042
Email: forresters@rethink.org
www.forresters.info

A unique centre that offers therapeutic care for people with mental-health problems.

JAMI

(Jewish Association for the Mentally Ill)
16a North End Road
London
NW11 7PH
Tel: 020 8458 2223
Email: info@jamiuk.org
www.jamiuk.org

The only Jewish charity in Britain concerned exclusively with mental-health issues.

MDF The Bipolar Organisation

Castle Works
21 St George's Road
London
SE1 6ES
Tel: 08456 340 540
Email: mdf@mdf.org.uk
www.mdf.org.uk

User-led charity aiming to support those affected by bipolar disorder and develop self-help opportunities.

MIND

PO Box 277
Manchester
M60 3XN

Tel: 0845 766 0163
www.mind.org.uk

Charity offering support and advice to people with mental-health problems. Raises public awareness. More than 200 local associations throughout England and Wales.

NHS Direct

Tel: 0845 4647
www.nhsdirect.nhs-uk

Rethink

(formerly the National Schizophrenia Fellowship)
5th Floor
Royal London House
22–25 Finsbury Square
London
EC2A 1DX
Tel: 0845 456 0455
Email: info@rethink.org
www.rethink.org

A mental-health charity working to aid those with a severe mental illness to recover a better quality of life.

SAD Association

(The Seasonal Affective Disorder Association)
PO Box 989
Steyning
BN44 3HG
www.sada.org.uk

Informs the public about the illness and supports sufferers.

SAMARITANS

Chris
PO Box 9090
Stirling
FK8 2SA
Tel: 08457 90 90 90; from Ireland: 1850 60 90 90
Email: Jo@samaritans.org
www.samaritans.org

SANE

1st Floor
Cityside House
40 Adler Street
London
E1 1EE
Tel: 0845 767 8000
Email: info@sane.org.uk
www.sane.org.uk

Charity aiming to improve the quality of life of people affected by mental illness.

YOUNGMINDS

48–50 St John Street
London
EC1M 4DG
Tel: 020 7336 8445
Email: enquiries@youngminds.org.uk
www.youngminds.org.uk

Established to help improve the mental health and emotional well-being of children and young people.

Notes

1 2CBs are a Class A drug, in effect much like ecstasy and amphetamines. 'At higher doses, users indicate that moving objects seem to leave "trails" behind them. Surfaces sometimes appear covered with geometric patterns and seem to move or breathe. Listening to music in conjunction with taking 2CB reportedly causes patterns, colours, and movements to be distorted.' (www.drugscope.org.uk) Dominic handed one of the pills over to his father but, because possession was illegal, we could not have it analysed.

2 A study of how insanity affected a broad church of artists and writers is to be found in Kay Redfield Jamison's excellent *Touched with Fire: Manic-Depressive Illness and the Artistic Temperament* (Simon & Schuster, New York, 1993).

3 It is a common, mistaken belief that smoking heroin is not addictive. It is. It is just as addictive as injecting but users fool themselves into believing otherwise. People with mental illnesses who present psychotic symptoms say that heroin makes them less anxious, calmer and less agitated. However, once withdrawal from the drug begins, the psychotic symptoms return much worse than before, leading to more agitation, more anxiety and more profound symptoms of mania. Much later, Zach contradicted himself and stated that of course smoking heroin is just as addictive

as injecting; it's simply less of a risk vis-à-vis infectious disease.

4 Ketamine is generally used as a veterinary tranquilliser, although in emergency medicine it is often the drug of first choice in order to render immobile a person who has had an accident. It is classed as a 'dissociative anaesthetic': in other words, it detaches the mind from the body. Those who enjoy it illegally find the near-death experience irresistible. It is similar to cocaine in that there is an initial rush but from then on the body goes into a slow dive. It impedes breathing and heart rate, and can lead to vomiting and loss of coordination, as well as hallucinations and delusions. It was labelled a Class C drug in the United Kingdom in January 2006. Ketamine is generally contraindicated for anyone suffering a mental illness. However, in 2006, an article in *Nature* magazine reported that the drug was being trialled by neuroscientists: 'They are finding that although ketamine makes some lose their minds, it might help others find their sanity.' Arguable. ('Depression: Comfortably Numb', in *Nature*, Vol. 443, 12 October 2006, pp. 629–31).

5 Recent research has indicated that there is a greater sensitivity towards stress found in people who have experienced *severe* adversity in early life. Consequently a larger proportion of those who have gone through 'neglect, separation and loss' develop bipolar disorder. ('The Stress Sensitization Hypothesis: Understanding the Course of Bipolar Disorder', in *Journal of Affective Disorders*, Vol. 95, 2006, pp. 43–9) That is not to say, however, that the separation anxiety experienced by Zach can be said to be the cause of his bipolar disorder or that every child who experiences such anxiety is likely to develop the condition.

6 Why is it that all psychiatrists appear to take their summer break in August, consequently leaving the mentally impaired at a loss as to how to deal with their various illnesses? I describe it as 'the deadly August break' because those vulnerable patients who have come to rely on a particular psychiatrist for help and a sense of security are left to fend for themselves. In the Woody Allen film

Play It Again, Sam, Woody's character bemoans the fate of every angst-ridden patient come the summer: 'If only I knew where my analyst was vacationing. Where do they go every August? They leave the city. Every summer, the city is full of people who are crazy till Labour Day.'

7 Pressured speech can be defined as talking rapidly and non-stop, generally in a loud and emphatic manner. The speaker is so driven that he is difficult to interrupt. Apparently, thoughts and ideas are travelling at such a pace through the brain that it is well nigh impossible to express them intelligibly or coherently.

8 See Appendix A, 'What is being sectioned?', 'For how long does a section last?'

9 How many times since has he stated exactly that? I've lost count. If only it were true.

10 *Midnight Express* (1978), from the book by Billy Hayes and directed by Alan Parker, depicts the arrest by the Turkish authorities of Hayes (played by Brad Davis) for drug smuggling. It is a searing portrait of an excessively harsh prison regime. At one point in the film, Hayes is sent to the prison psychiatric ward, where the treatment meted out to him is unnecessarily brutal. Force-fed huge amounts of antipsychotics, he is reduced to a vacant-eyed, drooling ruin.

11 For more than half a century, lithium has been used in the form of various salts to treat bipolar disorder. It reduces the frequency and intensity of mania that are hallmarks of the condition. It is also used in the treatment of severe depression. However, the side effects can be profound. It can induce tremors, blurred vision, weight gain, an increase in urination and a marked sensation of 'distance' – a feeling of being removed from reality.

12 Kay Redfield Jamison, *An Unquiet Mind: A Memoir of Moods and Madness* (Vintage Books, New York, 1996, p. 218).

13 See Frederick K. Goodwin and Kay Redfield Jamison, 'Alcohol and Drug Abuse in Manic-Depressive Illness', in *Manic-Depressive Illness* (Oxford University Press, Oxford, 1990, pp. 210–26).

14 A recent study into bipolar disorder and genetics found that 'Early-onset (age at onset [less than or equal to] 21) subjects had higher risks of drug abuse, alcohol abuse, rapid cycling, and suicide attempts'. The study concluded: 'Age at onset is associated with clinical heterogeneity in bipolar disorder and aggregates, possibly along with drug abuse, within families. These findings are consistent with the conclusion that age at onset reflects underlying genetic heterogeneity in bipolar disorder.' (Ping-I Lin et al., 'Clinical Correlates and Familial Aggregation of Age at Onset in Bipolar Disorder', in *American Journal of Psychiatry*, Vol. 163, Issue 2, February 2006, pp. 240–6)

15 A series of cult sci-fi novels by Robert Shea and Robert Anton Wilson. Steeped in '60s counterculture, *The Illuminatus! Trilogy* is a sprawling, fragmented epic of sex, drugs and conspiracy theories. Zach carried it around with him at all times and referred to it incessantly. He must have read it a dozen times. Obviously, the hallucinatory writing and frequent drug allusions were things to which he could relate.

16 From Zach's journal, July 2001.

17 Old friends from way back. Rickey would prove his mettle as the best of friends further down the line.

18 A considerable number of people still believe that 9/11 was indeed a Republican plot; there are myriad conspiracy theories about the attacks.

19 People with psychotic disorders have a far higher rate of drug abuse, and especially marijuana use, than others. Studies have conclusively determined that the greater the use of cannabis, the higher the risk of psychological impairment. A recent study found that in a sample of young people with recent-onset psychosis, 'The risk of psychotic relapse increased by approximately 6.4 per cent with each additional day of cannabis use within a 1-week period.' (L. Hides et al., 'Psychotic symptom and cannabis relapse in recent-onset psychosis: Prospective study', in *British*

Journal of Psychiatry, Vol. 189, Issue 2, August 2006, pp. 137–43.)

20 Francis Mark Mondimore, *Bipolar Disorder: A Guide for Patients and Families* (The Johns Hopkins University Press, Baltimore, 1999, p. 173).

21 Hypomania is a form of mild mania. The sufferer does not generally require hospitalisation nor does he display psychotic symptoms. Hypomania does not impair social or professional functioning. However, the mood is altered and, in Zach's case, it would eventually lead to flamboyant and outrageous behaviour.

22 Julius Millingen, *Memoirs of the Affairs of Greece* (London, 1831, p. 16), cited in Kay Redfield Jamison, *Touched with Fire: Manic-Depressive Illness and the Artistic Temperament* (Simon & Schuster, New York, 1993, p. 151).

23 D.A. Regier et al., 'Comorbidity of Mental Disorders with Alcohol and Other Drug Abuse: Results from the Epidemiologic Catchment Area (ECA) Study', in *Journal of the American Medical Association*, Vol. 264, No. 19, November 1990, pp. 2511–18, quoted in Francis Mark Mondimore, *Bipolar Disorder: A Guide for Patients and Families* (The Johns Hopkins University Press, Baltimore, 1999, p. 269).

Further Reading

Baker, Barbara, *When Someone You Love Has Depression* (Sheldon Press, London, 2003)

Barondes, Samuel H., *Mood Genes: Hunting for Origins of Mania and Depression* (W.H. Freeman and Co., New York, 1998)

Bentall, Richard P., *Madness Explained: Psychosis and Human Nature* (Penguin Books, London, 2003)

Berger, Diane and Lisa, *We Heard the Angels of Madness: A Family Guide to Coping with Manic Depression* (Quill, New York, 2002)

Bettelheim, Bruno, and Rosenfeld, Alvin A., *The Art of the Obvious: Developing Insight for Psychotherapy and Everyday Life* (Thames & Hudson, London, 1992)

Duke, Patty, and Hochman, Gloria, *A Brilliant Madness: Living with Manic-Depressive Illness* (Bantam Books, New York, 1993)

Dunn, Sara, Morrison, Blake, and Roberts, Michèle (eds), *Mind Readings: Writers' Journeys Through Mental States* (Minerva, London, 1996)

Fieve, Ronald R., *Moodswing* (Bantam Books, New York, 1997)

Goodwin, Frederick K., and Jamison, Kay Redfield, *Manic-Depressive Illness* (Oxford University Press, Oxford, 1990)

Gottesman, Irving I., *Schizophrenia Genesis: The Origins of Madness* (W.H. Freeman and Co., New York, 1991)

Greene, Graham, *A Sort of Life* (Penguin Books, London, 1971)

Hinshaw, Stephen P., *The Years of Silence Are Past: My Father's Life with Bipolar Disorder* (Cambridge University Press, Cambridge, 2002)

Jamison, Kay Redfield, *An Unquiet Mind: A Memoir of Moods and Madness* (Vintage Books, New York, 1995)

Jamison, Kay Redfield, *Exuberance: The Passion for Life* (Vintage Books, New York, 2004)

Jamison, Kay Redfield, *Night Falls Fast: Understanding Suicide* (Picador, London, 1999)

Jamison, Kay Redfield, *Touched with Fire: Manic-Depressive Illness and the Artistic Temperament* (Free Press, New York, 1994)

Karp, David A., *The Burden of Sympathy: How Families Cope with Mental Illness* (Oxford University Press, Oxford, 2001)

Laing, R.D., *The Divided Self: An Existential Study in Sanity and Madness* (Penguin Books, London, 1990)

Lam, Dominic H., Jones, Steven H., Hayward, Peter, and Bright, Jenifer A., *Cognitive Therapy for Bipolar Disorder: A Therapist's Guide to Concepts, Methods and Practice* (John Wiley & Sons Ltd, Chichester, 1999)

Marohn, Stephanie, *The Natural Medicine Guide to Bipolar Disorder* (Hampton Roads, Charlottesville, 2003)

Miklowitz, David J., and Goldstein, Michael J., *Bipolar Disorder: A Family-Focused Treatment Approach* (The Guildford Press, New York, 1997)

Mondimore, Francis Mark, *Bipolar Disorder: A Guide for Patients and Families* (The Johns Hopkins University Press, Baltimore, 1999)

Nasar, Sylvia, *A Beautiful Mind: The Life of Mathematical Genius and Nobel Laureate John Nash* (Touchstone, New York, 1998)

Nettle, Daniel, *Strong Imagination: Madness, Creativity and Human Nature* (Oxford University Press, Oxford, 2001)

Sacks, Oliver, *Awakenings* (Picador, London, 1990)

Sacks, Oliver, *The Man Who Mistook his Wife for a Hat* (Picador, London, 1985)

Solomon, Andrew, *The Noonday Demon: An Anatomy of Depression* (Vintage, London, 2002)

Steel, Danielle, *His Bright Light: The Story of My Son, Nick Traina* (Corgi, London, 1999)

Williams, Paul (ed.), *Psychosis (Madness)* (The Institute of Psychoanalysis, London, 1999)